Lᴏᴅɪᴀ Wᴇᴠᴇʀs has written widely on New Zealand and Australian literature. Her collection of travel writing about New Zealand, *Travelling to New Zealand*, the fruit of three years' research, appeared in 2000. She is currently Director of the Stout Research Centre at Victoria University of Wellington, a member of the Arts Board of Creative New Zealand and Chair of the Trustees of the National Library.

Country *of* Writing

Travel Writing and New Zealand
1809–1900

Lydia Wevers

AUCKLAND
UNIVERSITY
PRESS

for Alastair

First published 2002

Auckland University Press
University of Auckland
Private Bag 92019
Auckland
New Zealand
http://www.auckland.ac.nz/aup

© Lydia Wevers, 2002

ISBN 1 86940 271 5

National Library of New Zealand Cataloguing-in-Publication Data
Wevers, Lydia.
Country of writing : travel writing and New Zealand, 1809-1900 /Lydia Wevers.
Includes bibliographical references and index.
ISBN 1-86940-271-5
1. Travel writing—History. 2. New Zealand—Description and travel.
3. Travelers' writings, English—History and criticism. I. Title.
919.304—dc 21

Publication is assisted by a grant from the Marsden Fund, the Royal Society of New Zealand

Cover design by Christine Hansen
Cover image: Augustus Earle, *Against Truth*, n.d., Alexander Turnbull Library, A-279-002

Printed by Publishing Press Ltd, Albany, Auckland.

CONTENTS

ACKNOWLEDGEMENTS

This book would not have been attempted without the generous help of the Marsden Fund, which gave me a three-year research grant as part of the History of Print Culture Project, hosted by the Alexander Turnbull Library and the Humanities Society of New Zealand (HUMANZ). Initial work on the book was done with the aid of a non-fiction grant from Creative New Zealand or the Arts Council of New Zealand, as it then was, in 1995.

I owe immense thanks to the staff of the Alexander Turnbull Library and the National Library of New Zealand, who put up with my exorbitant requests for materials, a perpetual and overladen trolley, listened to chapters as they were drafted and were personally as well as professionally helpful. In particular, I would like to thank Marian Minson, Barbara Brownlie, the staff of the ATL research centre, Joan McCracken, Di Woods, Susan Bartel, Heather Mathie and David Retter.

My colleagues in the History of Print Culture Project – Brian Opie, Penny Griffith, Sydney Shep, John Thomson, Philip Rainer, Margaret Calder, Kathleen Coleridge, Ross Somerville and Stephen Hamilton – have been encouraging and helpful. I especially want to thank Penny Griffith, project manager, for her endless hours of help, and Brian Opie, whose innovativeness and determination made the project happen.

I am very grateful to Phil Parkinson for generously sharing his enormous original research with me. Many other people have been helpful and interested: Malcolm McKinnon, Ian Willison, Elizabeth Webby, the late D.F. McKenzie, Justine Clark, Vincent O'Sullivan, Mark Williams, Roger Blackley, Laura Kroetsch, Lyman Sargent, Jane Stafford, Linda Hardy, John Newton, colleagues at the Stout Research Centre. This book is immensely improved by the many hours of patient and scrupulous attention paid to the manuscript by Andrew Mason, whose editing skills are unrivalled. I would also like to thank Elizabeth Caffin and Katrina Duncan of AUP for their hard work on the text, and Ginny Sullivan for a very fast and good job on the index. My family, Alastair Bisley, Seb, Lizzie and Tom, have been wonderful.

Introduction

The most dramatic way in which the force of the encounter between Europeans and non-European peoples all over the world can be brought home to us two centuries later is via the print record. Simply as an illustration of the tidal wave that overtook an oral culture, collections of nineteenth-century writing about New Zealand – travel books, maps, emigration guides, ethnographies, newspapers, periodicals, shipping brochures, shipboard newspapers, journals, logs – are overwhelming in quantity and range. Print was the medium of permanent change, and Maori recognised the attraction of print and the power of literacy almost as soon as they encountered it.[1] *Country of Writing* surveys a particular tranche of print history – books which fall into the broad category of 'travel writing', itself composed of many different kinds of writing – to show what is transmitted to us by bookish travellers.

A community 'shapes and formulates its most fundamental experiences by deciphering the many texts it receives, produces and makes its own'.[2] This observation by the French historian Roger Chartier about the work of the New Zealand bibliographer D. F. McKenzie neatly summarises a set of relationships and effects that *Country of Writing* attempts to elucidate. By investigating the accumulation of texts about New Zealand which were produced and received by travellers, an idea of how 'the most fundamental experiences' were shaped and formulated reveals the constant play of projection and reflection, of cultural tension and anxiety, that both produces and characterises books by travellers, suggesting something about why travellers write books as well as the forcefulness of a print-based culture.

Benedict Anderson has characterised a dimension of European imperialism as 'print-capitalism'.[3] The many connections between travel as an expanding commercial enterprise in the nineteenth century, travellers' motivations, the market for books about travel, and the business opportunities revealed by travel writing's descriptions of new landscapes, plants and peoples, broaden Anderson's phrase out from its reference to the book trade to suggest what *Country of Writing* makes evident. The many fronts on which travel writing facilitates an intersection between a distant culture and a present enterprise, and the ways in which those intersections illustrate pressure points, assumptions and attitudes, are a constant theme of *Country of Writing*. As well as articulating and reinforcing a set of obvious comparisons between the traveller's culture and the place of travel based on ideas about civilised and savage peoples, 'waste' and overpopulated landscapes, degenerating and invigorating climates, and what constituted natural beauty, travel books are expressions of the effectiveness of print in putting the world on show and delineating a geography of power. There is a very long time-lag between nineteenth-century descriptions of non-European worlds and the Empire's reply, and for at least a hundred years the traffic in books, knowledge and people flowed out from Europe and not towards it.

The colour blue

In a paper delivered to the Hawke's Bay Philosophical Institute in the 1880s, William Colenso described one of the striking effects produced by the arrival of Europeans in the Bay of Islands.[4] He claimed that Maori had few natural materials with which to produce the colour blue. In the early summer young Maori would decorate their faces with light-blue fuchsia pollen, or use pukeko feathers and berries, but blue was a rare element of their palette until the arrival of Europeans, after which 'no colour was better known to them in all its shades than this one of *blue*'. Sailors wore blue jackets, blue shirts, blue trousers and blue caps; in the mission houses children wore navy blue cotton printed with tiny white dots, women wore blue linen and men blue woollen or striped cotton shirts and sometimes blue caps. It was a 'neat sight' to see the children and adult women sitting together at school clad in 'decent garments of English blue'. After the arrival of the American whalers there were twilled cotton shirts with a wider blue stripe and the 'famed American blue twilled cotton', which washed to a 'dull greyish-blue colour' and 'was known by the Maori as "tupapaku"'' (corpse).

One of the delights of reading travel writing is the discovery of details about the past. Colenso's recollections of the clothing worn in the Bay of Islands in the 1830s, including pre-Treaty denim, brings the whole scene into colour and focus as we look back to the visual impressions of a devout young printer recently arrived on the other side of the world. But Colenso's description is not travel writing as it is practised in the twenty-first century. His papers delivered to the Hawke's Bay Philosophical Institute and collected in the *Transactions . . . of the New Zealand Institute* were scientific, reflecting his continuing concern to describe and classify the world he arrived in fifty years before, and to preserve Maori knowledge, including his own observations of Maori. Most nineteenth-century travel writing saw its task in a similar way – the collection and dissemination of 'valuable and interesting Information'.[5]

Writing produced by travel followed precedents and protocols mostly to do with the transmission of geographic, ethnographic and environmental knowledge back to the sorting-house of Europe. New Zealand's extreme distance from Europe, literally the furthest away you could go, also conferred on it a special character: New Zealand as a wonderland of the new, a *terra incognita* of tremendous possibilities, was part of the response of travellers from the beginning. At the same time travel writing involved the author in what Mary Louise Pratt described as the 'anti-conquest': writing which represented travellers, explorers and naturalists as innocent investigators, motivated by their pursuit of knowledge, whose journeys happened to occur at the historical moment of European dispossession and appropriation.[6] For example, Colenso's recollections of the post-contact community of the Bay of Islands dressed in blue give a chromatic cohesion and a peaceful flavour to the scene of colonisation; many of his efforts to preserve Maori knowledge occurred after war, land confiscations, dispossession and depopulation. These effects of European expansion are excluded from or diminished in most travel writing, which focuses instead on its 'innocent' task of observation and the transmission of knowledge.

What to observe

In 1841 Colonel Julian Jackson, Fellow of the Royal Society, published *What to Observe; or, The Traveller's Remembrancer*. Previously published in Paris in 1822 under the title *Guide du Voyageur*, the book was reprinted twice in English (in 1845 and revised in 1861) and once in French (as *Aide-Mémoire du Voyageur* in 1834). Here Jackson laid out the duties and the profile of a traveller:

> The Object of this Work, as its title indicates, is to point out to the uninitiated Traveller what he should observe, and to remind the one who is well informed, of many objects which, but for a Remembrancer, might escape him. It will be seen, from a perusal of 'what to observe' what an immense field of Physical and Moral Research lies open to Investigation. The intending Traveller will be encouraged to exertion by the assurance that he can not only do much to enlarge the sphere of his own ideas, but acquire the means of communicating to others a great mass of valuable and interesting Information. It is superfluous to speak of the present facilities for Travelling. In proportion as these are great, the result will be beneficial, as regards a true knowledge of the Earth, and of the Laws, Religion, Manners, and Customs of Mankind, when Travellers shall have learned *how* and *what* to observe. The Work is intended for general use, and will be found serviceable alike to those who travel luxuriously over civilized Europe or America,

and to the adventurous and undaunted spirits who, in all climates, are content to brave obstacles and endure hardships in search of Knowledge.[7]

Jackson's was not the only observation handbook for the traveller. In 1838 Harriet Martineau published *How to Observe*, a book for inexperienced travellers that was described by Jill Steward as a 'vehicle for personal and social improvement',[8] and handbooks on travel etiquette became widely available later in the century. But the number of descriptive narratives about New Zealand which follow the Remembrancer's categories and divisions implies a wide circulation for the Royal Society model of scientific observation. Jackson was articulating a generic model for travellers' texts that was already well established by the nineteenth century, and amply illustrated in Pratt's analysis of the predominant streams of information and attitudes in eighteenth-century travel and exploration writing. It is notable, however, that a well-received description like William Yate's *An Account of New Zealand* (1835) follows the Royal Society model to the letter.

Descriptive and scientific travel writing of the eighteenth and nineteenth centuries was an agent for the spread of what Ian Willison terms the 'British sea-borne empire'[9] and introduced the non-European world into European knowledge systems and to the metropolitan imagination.[10] The attraction of reading about distant places and peoples was demonstrated in a healthy share of the book market,[11] the constant presence of writing about travel and travel destinations in metropolitan news media, and the ever-increasing flood of travel writing published as travelling became a pastime for large numbers of middle- and upper-class European tourists during the nineteenth century. Most travel books demonstrate an awareness of the conventions and precedents of travel writing, and an overriding consciousness of the comparison between home and abroad, self and other, here, there and elsewhere, which structures the traveller's 'search of knowledge'.

Country of writing

'Travel writing' is a deceptively homogeneous term for a genre defined by Joan-Pau Rubiés as that varied body of writing which 'takes travel as an essential condition for its production'.[12] In *Imperial Eyes* Mary Louise Pratt identifies a number of seminal conventions of eighteenth-century travel writing and two main genre streams: scientific and exploration. Travel writing about New Zealand in the nineteenth century is baggier and more mixed, and a potent archive of cultural history, recording a shift from eighteenth-century travel, with its heroic overtones of exploration, danger and singularity, to nineteenth-century tourism: a trip to see the world very often conducted in a crowd and organised by Cook's.

Of course, no archive can be neatly fitted into such broad generalisations. *Country of Writing* seeks to complicate the term 'travel writing' by suggesting a number of categorisations into which it might fall. As a general distinction, however, the travel writing discussed in *Country of Writing* addresses itself to an audience elsewhere, often one the traveller expects to rejoin, and is written by someone not intending to stay. The vast secondary literature produced around travel writing recently is spearheaded by a re-examination of the eighteenth-century literature of voyage and exploration, postcolonial interest in travel as an agency of colonisation, and tourism studies. It provides some of the framework and strategies for my investigation of the nineteenth-century New Zealand travel archive, especially through the work of Mary Louise Pratt, James Clifford and John Frow.

Writing seems to have been an inevitable adjunct of travel – a cultural duty and a framing intellectual habit – for most nineteenth-century travellers, as if mobility required a corresponding attempt at stability, at preservation, in the form of a textual record. The online National Library of New Zealand Catalogue, which does not allow you to select only nineteenth-century publications, lists 1806 items in the highest category of relevance for the subject phrase 'New Zealand description and travel'. More than half of these are collections of letters, journals or diaries published in the nineteenth century by travellers, many of whom, especially in the latter half of the century, wrote principally for their families and friends. The differences and similarities between these writers, who tend to go to the same places and have similar reactions, constitute a textual landscape. Travellers are usually readers and many refer to their reading in their own writing in order to agree or disagree, compare, extend or digress from their own experience. The travel experience is deeply textual – other travel books, brochures, maps, guidebooks all inform the traveller's progress, and almost all travellers notice and comment on the books, journals and wall illustrations they encounter as they travel. The traveller's eye for print reveals the high level of dissemination of information about different parts of the Empire circulating within it.

A great many questions flow from travel writing, beginning with the sheer size of the archive. Questions about who was travelling, and what they were reading and writing, give some idea of the social and cultural dimensions of the nineteenth-century travel boom, and comparing what travellers wrote shows their shared assumptions and attitudes. Recurring preoccupations reveal the tensions and ambiguities of travelling and of colonisation. A favoured travel route quickly becomes clear: the must-see, iconic sites of New Zealand, which become accessible through developing infrastructure. These sites – the hot lakes, the cold lakes and the mountains – stand for New Zealand as a landscape and as the projected site of European imperial civilisation, and are compared by many travellers and in the tourist brochures with the scenic wonders of the rest of world, locking into place a set of associations that help to define New Zealand as a country pleasing to European taste.

Reading

It is not possible to read this body of writing as if it is the transparent transmission from somewhere and somebody vanished from sight, as it frequently claims to be. But read through and with the distortions and crimps of the person, history, geography, gender, culture and race, travel writing nevertheless offers a way of recovering something of the world it seeks to describe. Through the self-reflexive representations of the text, it is possible to glimpse the kind of detail, like Colenso's comment on what everyone was wearing in the Bay of Islands in the 1830s, that brings history into material focus. Travel writing is not the transparent medium that practitioners claim, but the story it has to tell repays careful examination.

The preface to James Bruce's *Travels to Discover the Source of the Nile in the Years 1768, 1769, 1770, 1771, 1772 & 1773* (second edition, Edinburgh, 1805) articulates the appeal of eighteenth-century travel writing to its stay-at-home readership:

> In proportion as his dangers have been great and numerous, his activity and courage remarkable, his routes novel and interesting, we feel a correspondent interest in his fate. Books of travel are therefore read with a pleasure, which history, for the most part, is seldom able to excite. While they enrich the mind with new and interesting truths, they amuse it with all the graces of novelty, and all the attractions of personal adventure.

The personal dimension of travel writing, the celebration of the traveller and the journey which gives travel writing its narrative flavour, disguises the way in which it is also the expression of a social group characterised by both a cultural conviction that the experience and observations of European people should be recorded, and an economic and physical capacity to undertake long and often difficult journeys. In other words, the focus on the heroic, personalised aspects of travel conceals the fact that it is a class activity, enabled by financial status and cultural knowledge. Benedict Anderson has claimed that the community of the nation imagines itself into being by connections made across and by print objects in a common language.[13] The imagined community of the nation is asserted and reinforced by its encounter with peoples and lands outside its boundaries – physical, ethnic, historical and cultural. Preconceptions, attitudes and stereotypes in travellers' writing and reading delineate and confirm the imperial community, and continually reinforce the ways in which Europe understands itself as a norm. Travellers' books constantly mark out social and cultural differences from colonised peoples, differences which indicate the connections between the reader and the traveller.

The shape of the text

Country of Writing follows a chronological sweep through the nineteenth-century archive, to give a sense of its flavour and character. It is not a comprehensive survey of travel writing about New Zealand. Instead, it suggests the principal interests at work in travel writing, the different categories into which it falls and the print culture generated by travel. The book begins with the sudden and marked increase in the visibility of New Zealand as a way-station on a shipping route after the attack on the merchant ship *Boyd* in 1809, beginning in the columns of the *Sydney Gazette* and spreading out into a wide range of European publications. As the story of the *Boyd* accumulates detail and newsworthiness through its various versions, narrators and publications, New Zealand becomes a geographical space, a destination, with certain distinguishing characteristics. Captain Ceroni's watch dropped carelessly into a New Zealand harbour is a marker of the depths and repercussions of cultural misunderstanding that ripple out as the story of the *Boyd* circulates, and an instance of the way the print medium brings geography into focus and maps the morphing of a location. The place where the crew and passengers of the *Boyd* were killed is a marked location for travellers and travel writers for two hundred years, and the continuing currency of the story reveals a European readership's expectations of New Zealand as distant and exotic, a site of cannibalism and adventure. One of the consequences of the *Boyd* massacre was a delay in establishing a missionary presence in New Zealand, and when Samuel Marsden and J. L. Nicholas eventually arrived in the Bay of Islands, almost the first thing they did was travel to Whangaroa to discuss the massacre with some of the perpetrators and rehabilitate New Zealand as a place suitable for evangelical work.

William Colenso came to New Zealand as printer for the Church Missionary Society (CMS) settlement at Paihia in 1834. He interspersed his work as a printer and a lay missionary with extensive journeys into parts of New Zealand unexplored by Europeans. His journal account of the first of these trips, 'Journal of a Naturalist', is *Country of Writing*'s principal case-study of scientific travel writing in the heroic exploration mode. Colenso's papers show his awareness of genre conventions and models, and his extensive readings in the travel narratives of famous eighteenth-century African explorers like Mungo Park and Major Denham. Colenso's journey into Urewera country is represented as a journey into barbarous territory and is directed at both the reader of exploration narratives and members of the professional networks he aspired to join, led by scientists he met in New Zealand – Joseph Hooker, Charles Darwin, Allan Cunningham – who built collections of their specimens at Kew and achieved international reputations as botanists. Colenso's botanical work contributed to bringing New Zealand flora to Europe, including the dissemination of botanical classifications in print. The force of competition to identify species, attach names and stake out the field in print is evident from the 1830s and 1840s, as Colenso quickly publishes his account of his travels and sends to London a stream of specimen cases, book requests and impassioned letters querying the classifications and discoveries of other botanists.

Competition was not confined to naturalists. A number of travel texts produced in the first half of the nineteenth century arose from professional or commercial ambition. The three principal arms of the 'British sea borne empire' – church, army and commerce – produced travel texts with professional knowledge, particular agendas and different constituencies.

W. R. Wade, who like Colenso was a lay member of the CMS settlement at Paihia, published his *Journey in the Northern Island of New Zealand* in Hobart, where he became an ordained minister of the Baptist Missionary Society. Like Colenso's botanical journey publications, Wade's travel writing was intended to demonstrate something about his professional status beyond his role with the CMS. William Yate's *An Account of New Zealand* displays a breadth of geographical and ethnographic knowledge about New Zealand and its people, shaped to promote missionary activities. It disappeared from view, however, after an enthusiastic initial reception, when Yate was accused of homosexuality, including making sexual advances to young Maori men. Both Wade's and Yate's travel writing, for different reasons, is connected to church politics and sectarian imperialism, and uses the claim of the traveller to eyewitness authority to stake out the territory at issue.

A number of early and widely circulated travel texts, including E. J. Wakefield's *Adventure in New Zealand*, Ernst Dieffenbach's *Travels in New Zealand* and J. S. Polack's *New Zealand*, were associated with commercial interests. Polack was a British–Jewish merchant whose enterprises in the Bay of Islands were very successful, and whose journeys through remote New Zealand country describe a highly self-conscious and mock-heroic encounter between European trader and Maori. Both Wakefield and Dieffenbach[14] were connected with the New Zealand Company, whose history of promotional publication depended heavily on various kinds of travel writing intended to represent New Zealand as a place of opportunities for adventurers, settlers, farmers, scientists, businessmen and explorers. The Company's *de facto* claim to be the authority on New Zealand and its prospects also generated a steady stream of publications aimed at the intending colonist.

As the military presence and activity in New Zealand intensified, a number of travel accounts by soldiers were published in England. Focusing mainly on the adventurous aspects of an imperial soldier's life, accounts of New Zealand from a military point of view, like G. L. Mundy's *Our Antipodes* (1852), depict a relationship with Maori based on adversarial and patriarchal attitudes and engage intimately with the politics and administration of army life. Broadly speaking, military and commercial travel writing projected New Zealand as a colony in which British imperial interests were being advanced, indigenous disturbances quelled, and a stable, productive and prosperous society established.

Part of travel writing's attraction for a stay-at-home readership was its potential for sensationalism. A number of early travellers to New Zealand wrote journals or travel texts based on a way of life that was opportunist and circumstantial. New Zealand's reputation as a wild place outside the law and inhabited by cannibals attracted a white trash population described by both Charles Darwin and Joseph Hooker and denounced roundly and frequently in the *Sydney Gazette*. John Boultbee's *Journal of a Rambler*, handwritten and hand-bound in sailcloth (and subsequently edited by June Starke), describes his mobile life as a sealer and seaman among a lawless population in Bass Strait and around Stewart Island, and attributes his rambling life to a restless spirit. Boultbee's self-identification as a rover draws attention to the use of the term 'rambler' or 'rover' to describe a certain kind of undirected, opportunistic movement common in Pacific sea travel in the early part of the nineteenth century, familiar from Herman Melville's accounts of Tahiti and its sailors and beachcombers, and evident also in the writings of travellers like the artist Augustus Earle, the merchant Edward Lucett or the dilettante Edward Markham. The travelling adventurer's book typically mixes a personal narrative, often flavoured with sensational events, licentiousness and drinking, with eye-witness accounts of indigenous peoples and customs, and invariably makes an impassioned claim to truth. The boundary between travel writing and fiction, or between truth and lies, is constantly asserted by travellers with an extraordinary story to tell, or whose narrative relies on first-hand experience rather than scientific or ethnographic information. For all travel writers, but particularly the traveller/adventurers, a balance must be kept between the colourful story and the reader's credulity, which keeps the readership in the forefront – readers are addressed and imagined as a presence in the text.

The New Zealand Wars signalled an interregnum (though not a complete stop) in travellers who were not connected with the military coming to New Zealand. By the time regular travel routes were established in the 1870s, the size of the travelling population had boomed, thanks largely to the replacement of sailing ships by faster, more reliable and comfortable steamers. More tourists meant higher expectations of facilities and infrastructure, the development of an 'iconic' site route, increased pressure on the indigenous populations of key locations and the development of a cash economy, all of which are reflected in the preoccupations and reiterations of travel writing.

During the 1870s and 1880s two very distinct groups of travel writers exist. Travel writing has always been part of the repertoire of professional writers, not only professional travel writers but novelists, historians and public intellectuals, and, from the arrival of the young Charles Dilke in Hokitika in November 1866, a steady stream of professional writers – Anthony Trollope, James Anthony Froude, Constance Gordon Cumming, among others – included New Zealand on their itinerary. At the same time, the publication rose dramatically of travel books by ordinary tourists keeping a journal or writing letters for their families and publishing privately. The difference between these two groups of travellers might be expressed as the relationship between their writing and their travelling: were they travellers who wrote or writers who travelled? Almost everyone travelled the same route, encountered the same kind of experience and read other travellers' books, producing an increasingly mechanistic set of responses and attitudes about being a traveller. Points of focus and tension produce reiterated stereotypes and clichés, and an exhausted descriptive vocabulary is deployed around natural sights. What John Frow has called the 'structural role of disappointment'[15] becomes evident in many travellers' books.

As tourist numbers increase, guidebooks appear, some of which include travellers' narratives or provide chunks of descriptive writing that are recycled by travellers in their own texts. The leaking of categories of travel writing from one to another, and the recirculation of material from reader to writer, from guidebook to travel book, emphasises the centrality of print as the medium in which travel is processed, preserved, understood and given meaning. The re-distribution of travel writing and the knowledge it produces also results in increasingly fixed responses and judgements, especially about aesthetics, and all the orchestrated distinctions made by the 'West' about the non-West. Guidebooks provide the framework through which the traveller conducts his or her journey. They prompt responses, supply aesthetic discriminations and enable the traveller to make arrangements and determine a route. Consequently, the favoured routes become intractably lodged as providers of 'scenery', ethnicity and the picturesque, and overdescription of key sites such as the Pink and White Terraces becomes evident to the tourists themselves. Once a guidebook is available, travel becomes the domain of tourists, schooled to react and evaluate. Joan-Pau Rubiés has said that travel writing is a 'specifically Western discourse … organised around a vision of natural and historical diversity but also tied inextricably to universalist assumptions and aspirations'.[16] *Country of Writing* demonstrates this point in the context of a case-study of travel writing about New Zealand. The natural and historical diversity that travellers encountered in

New Zealand is always mediated through universalising practices, from systems of classification to naming of indigenous flora and fauna, and to making hierarchical discriminations about scenery, natural wonders and indigenous peoples. It is transmitted in a print culture that stored, circulated, recycled and reinforced Western formulations of knowledge about New Zealand, absorbing and appropriating the indigenous knowledge forms – as the traveller reaches for her writing desk or his weatherbeaten journal, a set of conventions and expectations kick into play. Travel writing works both to record and to process diversity. One of the most powerful tools for naturalising novelty and difference, travel writing is at the same time, and paradoxically, one of the few media for retrieving something of what it was like to be in Hokitika in 1866, or on the edge of the Pink Terrace in 1880. This book tries to show something of the landscape of print in which New Zealand was delivered to a distant readership.

CHAPTER 1

Captain Ceroni's watch

The beginning of the story

On 5 November 1809, the *Sydney Gazette*, a weekly paper six years old, reported the expected departure the next day of the vessel *Boyd*, under Captain Thompson, for the Cape of Good Hope, carrying coals, timber and cedar in logs and planks. The notice of the *Boyd*'s sailing appears at the top of page 2 as one of several apparently unrelated items of the colony's business, including a short list of commodity prices, a disclaimer about the number of skins carried by the colonial vessel *Unity* reported the week before (a 'wanton misrepresentation'), an account of the upcoming wheat harvest and a police notice of absentees, among whom are 'several Persons of very abandoned character with a preference to an idle and criminal course of life'. The notice finishes:

> By a recent arrival it is credibly reported that *Thomas Ray*, otherwise *Ratty*, who has been repeatedly advertised as an absentee under the head *Police Notice*, was some time since devoured by the natives at New Zealand, having effected his escape from hence, and afterwards deserted the vessel there to prevent his being returned hither; which the unfortunate man too late discovered must have been the inevitable consequence of his rashness.

The *Boyd* resurfaces as an item in the *Gazette* early the following year. On 10 March a letter from Alexander Berry, Supercargo of the *City of Edinburgh*, was published, having been left at Kororareka and sent to Sydney with Captain Chace in the *Ann*. It announced the

> melancholy information of the Boyd's capture by the New Zealanders under Tippahee, and the massacre of everyone on board except a boy, 2 women and a child, at a place called Whangaria, about twenty miles from the Bay of Islands.

Under 'Ship News' on 31 March 1810, the *Gazette* reported that Captain Wilkinson of the *Star* confirmed the 'melancholy' capture of the *Boyd* at the Bay of Islands and the 'atrocities attending that doleful event'.

As in previous issues of the *Gazette*, the column in which the *Boyd* item occurs is a mix of sale advertisements, price lists and various kinds of news. An item about the Governor of New South Wales, Commodore Bligh, appears in the same column as a story about a little girl who died falling in a fire, and a request for claims and demands against the Orphan and Gaol Funds. Such a flow both reveals the principal currents of interest in the colony and suggests a wash of information spilling over its many boundaries.[1] The tide of information enters by sea. Each issue of the *Gazette* carries announcements of shipping arrivals and departures, passenger lists, mail waiting to be collected and debts discharged, items offered for sale, commodity price fluctuations, and the flow of people in and out of the port and in and out of its institutions. There are also reports of small local events which suggest the many narratives of a penal and commercial colony, like the mysterious fire that afflicted His Majesty's store ship *Dromedary*, heating casks of spirits until they were nearly boiling. The story of the *Boyd* and how it was 'cut off' and blown up in New Zealand is one of these narratives, an event which puts New Zealand into the flow of news and information the colony receives, generates and recycles.

Before the *Boyd* episode there are only five references to New Zealand in the *Sydney Gazette* over six years; in 1810 there were five substantial articles, including a front-page leader. The attack on the *Boyd* brought New Zealand into focus. More importantly, as the story of the *Boyd* is told and retold over the next twenty years, it shifts emphasis and shape to serve conflicting interests. What follows is a mapping of the *Boyd* narrative as it moves out into textual history.

What happened to the *Boyd*

What happened to the *Boyd* took about three months to reach Sydney, and did so principally by way of the letter despatched by Alexander Berry to the *City of Edinburgh*'s owner, which recounts the first version of events. According to Berry, Captain Thompson had contracted with '*Tippahee*' [Te Pahi] for

> a supply of spars, the delivery of which was protracted for some days by plausible excuses; until at length the treacherous chief, who was assisted by his son *Mytye*, prevailed on Captain Thompson to send two of his boats manned to a distant part of the island under a pretext of getting the spars on board.
>
> Shortly after the departure of the boats, in one of which Captain Thompson went himself, the passengers and seamen left on board were attacked, and those on deck being prostrated, *Tippahee* with a speaking trumpet invited six seamen who had gone aloft to

'Tippahee, a New Zealand chief'
engraved by W. Archibald from
an original drawing by George
Prideaux Harris, London, 1827.
ATL A-092-007

return on deck, with a promise of security if they would cut the sails from the yards; and
being terrified into compliance, they were immediately bound hand and foot and sent
on shore for the purpose of being slaughtered and devoured, which sad destiny un-
happily fell upon them after protracted sufferings.

Tippahee was one of the few Maori names Sydney readers could be expected to
recognise, as the *Gazette* in December 1805 carried descriptions of his visit to
Sydney and reaction to what the *Gazette* called an Aboriginal war spectacle (he
was said to regard Aboriginal warfare with contempt). On the same page as
Berry's letter, the *Gazette* carried a reference to the previous week's notice of the
death of 'the Princess Atahoe, of New Zealand', who with her husband, George
Bruce, was returning home for 'the valuable purpose of collecting and cultivating
flax'. 'Princess Atahoe', or 'Mary Bruce', was Te Pahi's daughter, who had landed in
Sydney after being taken from New Zealand with her husband against their will.
No connection is made between Te Pahi and his daughter, nor is there any
reference to the quite different circumstances of their visits to Sydney; they
remain apparently unconnected narratives in the tide-like flow of the *Gazette*'s
information. The metaphor is used to suggest both the marine culture and

economy in which the story of the *Boyd* exists, and the way in which the *Gazette* as a print medium reflects it. The *Gazette* seems to scoop events from the pool available to it and report them in an unconnected and undifferentiated way, like objects randomly floating in on the tide, brought there by ocean currents of displacement, colonisation, commerce, opportunism and punishment.

On 21 April 1810, the *Gazette* published on its front page the full text of a letter signed by Simeon Pattison, Master of the *City of Edinburgh*, Alexander Berry and James Russell, the Mate. It opened with a warning to all masters of ships frequenting New Zealand not to admit many natives on board, 'as they may be cut off in a moment by surprise' (made possible by the fact that all ships carried boarding nets).[2] A longer account of the *Boyd* events follows, with Te Pahi remaining at the centre of hostilities, plus further detail of the visit made by the *City of Edinburgh* to Whangaroa after the attack and the names of those who were rescued. The letter finishes by noting that

> the natives of the spar district in this harbour have behaved well, even beyond expectation, and seemed much concerned on account of this unfortunate event, & dreading the displeasure of KING GEORGE have requested certificates of their good conduct, in order to exempt them from his vengeance, but let no man after this trust a *New Zealander*. We further certify that we gave *Terra*, the bearer of this, a small flat bottomed boat as a reward for his good conduct, and the assistance of getting us a cargo of spars.

A postscript by William Swain, of the *Cumberland*, states that 'Terra behaved very well, and all his tribe, for that reason I gave him several gallons of oil.'

The glimpse here of how Maori perceived the power of documents to negotiate their relationship to a rapidly changing world denotes a shift of balance towards what D. F. McKenzie called 'text-led European imperialism',[3] perhaps the most significant European cultural intervention in Maori life. The perceived superiority of a written over an oral culture to document truth is evidenced on both sides of the Tasman and the racial/cultural divide: a warning certificate to shipping is distributed through the *Gazette*, and the good conduct certificate is requested by Maori in the Bay of Islands in the expectation that it will assert the protective authority of a foreign written language against the incursions of a foreign and punitive military power.

Berry's letter and his attribution of a significant role in the *Boyd* episode to Te Pahi resulted in speedy retribution, reported in the following *Gazette*. On hearing of the attack, the captains of the *Perseverance, Speke, Diana, Inspector* and *Atalanta* took a party of seamen and sacked Te Puna, Te Pahi's island pa, during which it is reported that a seaman belonging to the *Inspector* was killed, and about eighteen 'natives'. Lieutenant Finucane of the *Experiment* commanded the party with equal spirit and forbearance, not permitting a single discharge to take place that was not actually necessary to the resistance of assault, and the conduct of the party was highly applauded by the Colonel [Foveaux], who bestowed on Lieutenant Finucane, the Captains and their people, the most satisfactory Eulogiums.

Consolidating the case against Te Pahi, the *Gazette* reports a passenger from the *Perseverance* claiming he had breakfasted on board the *Boyd* with Captain Thompson the very morning of the attack.

It was only about four months before Te Pahi's role in the destruction of the *Boyd* was revised, but exoneration came too late. His death was reported by Captain Samuel Chace in the *Gazette* of 25 August, together with the death of his son and destruction of his village, a destruction comfortably glossed for *Gazette* readers as the loss of 'a number of miserable huts into which the people crawl on their hands and knees'.

But the *Gazette* wasn't finished with the *Boyd*. The following issue carried another account, 'The Destruction of the Boyd', derived from Captain Chace, who said he got it from an 'Otaheitan' (Tahitian) in New Zealand, who 'as an *alien*, not being interested on the part of either the Bay of Islands or of the *Whangarooans*, may still more be entitled to credit'. This new account, purportedly derived from an eyewitness occupying the middle ground (with the authenticity of a native who is not a native) begins with motivation. The four or five New Zealanders, including 'George' [Te Aara], carried by the *Boyd* are said to have been displeased at their treatment on the voyage from Port Jackson and determined on revenge. The story continues:

On their arrival they communicated their complaints to their friends and relatives, who were of the *Whangarooa* party, and frequently at war with *Tippahee* and his subjects; and the design of taking the ship was formed in consequence. It being Captain Thompson's intention to take in a quantity of spars, he applied to the natives for assistance in procuring them, which they promised, but in order to entice him on shore, artfully objected to perform until he should accompany them to point out such as he might best approve. The Captain was thereby prevailed on to leave the vessel, accompanied by his chief officer, with three boats manned, to get the spars on board, the natives who had arrived in the ship being of the party, which was accompanied by a number of others in their canoes. The boats were conducted to a river, on entering which they were out of sight of the ship; and after proceeding some distance up, Capt. Thomson was invited to land and mark the spars he wanted. The boats landed accordingly, the tide being then beginning to ebb, and the crews following to assist in the work. The guides led the party through various parts of the wood that were least likely to answer the desired end, thus delaying the premeditated attack until the boats should be left by the effluence of the tide sufficiently high to prevent an escape; which part of the horrible plan accomplished, they

Front page of *The Sydney Gazette and New South Wales Advertiser*, 1 September 1810.
ATL B-K-503-FRONT

became insolent and rude, ironically pointing at decayed fragments, and enquiring of Captain Thompson whether they would suit his purpose or not? The natives belonging to the ship then first threw off the mask, and in opprobrious terms upbraided Captain Thompson with their maltreatment; informing him at the same time that he should have no spars there but what he could procure himself. The Captain appeared careless of the disappointment, and with his people turned towards the boats; at which instant they were assaulted with clubs and axes, which the assailants had till then concealed under their dresses, and although the boats' crews had several muskets, yet so impetuous was the attack, that every man was prostrated before one could be used. Captain Thompson and his unfortunate men were all murdered on the spot, and their bodies were afterwards devoured by the murderers, who, clothing themselves with their apparel, launched the boats at dusk the same evening, and proceeded towards the ship, which they had determined also to attack.

In Chace's report, the drama of the *Boyd* has moved from an event produced by 'treachery', consistent with an understanding of 'native' and 'savage', to take

on features of a formal narrative, with suggested motivation, dramatic recon-
struction of the principal scenes and a revenge plot, authenticated by being
filtered through a third party whose ethnicity and speech validate him as a
mediator between the opposing groups. The point of view is interesting. Captain
Chace's account is said to have been received from a Tahitian, and its detail
suggests that it was derived from firsthand accounts (which presumably were
Maori, as all the Europeans were killed), but it is recycled through a European
point of view. Who is commenting that the 'natives threw off the mask' and on
the 'opprobrious' terms in which they upbraided the captain? In its progression
from oral reports in Maori and 'Otaheitan' English to the front page of the
Sydney Gazette, the story has been dramatised and re-imagined from a British
point of view. The 'Otaheitan', known as 'Tom',[4] was later said by Alexander
Berry to have been a deserter from the *City of Edinburgh* on an earlier trip to
New Zealand. Berry describes him as 'a great favourite on board' who 'rendered
considerable service' from speaking both English and 'the New Zealand language
which is a dialect of his own'. Tom is all but invisible behind Chace's report, but
there is a drama in the narrative, missing from Berry's account, which conveys
the presence of Maori as agents in the landscape, displaying a superior knowledge

'Enlèvement du Boyd par les Nouveaux-Zealandais.' Engraving by Louis Auguste de Sainson,
Paris, 1839. ATL PUBL-0034-2-390

of the terrain and an ability to use it strategically, with a comprehensible motive for retaliation and, in pointing ironically at decayed fragments of trees, sophisticated social behaviour.

By the end of 1810, the *Boyd* has appeared eight times in the *Gazette*, twice on the front page, and is the only continuing narrative about New Zealand to circulate among a Sydney readership. As a narrative and a location, New Zealand had taken a place in the commodity market that was the *Gazette* – both news-as-commodity and commodity news. In this context, if you imagine the faint, written over but not quite extinguished Maori point of view on these events, there is a shadowed inversion of New Zealand as a location of commodities. A place where you go to fetch cargoes of spars and seals, which had been its principal textual presence in Sydney, and by inference the parent culture, might also be seen as a place in which commodities arrive. Is the *Boyd* episode a story about savages, treachery and massacre, or an opportunity to possess the ship's cargo and human freight, as well as take revenge for humiliation and maltreatment? As Greg Dening has observed about Tahiti, the question is who possessed whom?[5]

The versions of the *Boyd* which have come to us preserved in the fragile yet enduring medium of print dramatise the Maori as participants in a story which shifts, under pressure from competing European interests, from a dark landscape of savagery and inexplicable 'treachery' to an act of barbaric yet understandable reprisal. By the end of 1810, the story of the *Boyd* exists in two versions through several mouths, neither of which speaks directly for eyewitnesses but implies their reporting presence, at least suggesting another viewpoint from which the story can be told. In the pages of the *Gazette*, the story of the *Boyd* opens a window on a place where something has happened that has to be taken account of. It changes the narrative of British imperialism and colonisation, brings New Zealand into the regular flow of information, and dramatises it as a destination, a 'place'.[6]

The destruction of the *Boyd* became the general referent in the *Sydney Gazette* for any shipping casualty or report of cannibalism in New Zealand, and goes on being mentioned until the 1830s.

The circulation of the story

In 1810 a broadsheet appeared in London entitled 'A Short Account of the most cruel and barbarous Murder of Thirty British Subjects, belonging to the ship Boyd, from Botany Bay, by Savages of New Zealand, who afterwards brutally devoured them'. The broadsheet 'reluctantly' recounts the 'cruel and shocking vices which exist among some savage tribes and nations'. A perfunctory account of the *Boyd*, which claims the ship had put into New Zealand 'in distress', is

Broadsheet from the Fildes
Collection, Miscellaneous 1.

J.C. BEAGLEHOLE ROOM, VICTORIA
UNIVERSITY LIBRARY, VUW

followed by a potted history of allegedly cannibalistic occasions from Tasman
to Cook and the *Adventure* in 1773, when those who went to look for the missing
crew members are said to have

> witnessed the most horrid spectacle ever seen by any European – the heads, hearts, livers
> and lights of their own people broiling on the fire, and their bowels lying at some dis-
> tance, with several of their hands and limbs in a mangled condition, some broiled and
> some raw, but no other parts of their bodies, from which it appeared that the cannibals
> had feasted and eaten all the rest.

The broadsheet circles back home with the reflection that cannibalism has not
been unknown in the reader's own country. Quoting Gibbon, it notes that a
'valiant tribe of Caledonia' was accused by an 'eyewitness' of delighting in the
taste of human flesh.

> If in the neighbourhood of the commercial and literary town of Glasgow a race of
> cannibals has really existed we may contemplate, in the period of Scottish history, the
> opposite extremes of savage and uncivilized . . .[and] encourage the pleasing hope, that
> New Zealand may produce, in some future age, the Hume of the Southern Hemisphere.

Though its evident purpose is to sensationalise cannibalism, the broadsheet also naturalises the prospect of civilisation in New Zealand, bringing it both into Western history and as close as the Scottish border. Little is known about this broadsheet. It carries no imprint and only the name of the printer, though Ferguson's *Bibliography of Australia* records this and another broadsheet with the short title 'Cut off Ship Horrible Massacre!' published in the same year, which suggests the episode was a hot news item in London. Anne Salmond notes another broadsheet, 'Atrocious and Horrible Massacree' [*sic*], which reprints Berry's warning letter published in the *Gazette* in 1810 and finishes with a ballad about the *Boyd*, which Salmond says was 'circulated to sailors'.[7]

For the serious reader, an account of the *Boyd* appeared in 1811 in *The Philanthropist or Repository for Hints and Suggestions Calculated to Promote the Comfort and Happiness of Man*. *The Philanthropist* includes articles on the abolition of the slave trade, the civilisation of Africa, the treatment of the poor and vaccine inoculation in Mexico. It prefaces Chace's version of events, taken from the *Sydney Gazette* of 1 September 1810, with the comment that this account

> corrects the first details of this dreadful affair, which laid the blame upon a chief of that
> country, of the name of Tippahee, whom we are glad now to see fully exonerated from the
> base charge of cruelty and ingratitude; and lays it upon the conduct of the captain of the
> vessel towards some New Zealanders, who had acted as seamen aboard the ship.[8]

The owner of the *Boyd*, George Brown, was the brother-in-law of the Edinburgh publisher Archibald Constable, who published a letter from Berry in the *Edinburgh Review* and eventually in the fourth volume of Constable's *Miscellany* of 1827,[9] which bore the title *Adventures of British Seamen in the Southern Ocean displaying the Striking Contrasts which the Human Character Exhibits in An Uncivilized State*. As in *The Philanthropist*, the events surrounding the *Boyd* have become part of British anthropological, ethnographical and ethical discourse. Berry's 'Particulars of the Destruction of a British Vessel on the Coast of New Zealand' is substantially a letter he wrote from the *City of Edinburgh* at Lima in October 1810, amplified with a preface and his further recollections written ten years later. The preface refutes theories of the noble savage ('savage man has been found not only stained with all the crimes to which the most highly civilized society is incident, but abandoned to a fury and frenzy of passion'), glances briefly at exploration history and comments on the 'uncouth' names of the islands of New Zealand. It then focuses on Cook's account of 'the most savage race known in the world' – 'in almost every cove where Captain Cook touched, he found human bones lying near large fires' – though Cook's favourable reports of the domestic conduct of the Maori are also mentioned. Retrospectively, the preface establishes a sensationalist context for Berry's story of the *Boyd* which glosses 'savage' and pictures the place where savages live as covered with human bones.

Berry's longer version of the *Boyd* events in the letter from Lima is an account of his own actions rather than the warning to shipping that went to Sydney on the *Ann*. He says that, on hearing reports from natives of a ship being taken at Whangaroa, he determined to go there in spite of the danger. At the second attempt they were successful:

> We had this time better weather and reached the harbour without any difficulty. Wangeroa is formed as follows: First, a large outer bay, with an island at its entrance. In the bottom of this bay is seen a narrow opening, which appears terminated at the distance of a quarter of a mile, but, upon entering it, it is seen to expand into two large basins, at least as secure as any of the docks on the banks of the Thames, and capable of containing (I think) the whole British navy.[10]

Berry's depiction of the harbour as a future scene of British naval power retrospectively cancels the vulnerability of the *Boyd* and prospectively claims maritime protection for British ships.

> We found the wreck of the *Boyd* in shoal water at the top of the harbour, a most melancholy picture of wanton mischief. The natives had cut her cables and towed her up the harbour, till she had grounded, and then set her on fire, and burnt her to the water's edge. In her hold were seen the remains of the cargo; coals, salted seal skins, and planks. Her guns, iron, standards, &c. were lying on the top, having fallen in when the decks were consumed . . . Not to tire you with the minutiae of the business, I recovered from the natives a woman, two children and a boy by the name of Davies, one of your apprentices, who were the only survivors. I found also the accompanying papers . . .[11]

Berry's account to George Brown of what happened represents the *Boyd*'s captain as having been 'rather too hasty in resenting some slight theft', and has Te Pahi as the principal instigator because, along with a great many other Maori, he went aboard the *Boyd* and 'begged a little bread for his men; but the captain received him rather slightingly, and desired him to go away, and not trouble him at present as he was busy'. Berry concentrates on what he was told by the survivors of how they escaped and the horrid sights they saw (most of which are 'too shocking for description'), and he has no other explanation for what happened than Captain Thompson's treatment of Te Pahi. His account is focused on the viewpoint of a ship's owner and his own relation to events, including a wish to delimit his motivations:

> I think it is likely that I will receive little thanks for this ample detail of such a melancholy business; but I assure you it has been very unpleasant for me to write it; and I could only have been induced to do it from a sense of duty, and a desire to give you all the information in my power . . .[12]

However, Berry's letter is followed in the *Miscellany* by 'additional particulars' communicated at Constable's request – some profit was to flow from the loss of the *Boyd*. These 'particulars' include a prehistory of the events of 1808-9, especially the story of Te Pahi's voyage to Port Jackson (Sydney) with Captain Ceroni (or Ceronci) of the *Commerce*. At this point a completely different context and narrative viewpoint for what happened to the *Boyd* surfaces.

In May or June 1808 Captain Ceroni, master of a sealing vessel, called in at Te Puna in the Bay of Islands. Te Pahi persuaded Ceroni to take him to Sydney to visit his friends (how deliciously the prospect of international social life for Maori opens here), and first to go to Whangaroa, where he said the stores were much more abundant than in the Bay of Islands, which was exhausted from the continual visits of whalers. From his own account, Berry says, Ceroni was

> equally pleased with the harbour, the natives and their chief. As the natives of this district had then little knowledge of Europeans, many trifling articles in common use were to them equal objects of wonder and curiosity. A watch, however, was so much beyond their comprehension that they to a man agreed in calling it Etua (or God). Ceronci, proud of possessing an object of so much veneration, used to embrace every opportunity of displaying his Etua. In one of those vainglorious exhibitions, the redoubted Etua dropt into the water, to no small terror of the natives. Shortly after this unfortunate occurrence, he left the harbour, but, for some reasons best known to himself, he departed during the night, and without taking leave, which confirmed the natives in their opinion that he had done them an irreparable injury by leaving his Etua behind as a demon of destruction. Shortly afterwards, a violent epidemic took place amongst them, which carried off great numbers, and amongst others, their adored Kytoke. This they attributed to the devouring spirit left amongst them, and the survivors vowed revenge against the white men, the supposed authors of their calamity.[13]

The careless Captain Ceroni turns up again in Berry's narrative as a passenger in a voyage by the *City of Edinburgh* to the Bay of Islands in 1809, during which friendly relations were established with Tara and Tupi, the local chiefs at Kororareka, and successful commercial transactions took place. Having extensively praised Tara and Tupi and their friends, Berry continues:

During our first stay in New Zealand, we heard nothing of the story of Ceronci's watch. On leaving the harbour however, with all our friends on board, with a singular fatality, he again dropt a second watch overboard. The venerable Tarra, who was near him wrung his hands and uttered a shriek of distress, exclaiming, that Ceronci would be the destruction of the Bay of Islands as he had already been of Wangeroa.... On our second return to New Zealand Ceronci was not on board. As our intentions were to load with spars, we again determined to give the preference to Wangeroa. On approaching the land our intentions became known to the New Zealanders on board. They immediately came in a body and requested we would desist, detailing at great length the history of the watch, and when they found we were determined, they even burst into tears.[14]

In the event, the wind compelled the *City of Edinburgh* to enter the Bay of Islands, where, with a half-loaded ship, they learned about the *Boyd*.

The story of the *Boyd* as it filters through from the *Sydney Gazette* to Constable's *Miscellany* gathers layers, contexts and complications. As the sources of information widen and another (Maori) point of view is implied, so the story broadens out from the initial tabloid headline, atrocity and massacre, to a narrative with dramatic actions and interactions, historical determinism, internal tribal politics, vested commercial interests and cultural imperatives. The instability of the narrative reveals the difficulty of comprehending, assimilating and detoxifying such a story, and the contrary desires and impulses it embodies. Similar stories about Maori cannibalism and their treatment of Europeans had reached the wider world before. The murder of Marion du Fresne in 1772 is a well-known example, and throwaway paragraphs such as the *Sydney Gazette*'s reference on 5 November 1809 to the supposed fate of Ratty in New Zealand indicate that the association of murder and cannibalism with New Zealand was relatively commonplace. The fact that the possible devouring of a police absentee by the natives of New Zealand is a peripheral event in the pages of the *Gazette* suggests that, from Sydney in 1809, New Zealand is a transgressive but little-known and unimportant place, controlled by distance and an appropriately retributive boundary marker: the Maori reputation for cannibalism. Rats who leave sinking ships are asking for trouble. As the story of the *Boyd* unfolds, a sharper, more particular and more disturbing focus on New Zealand develops. From being a place which marked the broken edges of control, confirming the boundaries of the developing penal colony, and existing in the minds of Sydney merchants (if they thought of it at all) as an opportunity for commerce in profitable but irregular transactions, New Zealand has claimed an active role and disclosed itself as retaliatory and damaging.

There is a noticeable shift in emphasis and a redramatising of the story of the *Boyd* over the several versions provided by Alexander Berry, the reports from Captain Chace and other published accounts. While the 'massacre of the *Boyd*'

A view in Whangaroa Harbour, 13 November 1841. Pencil and watercolour by Richard Taylor.
ATL E-296-Q-021-2.

(to use the description which achieved the widest circulation) remained a marker of atrocity in broadsheets and similar precursors of the tabloid press, other accounts redescribe it in more acceptable terms, notably by attributing blame to the European Captain Thompson, and relocate it in a discourse that to an extent rehabilitates the dark events too shocking to describe, the tradition of the revenge narrative.

The particulars of the story

In Alexander Berry's 'particulars', written ten years later, much greater attention is paid to the Maori, and several people appear who were not present in the earlier version, especially his trading partners, Tara and Tupi, from the Bay of Islands. Berry's previous acquaintance with Te Pahi and his relations with the local community are recounted and contextualised, as are the local tribal politics. He reports getting lots of advice from local Maori who refused to go with him to Whangaroa to investigate, saying 'such a thing would infallibly embroil them with the natives of Wangeroa'. Berry didn't have enough muskets, so he borrowed all those of Tara and Tupi; and after his first aborted attempt to go to Whangaroa, he returned to find Tupi and Tara had 'come on board for the safety of the ship'. Berry's own politics were strategic. He used the incident of the deserting

'Otaheitan', Tom, to accuse a local chief and established friend, 'Metenangha', of deliberately enticing sailors to desert, and succeeded in coercing him to go to Whangaroa as proof of his honour. Berry's dealings with the chiefs at Whangaroa were facilitated, and perhaps made possible even, by 'Metenangha'. On their arrival they were met by chiefs dressed in canvas from the *Boyd*.

> The conversation soon turned upon the capture of the ship, which, far from avoiding, they delighted to dwell upon, evidently regarding it as a most heroic exploit, in the same way as a party of British tars look back with pleasure to some successful attempt against an enemy's ship of superior force. They readily mentioned the name of the ship and captain, the number of men and guns. I then asked the reason of the attack, 'Because,' they replied, 'the captain was a bad man.' On inquiring what he had done, they answered, that one of their chiefs having secreted the carpenter's axe beneath his clothes, the theft was detected before he left the ship, in consequence of which, the captain tied him to the capstan, where he kept him for several hours, and threatened to flog him. On my remarking that the conduct of the chief merited the treatment he received, they replied, that any indignity offered to a chief was never forgotten.[15]

Berry traded the survivors, who were being kept prisoner, for axes and muskets and, in a show of strength, compelled one of the Whangaroa chiefs to get into his boat and guide them up a 'winding tide river, so narrow as hardly to leave room for a boat to turn' between low banks covered in mangroves.

> On our passage up, the natives, concealed among the mangroves, saluted us with their muskets, whether with a view to honour our arrival and celebrate their reconciliation with the white man, or to convince us that they were as well armed as ourselves, I did not know.[16]

Invited to stay the night, Berry, 'though perfectly assured of my own safety and the firm friendship of Metenangha and his friends', still 'thought it preferable to sleep with our own men on a small island near the remains of the *Boyd*'.

> I had so much confidence in Metenangha and Towaaki that I believed we might have accepted their invitation to sleep in the midst of the natives with safety; but as there was nothing to gain by such a step, I thought it unwise to incur any risk. On the other hand we had just examined the miserable remains of the Boyd; we had seen the mangled fragments and fresh bones of our countrymen, with the marks even of the teeth remaining upon them; and it certainly could not be agreeable to pass the night by the side of their de-vourers. The island where we took up our abode for the night was a small perpendicular rock, where we could have defended ourselves against any number of New Zealanders.[17]

In these later 'particulars' Berry's recollections of his visit to Whangaroa have complex nuances. For the first time he appears to 'see' the physical location, though the landscape he sees is dense with strategic and tactical signs: the winding river too narrow for turning, the peopled and sounding mangroves, the defensive island. In describing his conversation with the chiefs, Berry's figure of speech recasts their action, if not as an exculpation, at least in the familiar terms of military exploit: they are like a 'party of British tars'. The simplicities of 'the captain was a bad man' offer a view behind the more brutal simplicity of the event which overtook him. Both Berry's conversation with the Maori and his overt bullying reveal the cultural imperatives at work in his treatment of them. He figuratively includes the massacre of the *Boyd* in British maritime warfare, 'naturalising' it as a scene of contest, while in his indiscriminate bullying of friend and foe he emphasises a boundary of race and forces a recognition of strength. However, the vulnerability of his position, again a question of race and strength, is acknowledged in the choice of a perpendicular rock on which to spend the night.

Boyd effects

The *Calcutta Gazette* carried Berry's letter of October 1810 in its supplement of 21 March 1811, adding the detail that Thomas Davison, a survivor, 'owed the preservation of his life to his being club-footed, the natives taking him for a son of the devil!'[18] A direct result of the attack on the *Boyd* was the delay in the arrival of Samuel Marsden and the missionary presence in New Zealand.[19] When Marsden did arrive in 1814, he directed much of his initial effort to travelling to Whangaroa and confirming a version of the *Boyd* that exonerated Te Pahi, whom he had known in Sydney. Marsden's letters and J. L. Nicholas's account of their meeting and discussion at Whangaroa supply an 'other' – Maori – explanatory viewpoint on the massacre of the *Boyd*. Before the civilising presence of the mission can be established, the story of the *Boyd* is re-examined and explained.

The *Boyd* and its effects are present throughout Nicholas's narrative of his travels in New Zealand during 1814 and 1815. Everywhere he goes he keeps an eye out for evidence of the *Boyd* and finds it in the dispersal of objects from the ship through the wider Maori community – dollars hung around the necks of Maori at Whangaroa and also at Bream Bay, the letter Berry left at the Bay of Islands warning ships about Te Pahi, a fragment of a letter addressed to Captain Thompson, given to Marsden at Waitangi, and at Te Puna, Te Pahi's destroyed village, a substantial iron object

> technically termed a knee, taken from the Boyd; and as it could be of no possible use to the natives, and as the trouble of bringing it thither must have been very great, I should suppose their motive in removing it was to sell it to any of the ships that might enter the harbour.[20]

The attention paid by both Marsden and Nicholas to the *Boyd* reveals an anxiety about the event that marks it off from previous European encounters with Maori, and from other casual references to the practice of cannibalism in New Zealand. In Nicholas's account of the visit he made with Samuel Marsden to Whangaroa in 1814, the two men accepted an invitation to spend the night and 'feared not to close our eyes in the very centre of cannibals'. Marsden's description of the visit, in the *Missionary Register* for November 1816, comments:

> I viewed our present situation with sensations and feelings that I cannot express – surrounded by cannibals who had massacred and devoured our countrymen, I wondered much at the mysteries of Providence, and how these things could be! Never did I behold the blessed advantages of civilization in a more grateful light than now![21]

But once the smoke of Berry's accusations against Te Pahi cleared, most reporting visitors, from Nicholas on, were concerned to represent the *Boyd* as the product of Captain Thompson's bad judgement, understand the Maori motivation and construct an explicable moral landscape.

> We wished to learn, if possible, from the tribe of Wangeroa, that which had so cruelly cut off the Boyd, some details respecting that horrid catastrophe, and the motives that impelled them to it.[22]

Turnbull's *Voyage Round the World*

The earliest account of the *Boyd* to appear in a book, one often referred to as a source by later writers, was the appendix to the second edition of John Turnbull's *A Voyage Round the World* (1813). Turnbull was Supercargo on the *Margaret*, which undertook a speculative commercial voyage around the Pacific between 1800 and 1804. He wrote an account of the voyage and descriptions of the countries he visited for 'the amusement and information of his private friends', but was soon persuaded to 'lay them before the public'. The appendix, which gives 'some account' of New Zealand, was added for the second edition. Turnbull's interest in the *Boyd*, which he describes as a 'melancholy fatality, over which humanity mourns', is generated because it interrupted the 'active and friendly intercourse' taking place between Port Jackson and New Zealand, based on the movement of the whale and seal fishery from New South Wales to New Zealand when the Australian coast was fished out. According to Turnbull, these early ships found the Maori were hostile only if provoked. For Turnbull, the important contexts to the attack on the *Boyd* are the visit Te Pahi made to Sydney, which he recounts in full from the *Gazette*, and the abduction of Te Pahi's daughter and her husband by Captain Dalrymple of the *General Wellesley*. Te Pahi was known for his 'kind offices' to South Seas whalers and, as the most important chief at the Bay of Islands, was treated to gubernatorial hospitality, like a visiting head of state, on his trip to Port Jackson. Maori expressed anxiety about the treatment of indigenous peoples by the British, perhaps as a result of information gathered on Te Pahi's visit to Port Jackson, supplemented by the traffic between the Bay of Islands and Sydney in later years.[23] Turnbull reports that Te Pahi was sent home in a ship specially fitted out by the governor, but took sick on the voyage. A young man from the ship's company was ordered to wait on him, which he did so well that Te Pahi asked that he be left with him. The young man, George Bruce, remained in New Zealand when the ship sailed, and became perhaps the first Pakeha Maori. He learned to speak Maori, was tattooed, and married Te Pahi's daughter, Atahoe, who became known as 'Mary Bruce'. Turnbull's source for the subsequent story of George Bruce is attributed to 'the Calcutta journals', which related 'in substance' the 'afflicting narrative'.

Turnbull makes no direct comment on the events of the *Boyd*, but is concerned to combat the representation of the New Zealanders as a barbarous people by telling stories which suggest otherwise. We must 'indulge our hope' that the 'patient benevolence of our countrymen' will restore the interrupted intercourse which both promised the 'civilization of a so large a country' and 'opened a market'. What New Zealand needs are a few 'honest and industrious artificers' who would soon animate all the 'hidden energies of the soil and climate', although, Turnbull warns, reverting to moral philosophy, 'human policy should ever be united to sound morality and genuine philanthropy'. Beyond these pious utterances, Turnbull doesn't allude to any coercive or persuasive process that might bring the Maori into accord with his grand visions. The connection between his projection of the valuable place New Zealand might become and the problems that lurk under the surface of his plans is shadowed when he finishes with a speculative fantasy about the things 'Mary Bruce' ('Princess Atahoe') might tell her countrymen about Calcutta if God allowed her to return to New Zealand. The list is striking for its sequence, which imaginatively follows the astounded stare of the listening New Zealanders and brings them, detail by detail, from wonder and desire to an instructive conclusion. The

> height and magnitude of the houses and their interior splendour, the magnificence and majesty of some of its inhabitants, the richness of the country, the money lying in heaps in the streets, the costliness and variety of the goods in the shops, the deliciousness of the fruits, the tremendous size of the animals, as big as a New Zealand house, the great number of English ladies seen on the esplanade in their curricles, carriages, palanquins, &c., Fort William, with its astonishing ramparts, its great guns, its innumerable soldiers, will make the New Zealanders stare with astonishment.[24]

Atahoe died in Sydney on her way home and was unable to tell her countrymen of the wonders in store for them. Turnbull's version of the *Boyd* episode is skimpy, and implicitly accepts Berry's assertion of Te Pahi's guilty participation, but works to position the attack in an ameliorating context of previous wrongs and good behaviour, and moves quickly forward from that into a vision of what New Zealand could become. It is a kind of letter of instruction for his country-men about their objectives, their morality in relation to the Maori and the process of seduction whereby everything can be achieved, in which the *Boyd* is represented as an unwelcome and atypical event.

The *Boyd* as melodrama

In 1845 a pamphlet was published in England which featured the attack on the *Boyd* (a massacre by cannibals) as the leading item among the stories it adver-tised: 'John Williams, a runaway convict at Norfolk Island', John Crossland, the Derby hangman who 'executed his own brother and father', and 'Ravillac, who assassinated King Henry the fourth of France'.[25] These narratives embody a fetish-ised and exoticised culture of punishment and violent death, shifting between what happened to a British ship in foreign waters and events sanctioned or pro-duced by institutionalised procedures. What is suggested by the *Boyd*'s inclusion in this list of stories?

The differences in circumstances, motivation and geography in these inci-dents are overridden by what they share: all are transgressions against law or custom, which confirm the powerful presence of discipline and punishment. The *Boyd* is headlined and distinguished from the other examples by being geograph-ically remote and accompanied by various representations and artefacts – the story is 'embellished with a representation of the real head of Watangheon, the principal murderer, and a frontispiece copied from the grand painting exhibited in the Royal Liverpool Museum' – which turn it into something between a curio and an exhibit. The incorporation of the story of the *Boyd* into a publication aimed at the ever-hungry market for sensational and murderous events also neatly suggests an appropriate retribution. The transgressor becomes a commod-ity, and an event that occurred outside the boundaries of European prohibition is brought by association into a familiar social and cultural context, where the limits of transgression are predetermined – that is, they happen in relation to the law. The pamphlet's depiction of the events of the *Boyd*, which is grossly inaccurate and ignorant of geography and anthropology,[26] represents the crudest version of the world-as-exhibition,[27] reduced to a one-dimensional picture.

Similarly, the pamphlet's brief written account, 'The Narrative of the Boyd', reduces the episode to sensationalism and crude melodrama: 'At length all was silent – murder had been committed by wholesale, and the murderers were

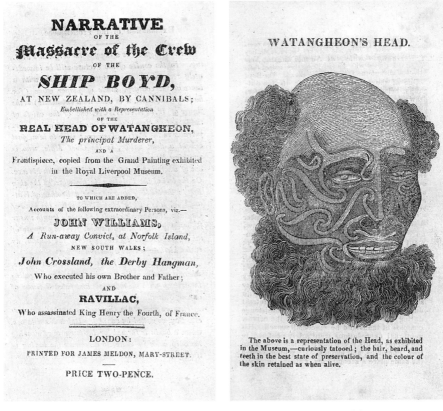

From 'Narrative of the massacre of the crew of the ship Boyd', London: J. Meldon, ca 1845, p.3 (left) and p.7 (right). ATL B-K-108-003; ATL B-K-108-007

weary of their labour!' It also claims to recount the fate of 'Watangheon', who, enticed on board a vessel twelve months after the massacre, 'became outrageous . . . and attacked every person who came near him. At length it was found necessary to dispatch him', whereupon the two others taken with him preserved his head 'by a process peculiar to the natives of New Zealand'. These events are entirely at odds with any account like Marsden's of what happened, but poetic justice is achieved.

Readers and the *Boyd*

Alexander Berry made one last visit in print to the site of the *Boyd* not long before he died, at an advanced age and in possession of considerable wealth, in Sydney. In his *Reminiscences,* published in Sydney in 1912, he gives a much-reduced account of the affair of the *Boyd,* and says simply that he resolved to visit Whangaroa and on arrival found a large ship lying in shallow water, burnt to the water's edge – and the bones of the crew lying over the beach. By the assistance of Metenangha, I succeeded in recovering the few survivors . . . & the duplicates of bills and other documents which I had left with Mr Lord for transmission to England. . . . Thus my enterprise was not a mere quixotic adventure to save distressed damsels from the hands of giants and ogres, but was attended by very beneficial consequences to myself.[28]

So much for massacre, murder and destruction. A hundred years later the story is lodged between fairytale and good business practice.

As the *Boyd* develops into a major topic and location for travellers who are trying to understand and typify something about New Zealand, the transactions implied by its frequent appearance in print over almost 200 years are part of a cultural process. In this process, which connects travel writing, imperialism and colonisation, peoples, events and places are transmitted by print and filtered through narrative. Incomplete, overlapping, revised, reviewed, the story of the *Boyd* grows into a cultural history and a textual landscape – volatile, moulded and eroded by the pressure of competing discourses, narratives and interests, as powerful as glaciation or deforestation.

In its complicated retellings, the massacre of the *Boyd* marks the beginning of the colonisation of New Zealand in texts, continuing the impetus of 'text-led European imperialism' established in the publications relating to Cook's voyages. An event which registers first on the front pages of the *Sydney Gazette*, and is then recycled in broadsheets, pamphlets, miscellanies and travel accounts, takes its place among the newsworthy events of the world and, scoring whole chapters to itself in nineteenth- and early-twentieth-century histories of New Zealand, has begun a process which brings the unfamiliar into discourse. Before the *Boyd*, New Zealand appeared in the *Gazette* as the Bay of Islands, scene of the flax, spar and seal trade, outfitter to whalers, convenient outpost for spillage from the penal colony. After the *Boyd*, New Zealand was no longer a way-station between fixed points on the map. A location somewhere off the edge of major trade routes and regularised social and penal codes, where anything might occur and often did, it became characterised by an event whose scale and breaking of social prohibition required an effort to comprehend and assimilate. Among other things, what the New Zealanders did in burning the *Boyd* and killing and eating its passengers and crew was *reply* to the opportunistic and punitive behaviour of a frontier society.

Before 1810 New Zealand's marginality is amply illustrated in its comparative invisibility in the *Sydney Gazette*. But, like Captain Ceroni's watch dropped into the waters of Whangaroa harbour, an event which seemed of little consequence to its perpetrator but was of far-reaching personal and symbolic significance to the culture into which it had so carelessly been let fall, the *Boyd* episode was the splash which signalled a weight shifting, whose ripples spread outwards across the Tasman to London, a displacement charted in print for at least forty years. When Marsden wonders at the mysteries of Providence while surrounded by cannibals, and publishes his wonderings in the *Missionary Register*, he brings the physical space of New Zealand into textual space and into Western Judaeo-Christian discourse. The 'grateful light' of civilisation illuminates a dark landscape of murder, cannibalism, exploitation and cultural conflict, revealing a missionary and his companion waking at dawn to see 'an immense number of human beings, men, women and children, some half naked, and others loaded with fantastic finery . . . stretched about me in every direction … the warriors with their spears stuck in the ground, and their other weapons lying beside them'.[29] The conquest of New Zealand has figuratively occurred.

CHAPTER 2

Adventures of the printer

One Friday morning in November 1841, thirty-year-old William Colenso, printer for the Church Missionary Society at Paihia, embarked on a little vessel bound for Poverty Bay. It was not his first journey outside the Bay of Islands; with other missionaries he had been on several trips over the northern peninsula and to the East Coast in 1838.[1] But it was his most ambitious attempt to travel through the country he had settled in, and became his most successful botanical journey. From his landing-point at Hick's Bay near East Cape, he walked south to Poverty Bay, across country to Waikaremoana and on to Rotorua, Matamata, the Waikato river, Manukau in Auckland, the Kaipara and back across the peninsula to the Bay of Islands. It took him just over three months.[2] During his trip he collected almost a thousand botanical specimens and forwarded 600 of them to Sir William Jackson Hooker at the Royal Botanic Gardens of Kew. In 1844 his account of this journey was published in the London *Journal of Botany* (edited by Hooker) as the 'Journal of a Naturalist in some little known parts of New Zealand'. Later in the same year a slightly modified version was printed in Launceston as a pamphlet, *Excursion in the Northern Island of New Zealand in the summer of 1841–2*, and a year later in the *Tasmanian Journal of Natural Science.*

Colenso's published accounts of his journey make no mention of the missionary activities which were the reason for his travels, focusing entirely on his role as a botanist and explorer. His story conforms to the conventions, purposes and practices of what Mary Louise Pratt has described as 'one of Europe's proudest and most conspicuous instruments of expansion, the international scientific expedition'.[3] Colenso's trip around the East Coast and inland through country previously untravelled by Europeans is not only presented primarily as a botanical expedition, but also employs many of the set-pieces and conventional tropes of exploration narratives. In his text Colenso stands somewhere between Mungo Park and Joseph Banks, surveying the landscape from the heights of the Ruahine ranges with all the possessiveness of a new monarch, and walking with his eyes on the ground ready to pluck out another plant to send to Kew.

In a paper read to the Hawke's Bay Philosophical Institute in 1887 and later published as 'Ancient Tide Lore and Tales of the Sea from The Two Ends of the World', Colenso recalled his early travels on the East Coast. Alone on a sea beach in the 'exceeding stillness' of a New Zealand night, he identified with a group of men whose exploits and writing shaped and were shaped by the powerful outward pressure of European expansion. Colenso identified with them as a sentimental hero, whose solitary presence in a place remote from Europe imprinted on it deep traditions of Western sensibility, gathering it into the broad transforming stream of Western intellectual and print culture.

> Sometimes, on such occasions, – in such moments of utter loneliness – standing on the beach, the only person there, with the whole expanse of Hawke's Bay before me, – I have been led to think of the famed African traveller Mungo Park, and of the death of the Explorer Capt. Clapperton in the African desert, and his burial in the sand by his faithful and only surviving attendant the young Cornishman, Lander, whom I also knew; – for Lander too, had 'stood alone!'[4]

In a footnote to this paragraph, Colenso observed that when young he read

> (devoured!) diligently and repeatedly every work on African travel I could obtain – from those of Bruce and Mungo Park downwards; these later ones of Major Denham and Captain Clapperton (then fresh) were causing a kind of stir in the world. All such had a wonderful influence over me, amounting to fascination! I had very nearly devoted myself to carry on that enquiry-research in Central Africa.[5]

Work, work, work

William Colenso first arrived in New Zealand on 30 December 1834, having just turned twenty-three. Less than two months later, he pulled the proofs of the first book to be printed in New Zealand, William Williams's translation of the Epistles of St Paul to the Philippians and the Ephesians, and began in earnest his epic labours on the press: 'I may say that for years I never knew a day of rest: Sunday and weekdays, day and night, it was work, work, work'.[6]

A year after Colenso's arrival at Paihia, the Bay of Islands was visited by the first of several scientific expeditions to call in at New Zealand in the early years of European settlement: the voyage of the *Beagle*, carrying Charles Darwin.[7] These expeditions extended what Pratt has called the web of imperial meaning-making: complicated and interdependent intersections of exploration, colonisation, production and dissemination of knowledge which were advanced through scientific societies, missionary societies, readerships, explorers, collectors, administrators and developers. Colenso's skills, beliefs and interests involved him in some of the most significant areas, in both knowledge and executive power, of nineteenth-century imperialism: literacy, religion, exploration and science. His own reading of exploration narratives and his ambition to distinguish himself as a naturalist shape his accounts of travel in New Zealand, and reflect his wish to delineate himself in terms which establish a claim to authority less problematic than his actual status as a printer, lay missionary and dissenter in a High Church Anglican mission.[8]

Darwin was the first of several important naturalists Colenso encountered in New Zealand. Allan Cunningham, the Colonial Botanist of New South Wales, visited for three months in 1838 and made several excursions around the Bay of Islands, some of them in Colenso's company. Colenso corresponded with him, sending botanical specimens, until Cunningham's premature death a year later. Lady Jane Franklin visited briefly with her husband in 1841, though her activity was constrained by a sprained ankle,[9] and sent Colenso a botanical microscope. On his trip around East Cape a year later, he named a fern after her. The most important connection for him was Joseph Dalton Hooker, son of Sir William Hooker, who visited on his way to the Antarctic on the *Erebus*, under the command of Captain James Ross, in 1841. Darwin and Joseph Hooker, close friends, colleagues and collaborators, between them transformed the natural sciences. Hooker's expeditions to Antarctica, India and South America, and his succession as Director of the Royal Botanic Gardens of Kew after the death of his father, made the Kew collections a primary site of botanical knowledge for the planet. This knowledge he used to formulate his theories of plant distribution, as well as transforming the gardens of suburban England by introducing new ornamental plants from distant parts of the world, most notably rhododendrons from his expedition to Sikkim in the late 1840s. The 1848 guide to Kew Gardens included as its epigraph verses extolling 'Imperial Kew . . . enthroned in vegetable pride', centre of a universe from which 'Obedient sails from realms unfurrow'd bring/For her the unnamed progeny of Spring'.[10]

Colenso was one of innumerable correspondents sending specimens and seeds to Kew. David Mackay has identified 126 collectors working in the non-European world up to 1820 who sent specimens to Joseph Banks,[11] and this number increased with the expansion of Kew Gardens under William Hooker. In the preface to his *Kew Gardens*, Hooker appealed to

> travellers or merchants who hold intercourse with various parts of the globe, and who would gladly contribute to this great national collection. Brief instructions may be had of the Director . . . Large though our stores assuredly are, there yet remains much to be obtained from almost every distant part of the world.[12]

Colenso, who accompanied Joseph Hooker on several of his New Zealand botanical excursions, and who corresponded with him for fifty years, became an ardent contributor to the Kew herbaria. He owned an annotated copy of William Hooker's teaching text, *Botanical Illustrations*, given to him by the author, and addressed his first important account of his botanical discoveries to Hooker. It is hard to open a page of Joseph Hooker's *Handbook of the New Zealand Flora* without Colenso's name on it. When Joseph Hooker first visited Colenso at Paihia, on 19 August 1841, he saw in the sitting room 'a portrait of poor Allan Cunningham and a pretty Zinc tree in a bottle, as also some of my Father's botanical works on a table'.[13]

The network between scientists, explorers and commerce in the eighteenth and nineteenth centuries makes it clear how expansive and concerted their efforts were. William Hooker was a protégé of Joseph Banks, as was Mungo Park. One of Hooker's purposes in establishing the Kew herbaria, which collected and renamed the plants of the world in a global, European-centred taxonomy, was to establish a 'collection of interesting and economic vegetable substances . . . In a short time this will constitute a highly important feature of the Gardens'.[14] The Museum of Economic Botany was an important feature of Kew by the mid-1850s. One of Park's objectives as he made his arduous way towards the Niger in the 1790s was to note useful plants and trading opportunities. His brother-in-law, James Dickson, was a distinguished botanist and one of the founders of the Linnaean Society, and Park's *Travels in . . . Africa*, one of the best-selling books of the nineteenth century, is full of botanical descriptions and identification of African plants, later recalled by Major Dixon Denham as he comes across trees he recognises from Park's descriptions.[15] When Denham met the Sultan of 'Sackatoo' in 1824, after an arduous journey from Kano in present-day Nigeria, they had

> a long conversation about Europe . . . He asked me to send him, from England, some Arabic books and a map of the world. He also spoke of the gold and silver to be obtained in the hills of Yacoba and Adamowa; but I assured him that we were less anxious about gold mines than the establishment of commerce, and the extension of science.[16]

The extension of science and the establishment of commerce are the objectives of exploration journeys. Mary Louise Pratt has described the exploration literature mentioned by Colenso as 'anti-conquest narratives', literature which underwrote colonial expansion while avoiding the rhetoric of subjugation. Personal adventure and experience – what Pratt calls the 'narcissism of the sentimental' – characterise the explorer as he makes his way through the landscape and through the complex and obscure negotiations of European expansionism with African and Islamic politics.[17] Denham describes his entry into Sockna with loving attention to his clothing.

> I rode on his right hand dressed in my British uniform, with loose Turkish trousers, a red turban, red boots, with a white burnouse over all. This, though not strictly according to order, was by no means an unbecoming dress.[18]

Some subtle shifts of attitude occur with Colenso. He is the intellectual product of Romanticism, a missionary, and he is dealing with an indigenous people who were generally willing to receive his teachings and accommodate his presence. The hostility encountered by Park and Denham in Moorish Africa is very different from the contact zone of Maori and European. Colenso's progress through Maori country negotiates tribal differences and territories within a single cultural entity; nevertheless, to adapt a point about perception made by Peter Beilharz, while difference is fundamental, humans think through similarity.[19] Colenso's perception of landscape was heavily influenced by the European literary tradition of landscape writing and by his passion for exploration. Denis Walker, drawing on Edward Said, calls Colenso's way of describing the natural world he travelled through as his 'textualised vision'.[20] Colenso's drive to document and contextualise what he saw and experienced projects shared cultural expectations, and lays claim to the prestige of being the first European to record that journey. In some important ways, Colenso's travel narratives of the 1840s reproduce the exploration narratives he devoured in his youth.[21]

Plant epiphanies

One of the best-known episodes of Mungo Park's journey, featured as the title page illustration of the 1860 edition of *Travels in the interior districts of Africa*, was just after he had been plundered by a group of bandits in a wood. Having stripped him of all his possessions, most of his clothes and his horse, the bandits left Park in a state of

> amazement and terror . . . I saw myself in the midst of a vast wilderness in the depth of the rainy season, naked and alone . . . I considered my fate as certain and that I had no alternative but to lie down and perish . . . At this moment, painful as my reflections were, the extraordinary beauty of a small moss in fructification, irresistibly caught my eye . . . Can that being (thought I) who planted, watered and brought to perfection, in this obscure part of the world, a thing which appears of small importance, look with unconcern upon the situation and sufferings of creatures formed after his own image?[22]

Park's moment of epiphany conquers despair, and he travels on to encounter some friendly shepherds with whom he arrives safely at sunset in the town of 'Sibidooloo'.

When Colenso arrives at Hick's Bay in the evening of Monday, 22 November 1841 at the outset of his journey, and is landed on shore through the breakers, he finds that in the rush he has left on board the disappearing vessel his package of specimen paper. Night is closing in and he is exhausted after three days of sea sickness, but just before the light goes he notices, growing on the sand hills near the shore, a 'small shrubby plant with fleshy leaves and erect succulent stems . . . a species of Euphrasia . . . that species having been found in similar situations a little further south, by Sir Jos. Banks in 1769'.[23]

According to Pratt, arrival scenes are a 'convention of almost every variety of travel writing and serve as particularly potent sites for framing relations of contact and setting the terms of its representation'.[24] Colenso's arrival at Hick's Bay in 1841 is framed as a naturalist's – his gaze is concentrated on the departing ship carrying the specimen papers, and then on the ground in front of him. His moment of naturalist's epiphany, while not exactly comparable with Park's, is in the same mode. Arriving at a place of physical deprivation, solitude and alienation, he regroups by focusing on a detail of the natural world. In Park's case the sight of the moss prompts him to invoke the protective structure of belief systems that re-establish his own place and role in the landscape, his existential purpose. In Colenso's a small shrubby plant is a sign of his arrival as a botanist, and allows him to establish precedent by invoking Joseph Banks, representative of the botanical systems, institutions and patrons which validate Colenso's presence, at night, cold, wet, sick and alone, on an alien shore. It is the signature moment of the explorer/traveller.

'William Colenso, botanist-printer.' Photolithograph of scraperboard illustration by George Woods, ca 1945. ATL E-205-Q-017

Two of Colenso's published accounts of the 1841 journey vary a little in their detail. In the pamphlet *Excursion in the Northern Island of New Zealand*, Colenso's appearance on shore is met by '[S]everal natives [who] ran down to see the foreigner who had so unceremoniously landed on their shores, by whom I was conducted to their village of miserable hovels among the sand hills'.[25] In the version Colenso sent to William Hooker, there is no one present but himself, and he appears to spend the night on the beach.

As published, the 'Journal of a Naturalist' is contextualised by Hooker's preface, which introduces both Colenso and New Zealand to the scientific network and the larger European metropolitan public, and sets the terms in which they are to be read – terms which are mostly taken from an article by Allan Cunningham published by Hooker in the *Companion to the Botanical Magazine*. New Zealand has been the subject of 'lively interest' since the publication of Cook's *Voyages*. Despite a large increase in colonisation, it is still 'very much a sealed country' to the naturalist. The focus of attention is on pulling aside the veil so tantalisingly described in this quotation from Cunningham:

> . . . when we glance at the map and perceive its snowy peaks, and especially that of Mount Egmont on the immediate western coast, the apex of which towers 14,000 feet above the ocean, whose waves wash its base, the upper part from the peak downwards to the extent of 5000 feet being clothed with eternal snows; in fine when we reflect upon the fact that (excepting at its northern shore in Cook's Strait and at Dusky Bay on its south western coast) the Botany of the large or middle island is, to this day, veiled from our knowledge, we cannot but exclaim at the rich store of vegetable productions which yet remains to be laid before us![26]

In Colenso's accounts of his journey, the Maori with whom he travels, whose knowledge of the country and its routes enables him to move through it and whose provision of food keeps him alive, are mostly contained within the explorer/indigene frame so familiar from African exploration narratives: unnamed natives who service the explorer's needs. If anything, Colenso's 'natives' are even less differentiated and personalised than Park's. However, there are moments when the anxieties and sentiments of an explorer pursuing a journey through alien terrain and among a possibly hostile people break through Colenso's self-representation as the meticulous man of science in an objectivised landscape dotted only with specimens. The landscape he travels through is generally described in visual and analytic language, but occasionally he raises his head from the ground and reflects on his situation, or takes in a wider view and becomes conscious of himself in ways that complicate the simple conversion of 'nature' into 'natural history'. The landscape presents him with various obstacles. It is steep, exposed, and hard work. As he pitches his tent at Te Pito, a few days into his journey around East Cape, pouring rain makes him 'glad enough to obtain shelter anywhere', but the wider prospect that opens for a moment is too vast and comfortless to be looked at for long:

> ... in our present position, on the side of a very steep hill quite open to the South Pacific which rolled its immeasurable billows to our feet, both shelter and food were anything but obtainable.[27]

Pelion on Ossa

One of the set-pieces of the exploration narrative has been called by Pratt the 'monarch of all I survey scene . . . a brand of verbal painting' which produced for the home audience the 'peak moments at which geographical discoveries were "won" for England'.[28] At such moments the explorer, who has found his way with the help and knowledge of the local people, proceeds to discover what they already know. Written in the 1840s, Colenso's work is not in the later tradition of British exploration writing which featured extended descriptions from viewpoints, like Richard Burton's famous and detailed first sight of Lake Tanganyika in the 1860s. But his presence as the observer, the traveller in visual command above a spread-out landscape, the perspective through which the reader sees the 'sealed country' of New Zealand, is established at several points in his narrative.

After leaving Kaupapa, William Williams's mission station at Poverty Bay, Colenso rises early one morning and, on gaining the summit of the hill before him,

> had an extensive view of the interior. Hill rose on hill, Pelion on Ossa, in continuous succession as far as the eye could reach. To the left was Wakapunake, an immense table topped hill, or rather mountain; while far away in the distance to the right, a peculiarly precipitous mountain cast its bold outline in fine relief into the sky: this my native guide informed me was Waikare, to which we were going. Time however would not permit a lengthened gaze; so, descending the hill, we proceeded onwards.[29]

A day or so before this Virgilian view of piled hills, Colenso has had a prospect of Poverty Bay 'with its romantic headlands'. This prospect, for a different reason, is also cut short.

> The atmosphere . . . was so filled with smoke arising from the fern which was burning furiously to windward, that it was only with difficulty that I discovered a single distant object.[30]

In both scenes, Colenso has an expansive moment of looking outwards and casting himself in the mould of contemplative possessor of the scene before him, a mode of descriptive writing common since the Romantics and known as 'promontory description'. Yet something cuts off his gaze as if it must not be allowed to linger. When he is looking towards Poverty Bay, his ability to see is curtailed by the rising smoke which veils the country, and keeps it veiled. It is only in the restricted space of a small stream in a desolate wild valley where he stops for the night that he begins to see again, and spot the tufts of *Epilobium* growing among the fern.[31] A few days later, when he reaches the summit of the hill and looks inland to see spread before him 'Pelion on Ossa' (Virgil's phrase – by way of Cowper – to describe a rugged terrain), the landscape is at once recast into indigenous geography by his – unnamed – native guide, who names the principal peaks. As if this has caused some anxiety to Colenso, he stops looking out and proceeds downhill. He is rewarded by some interesting specimens as he goes, one of which, a *Coriaria*, is 'disputing for possession of the soil with those very common occupiers Pteris esculenta and Leptospermum scoparium'.[32] Colenso names the new plant after his 'much respected friend, Capt. P. P. King, R.N.', one of the recent cohort of friends and colleagues introduced by Allan Cunningham.

Into the Mahometan Elysium

After lunching on roast potatoes at Hopekoko, a small stream, Colenso and his party arrive at a

> small cataract, down which the water fell perpendicularly about twenty feet into a deep and dark basin. The only ford at this place was on the very slippery edge of the fall . . . over which I was obliged to be carried, for I dared not trust my own footing on that perilous and uncertain path, which forcibly reminded me of the bridge to the Mahometan Elysium. As it was I very nearly fell, through nervous excitement, into the gloomy depth below.[33]

As Colenso travelled further from the mission station at Poverty Bay, he turned inland towards Waikaremoana and Rotorua on a route he claimed no European had traversed before. Within the constraints of his objectives as a naturalist, his account of the landscape starts to reflect some of his apprehensions about what he is doing. Descending into a terrain which has become darker and more dangerous, it reminds him 'forcibly' of 'the bridge to the Mahometan Elysium'. On that perilous and uncertain path his physical powers fail him, and like the dead he is carried into the country of the infidel, where through nervous excitement he 'nearly falls'. Colenso's language has shifted here from objectivist listing of botanical characteristics and identification of species to personal experience and adventure, and makes his situation and emotions the focal point and point of meaning in the landscape. His reference to the 'Mahometan Elysium' links back to the paradigm of African exploration narratives and to the history of European Orientalism, engaged in conflict with the perennially ambiguous figure of the infidel. The landscape he crosses, including its plant cover 'disputing for possession', is described in language that suggests a potent mix of contesting ideologies, possessions and emotions. There is also a lot of boundary and threshold imagery, climaxing with the image of crossing a perilous ford on the slippery edge of a waterfall.

When Mungo Park arrived in Benown, residence of the most powerful local Moorish potentate, Ali, the Moors at first took great interest in the unfamiliar sight of a Christian. Park entertained them for a whole afternoon taking off and putting on his clothes to show how they worked. The interest, however, soon turned to insults and teasing. Park reflected:

> I was a stranger, I was unprotected and I was a Christian; each of these circumstances is sufficient to drive every spark of humanity from the heart of a Moor; but when all of them as in my case, were combined in the same person, and a suspicion prevailed withal that I had come as a spy into the country, the reader will easily imagine that, in such a situation, I had everything to fear.[34]

He was kept prisoner for several months in increasing deprivation and abjection.

Colenso's entry into the country inland of Poverty Bay is reminiscent of Park's experiences in Moorish Africa. His gesture towards the Mahometan Elysium sets the frame of reference for his arrival at villages on the way to Waikaremoana. He is entering country where he is a stranger, unprotected and a Christian. His first stop, Te Reinga, is reassuring. Beside a large waterfall, Colenso finds the roar of the waters soothing as well as solemn. His day opens with prayers and breakfast, and his visit to the 'exceedingly romantic' waterfall is described at length. Part of the reassurance comes from the way the waterfall scenery accommodates itself to pictorial and aesthetic conventions.[35]

> The waters fell from rock to rock ... several times, ere they were swallowed up in the dark eddying gulph below. The deep gloom of the river in the gorge beneath, the different hues of the dense masses of foliage on either side, the sunbeams peering downwards through the tops of the trees, the enormous bed of rock above, white as snow, with the natives who accompanied me perched here and there upon the same, and the little village in the back-ground, contributed to give the whole an enchanting effect. In the height of the fall only was I disappointed. I attempted a hurried sketch, but could not do the scene justice. In fact, I had too many things upon my hands at once, consequently I did nothing well. I wished, afterwards, when it was too late, that I had remained a day at this place, instead of pressing on, post-haste, in the manner I did.[36]

'Te Reinga Falls, near Gisborne, N.Z.' Pastel drawing by Edward Roper Sandys, ca 1888.
ATL C-075-013

Again Colenso's experience is at the centre of the scene. From his perspective the village and the natives look tiny and enchanting, and they become part of what is clearly a scene from a Romantic landscape – each feature falls into place as part of an aesthetic effect. Colenso also figures himself here in doubt and regret, fleshing out for a moment (very much in the manner of Park, who constantly apologises to his readers for his decisions about whether to go on or turn back) the mixed, erratic, anti-heroic, emotional country in which any journey takes place, even one as sternly focused on its task as that of a naturalist.

The journey of the scientist is increasingly pressured by the adventures and anxieties of the explorer as Colenso journeys inland, and the country he is travelling in and the people who inhabit it become more and more difficult to separate as he approaches Lake Waikaremoana.

Fern all round

With his unnumbered 'guides and Baggage bearers' he heads upriver on a very hot day into steep hills covered with fern, gaining 'nothing new in the whole of this melting day's horrid march; fern, fern, nothing but dry, dusty fern all round!' As they progress into the interior it becomes increasingly barren, the vegetation scanty and stunted, the soil dry and dusty, the hills denuded by winds so strong no person could keep their footing in a southerly, the plant specimens diseased. Arriving at the Waikaretaheke, a rapid stream exiting from the lake, they find a bridge of trees 'thrown across the foaming torrent' – another boundary – which, though strongly secured together,

> seemed as if every rush of the bounding water would have carried it away. A nervous person would not have hazarded himself on such a vibrating and precarious footing.[37]

Colenso's experience at Waikaremoana is figured as an imprisonment. Arriving at the village of Onepoto, he finds the gateway 'embellished with a pair of huge and hideous clumsily carved figures, besmeared with red pigment and grinning defiance on all comers'. The wind blows so strongly it is not possible to cross the lake, and he finds it hard to pitch his tent owing to the 'great unevenness' of the ground: 'Here I was confined a prisoner until the morning of the 29th, when, the wind lessening, I effected my escape, crossing in safety to the opposite shore.'

Several displacements occur in this scene. Although Colenso arrives in a party, there seems to be no one present but him. The village is no more than a gateway, near which Colenso pitches his tent, and the 'huge and hideous figures' show no sign of their makers, or the community they guard. The landscape is so unpeopled in his text it might as well be empty, except that it is full of signs of presence. It is this empty landscape, replete with natural hostility, which imprisons him, enacting what the phantom people only represent in their carved figures. The 'natives' reappear only when Colenso has turned his attention back to botany, and then solely to provide information about the fruiting of the ta'wai, which Colenso discounts.

Father Baty

A blank in Colenso's published narrative, a space which like the unpeopled landscape is thick with presence, is his meeting with Father Baty at Onepoto. Father Baty had landed at Mahia with Bishop Pompallier on 30 September 1841, intending to stay on for a few weeks after Pompallier's departure for Akaroa. The murder of Father Chanel at Futuna diverted the mission schooner to the Pacific, however, and it was almost a year before Father Baty returned to the Bay of Islands.[38] He occupied his time travelling and working in the area, and as Colenso advanced on Waikaremoana he learned that he was preceded by a Catholic priest, who was ahead of him by a few hours and on his way to visit the same villages.

In his journal, copied and sent to the CMS, Colenso heightens the drama of the encounter by anticipating the day before that 'I should be obliged to hold a controversy with this man', and as he crosses the Waikaretaheke on the native bridge, moving towards his controversy with Father Baty, he again invokes 'a nervous person' who 'could not have dared to attempt the crossing over it, although perfectly safe'. Arriving at Onepoto, Colenso was met outside the pa by 'a young Chief with New Testament in his hand', who told him that Father Baty and his large party of Maori from Hawke's Bay were inside the pa and asked Colenso to pitch his own tent outside the stockade. The following day, Christmas Eve, Colenso found the Maori from Hawke's Bay 'about 20 in number decorated with Crucifixes and Medals and looking anything but sweetly on me' in the chief's house. When he began talking to them, 'remarking on their tokens', they sent for Father Baty and the conversation was transformed into a

> discussion on the peculiar doctrines of the R. Church . . . in Native which lasted for 3 hours . . . The Natives got weary of listening, and drew off, on which we entered into conversation (in English) on some of the most prominent of the Doctrines of the Ch. of Rome; which occupied more than an hour.[39]

The next day, as Colenso was preparing to leave, for there was not enough food at the pa to support all the visitors, he sent one of his Maori companions, 'Abraham', to ask for a pig. Father Baty got his own back for all Colenso's observations about black robes, crucifixes and images by remarking that missionaries cannot live without pork.

Colenso's omission of the encounter with Father Baty from both the 'Journey of a Naturalist' and *Excursion in the Northern Island of New Zealand* can be explained by the simple editing of non-botanical material. His published text does, however, leave the distinct impression that Colenso is not only the lone European present in a landscape and human environment repeatedly figured as hostile and alien, but also that he is the first European traveller to go on that route, when in fact he is the second, even if only by a few hours. Colenso's heroicising narrative explicitly draws attention to his exploits by invoking a nervous person who could not do what he is doing, and implicitly to his ideological and professional position. The black-robed priest is doubly effaced, first by Colenso's geographical reference to the 'Mahometan Elysium', which gives a very different picture of what he might have encountered, and second by the 'huge and hideous' carved figures over the gateway to the pa. Both these references point the reader to the links between difference in belief and 'civilisation'. In his journal Colenso dramatises the doctrinal issues that surface in his meeting with Father Baty, and these are the substance of his reporting to the CMS, but the drama of his botanical and adventure narrative is so closely modelled on exploration narratives, especially those of African explorers, that his actual encounter with the doctrinal difference of the Catholic priest disappears from his account in favour of a far more ambiguous set of references that connect the possibility of a Muslim with an image of Maori as savages. The different parties of Maori who follow the Roman or the Anglican way vanish from the published text as if the Maori can be present only in certain strictly defined and confined roles – as guides and baggage bearers, as the invisible component of Colenso's 'we', as nameless groups who complete tasks for him, like climbing trees for flowers or producing food or providing canoes.

The aspects of his situation that produce anxiety are invested in the physical landscape, in his reflections about what a nervous person might do, or in depicting an effect of the weather as an imprisonment in a defiantly non-European environment. When he is diverted from his botanical work, the landscape he sees represents other strands of the web of imperial meaning-making: artefacts whose clumsy execution denotes savagery equally with what they represent; waterfalls and lakes and gorges and headlands which make Colenso reach for his sketch-pad in recognition of an aesthetic response; or long stretches of the featureless country encountered by every imperial traveller who cannot discern there the marks of his cultural interest.[40] If what you want to see is not visible, nothing is visible. It is not until he is about to leave Waikaremoana, having already escaped across the lake, that Colenso refers to the Maori at the pa, a reference that supports and continues his chosen self-dramatisation. He sees some wonderful tree ferns, *Dicksonia* with especially long fronds, and half-wishes he could stay longer.

> Had I not been very anxious to prosecute my journey I might have spent an agreeable time at this romantic spot; such, however was not the case. I was among a tribe noted for their reckless ferocity; to whom, secluded as they are in their mountain retreats, a white man was indeed a stranger.[41]

Learning from Maori

Yet it is apparent throughout Colenso's narrative how much he is hearing and learning from Maori. 'Journal of a Naturalist' differs quite markedly in this respect from *Excursion in the Northern Island of New Zealand* and Colenso's much later pamphlet, *My First Visit to Lake Waikare*. In the 'Journal' Maori are an anonymous collectivity. Occasionally Colenso reports their speech, as when they tell him the ta'wai doesn't always fruit when other trees do, a piece of botanical knowledge he discounts, but he never reports their names. His transactions with them are hidden in the verb 'obtained' – he obtains canoes, guides (with difficulty) and provisions just as he obtains specimens of plants or shellfish – and whenever he arrives somewhere the 'we' of arrival slides quickly into the 'I' of presence. The *Excursion*, however, is a much ampler narrative, and includes more of the adventure of travel. In it Maori are still mostly unnamed, being referred to

'Asplenium.' Herbert Boucher Dobie;
from *New Zealand Ferns* by
Marguerite Crookes, 1963, p.337.

collectively as 'the natives' or 'my natives'. They behave in ways that do not conform to European codes, and most of the time are simply invisible. By including
more of his non-botanical experience, however, Colenso suggests much more
about a Maori landscape, Maori knowledge systems and Maori history.

Take fern. Colenso is disheartened by the hills of fern he treks through on the
way to Waikaremoana. There are no new plants and his interest in fern is
confined to the discovery of new species which can be numbered and sent to
Kew. But when he records the response of the Maori as they emerge from dense
bush onto a ferny plain near Ruatahuna, a response not recorded in the 'Journal',
a different perception of the landscape appears:

> Towards evening we emerged from the dense forests, in which we had for some days been
> confined, to a large plain covered with fern, the first fern we had seen for several days.
> My natives rejoiced at the sight, vociferating loudly their being privileged to see a 'koraha
> maori' . . . again! Their uncontrolled joy forcibly reminded me of the rejoicing of the 'ten
> thousand' Greeks on their again seeing the sea.[42]

Again Colenso is 'forcibly reminded', just as he was of the 'Mahometan Elysium',
but this recollection invokes a prospect of civilisation for Maori, for his figure
identifies them with European history, not with an enemy of Europe. It is quite

clear that Colenso is in dialogue with them, however lightly this is represented in his narrative.

Oh, Solitude!

The next day, he climbs to the summit of a hill above the Whirinaki to look at the view:

> an extensive plain extended E. and W. as far as the eye could reach; beyond which a chain of lofty table-topped mountains bounded the range of vision. Here, notwithstanding the pleasurable height to which my imagination had been raised whilst engaged in contemplating the magnificence and extent of the prospect before me, it soon sank below its ordinary level, on finding that not a human being dwelt in all that immense tract of country on which my eager gaze rested! The grass grew, the flowers blossomed, and the river rolled, but not for man! Solitude all!! Even the very little birds, few though they were in number, seemed to think with me; for they flew from spray to spray around and about my path with their melancholy 'twit twit' as if wishing to have all they possibly could of the company of a passer-by. Their actions were quite in unison with my feelings, and I could but exclaim – 'Oh Solitude where are thy charms?' etc. Descending to the banks of the river Wirinaki, I was rewarded with the discovery of a few new plants.[43]

This has become an intensely personalised landscape. Here is Colenso, on mission work, one of a small group of people, looking at the magnificent view of the volcanic plain, suddenly struck by his aloneness, a stranger in an alien land. His response is highly textual and literary. He adopts a Romantic pose, his language takes on a poetic syntax, the natural scene is in sympathy with his emotions, and he quotes William Cowper. His apprehension is converted into a rhetoric that would be instantly recognisable to his readership: man and nature straight back to Adam.

The line of verse that comes to Colenso on the hill above the Whirinaki is interesting. The full text is:

> I am monarch of all I survey,
>   My right there is none to dispute;
> From the centre all round to the sea
>   I am lord of the fowl and the brute.
> Oh, solitude! where are the charms
>   That sages have seen in thy face?
> Better dwell in the midst of alarms
>   Than reign in this horrible place.

These are Cowper's 'Verses supposed to be written by Alexander Selkirk', whose famous account of his trials and adventures on Juan Fernandez became the basis for Defoe's *Robinson Crusoe*. In the 1850s the New Zealand government commissioned and published translations into Maori of *Robinson Crusoe*, along with Bunyan's *Pilgrim's Progress*.[44]

The flip side to the 'monarch of all I survey' experience is loneliness, a common feature of exploration narratives. This kind of solitude does not recognise the presence of others because they are 'natives', and its emotional effect depends on the assumption that there is no dispute about possession of the territory in view. How did Colenso know there was no human being in all that 'immense tract of country'? Who identified the peaks for him? Who showed him the route? The hard information in this passage is geographical, and must have come to Colenso from one of his companions. His personal response is entirely learned. He responds as a highly literate European whose attitudes are shaped by the intellectual and print cultures of his time, and who is able to ignore his actual social circumstances to the extent that the people he is with, and who are informing him, vanish from the scene, their history reduced to names of geographical features, and their culture, their country, overlaid with the apprehended solitude of one white man. In all these ways Colenso reproduces the narrative conventions of the exploration literature of his time, and reflects the prevailing expansionist and imperialist attitudes which drive both the physical journeys and their representation in print culture.

The runaway guide

A later episode emphasises the gap between Colenso's expectations of Maori and their behaviour towards him. Throughout the 'Journal' and the *Excursion* he seems to take it for granted that Maori will carry his bags, guide him and supply food, even though he refers to the difficulty of persuading people to leave their villages and accompany him. Just as the plants exist to be admired and become specimens, catalogued and numbered in a system that takes no account of their indigenous names or ordering, Maori exist only in relation to him. On the last day of 1841, deep in the sodden bush with almost no food left, Colenso wakes with 'the rain still incessant and our cold, wet, lonely and all but starving situation was anything but pleasant; when, as if we wanted somewhat more to taste of the very acme of cheerlessness, our only guide deserted us, returning to Waikare'. The guide had intimated as much the evening before and Colenso had a watch kept over him, but he had 'easily' found an opportunity of leaving. Shivering in his summer clothing and holding an old umbrella over his head to keep the rain off, Colenso and his remaining Maori, who were all from other parts of the country and had no more idea of the route than he did, resolved to proceed on their journey regardless – 'a determination to which we were compelled through hunger, having consumed our last scanty meal'.

About noon the next day the 'runaway guide' overtook them, 'bearing a large basket of fine potatoes on his shoulders, for which he had purposely gone back all the way to Waikare . . .'. Triggered by this event, Colenso embarks on another 'standard apparatus of travel writing',[45] the ethnographic portrait.

> I could not but applaud the man's kind consideration, whilst I disapproved of his leaving us in the manner he did, without saying a syllable as to the object of his returning. This, however is quite in keeping with the national character of the New Zealander. Prompted incessantly by an ever-restless and indomitably independent principle of doing some capricious work of supererogation, their defined duties are left unperformed, they often sadly try to the utmost the patience of those by whom they are employed. In their own language they have a word (pokonoa), which, while it fully conveys the force and meaning of the foregoing remark, is, from the frequency of the occurrence of such behaviour, in daily if not hourly use by every native of New Zealand. Nor is this capricious way of acting confined to those who are still in their novitiate; on the contrary, those who may have been for years in your employ are equally, if not more prone to such conduct.[46]

The kind act of Colenso's guide in returning over difficult ground in terrible weather to fetch food for his distressed party becomes the occasion for Colenso to homogenise the guide's behaviour into a collective 'they', describing the employment relationship between Europeans and Maori. The guide's kindness is transformed into a 'capricious act of supererogation' characterising the way in which Maori collectively default on their 'defined duties'.

Colenso's reference to the Maori word 'pokonoa' suggests that this behaviour is characteristic of Maori and links Maori and European cultural practice as normative, as if Maori too have expectations of performance based on an employment contract. H.W. Williams's *A Dictionary of the Maori Language* (1971), the seventh edition of William Williams's epic work of 1844, defines *poka noa* as 'do anything at random or without authority'. Certainly the guide's departure was without European authority: Colenso was not asked for permission and explicitly did not give it. But was it random and was it without Maori authority? The guide's perception of crisis must have been due partly to Maori ideas about hospitality and responsibility to guests, which included provision of food for travellers through tribal lands, and his departure, far from being a random wish to abandon them, was a response to extremity. Colenso's response is to override his initial recognition of the guide's kindness and consideration (a recognition that carries an involuntary negative, 'I could not but applaud'), to reassert the primary relationship between explorer/traveller and native – the servant who is not worthy of his hire and whose own cultural practices, far from being acknowledged or investigated, inconveniently disrupt the legitimate expectations of European authority.

The guide's absence, Colenso's own hunger, incessant rain and the distress of his companions are not permitted to interrupt his botanising – among other discoveries he finds a large climbing fern which he dedicates 'in memory of that very zealous botanist, my much lamented friend, the late Allan Cunningham Esq'. Colenso's denial of coevalness to the Maori is seen also in his botanic praxis. Natives are always a poor second to plants in his apprehension of a landscape, a landscape which is quickly distinguished with markers of the botanist's presence. As he progresses through the pelting rain, removing interesting specimens from their mossy beds to his cloak, he displaces the Maori as proprietors and inhabitants and literally and cognitively pushes forward the expanding frontier of Euro-imperialism, reordering, renaming, rewriting.

The botanist's frailties

Problems with departing guides recur in 'Journal of a Naturalist'. Guides are in a different category from the Maori accompanying Colenso, though he is not specific about who these are, referring to them always in the collective and possessive: 'Whilst my natives were pitching my tent, I obtained a few specimens of Jungermannia.' Guides are locals who know the surrounding country and landmarks, and presumably have their own reasons for travelling with Colenso or are bound by cultural or financial obligations. It is clear that parties of Maori are moving around the country on their own business. After crossing the inner harbour at Tauranga and heading inland, Colenso and his party

> bivouacked for the night by the side of a small stream where we were incessantly tormented with mosquitoes; and to add to our misery, my guides returned sans cérémonie, leaving my baggage in the desolate wild; through which conduct we were obliged to remain supperless, not having had any food since our early breakfast. The next morning, after some delay from our want of guides, who were eventually obtained from a party of natives in the neighbourhood, we again proceeded . . .[47]

In the 'Journal' Colenso's dependence on Maori knowledge and labour and the nature of his transactions with them are recorded but lightly passed over, along with other physical irritations like the multitudes of mosquitoes and lack of food, in the interests of an objectivist account of his botanical discoveries.

There is, however, a clear trajectory in Colenso's narrative which follows his progress inland. As his journey wears on and wears him down, his relations with Maori become more fractured, the conditions worse and the food very scanty. Fatigue and confusions about the route increase, there are fewer plants 'worth noticing', and the labour of gathering and carrying specimens sometimes gets beyond him. As soon as he is without guides the country becomes a 'desolate wild', and as he gets closer to the end of his journey the plant specimens decrease and the human experience of the journey becomes more prominent. At certain points the physical cost of his travel becomes evident, and the man of science is overtaken by the human body.

When he arrives at Tarawera, feverish, stiff, sore and ravenously hungry, he sets off, while breakfast is being prepared, to visit a boiling spring. After climbing a hill without finding it, and being 'almost exhausted from want of food', he returns to the village. In the little apologia that follows, Colenso distances himself from the way in which his collector's zeal has given way to the stressed and exhausted body of the traveller, physical extremity overcoming the careful habits of the naturalist.

> I have several times been surprised at the great carelessness which I have exhibited towards rare natural productions, when either over-fatigued or ravenously hungry; at such times botanical, geological and other specimens, which I had eagerly and with much pleasure collected and carefully carried for many a weary mile, have become quite a burden, and have been sometimes one by one abandoned; to be, however, invariably regretted afterwards.[48]

The further you travel, the less you remember. During the later stages of his journey, Colenso successively touches base with three major botanical figures. He dedicates a species of *Aspidium* to Allan Cunningham, 'my much lamented friend'. A 'carelessly plucked' pendulous fern, which he later thinks is a distinct species, is named *Asplenium Forsterianum* 'in honour of that celebrated Botanist, whose name should ever be held in remembrance by all persons botanizing in the forests of New Zealand'. A few days later, while travelling through a 'romantic valley called by the natives Hinuera', he discovers an elegant *Asplenium* under a rock 'very near in habit and affinity to A.Colensoi'.

> I did myself the honour and pleasure of naming this graceful Fern in compliment to my much respected and talented friend J.D. Hooker, Esq., M.D., who, in the capacity of Naturalist, visited these islands in H.M.S. 'Erebus', (one of the Antarctic Discovery Ships) in the winter of 1841.[49]

Colenso's naming practices are like flags planted in the country of his forgetting. They remind him of why he is there, who stands behind his work, and the origins and scale of the project he is engaged on. Cunningham, Forster and Hooker articulate his credo, his knowledge, his intellectual debts and his social and professional ambitions, and they act as points of reference to which he can connect his selfhood. In danger of succumbing to exhaustion, solitude and carelessness, Colenso peoples his journey and the landscape with the names that remind him of what is at stake, a patrimony of names with which he can map his surroundings and his relation to them. All the plants he names are ferns.

After crossing the Waikato river, Colenso and his party come to extensive swampy plains colonised with docks. He reflects on the way European weeds proliferate so fast they crowd out 'the original possessors of the soil'. Maori in Poverty Bay had told Colenso that dock seeds were sold to them by whites as tobacco seed. The plains around the mission at Otawhao afford little entertainment for the botanist, and in any case time is pressing. Colenso frequently regrets that he cannot linger in interesting or beautiful places. He is called onwards – by the Sabbath, by his need for food, by his pressing timetable and obligation to be back at the mission, at the press, sometimes just by impetus. When he failed to make that satisfactory sketch of the falls at Te Reinga, he wished 'afterwards, when it was too late, that I had remained a day at this place, instead of pressing on, post-haste, in the manner I did. I just glanced at the vegetation here.' In the Waikato his regrets become a refrain, but not even his conviction that the dense humid forests along the banks of the river will contain many new and interesting plants permits a delay. He is entering a more populous landscape, with some enchanting scenery breaking up the weary miles of 'desolate wilderness'. The Waikato carries river traffic and for a little tobacco Colenso buys a beautiful bird ('as far as I am aware an entirely new and undescribed species' but in fact a coot or heron) from a 'native in a canoe'. Intending to stuff the bird, he keeps it until they land. But it is so lovely 'I could not make up my mind to put it to death, so I let it go'.[50]

The culture of botanising

Colenso's botanising was given great impetus by his meeting with Allan Cunningham in 1838. After Cunningham's return to Sydney and until his premature death in 1839, he and Colenso corresponded about botany and he sent Colenso a number of books, as well as his own vasculum for collecting plant specimens and other tools of the trade like glass-stoppered jars and acid. On 4 December 1838 he wrote to Colenso to introduce Captain Philip King and commented on the physical costs of being a botanist.

> My excellent friend Capt P.P. King R.N. sails across to you with Captn Harding in the Pelorus. He is in indifferent health, and has thought that a cruize at sea might benefit him. Might I beg you, when you paid the Bishop your respects on landing, to receive Capt K and show him, as if he were my brother such little civility as may be in your power . . . he is an old Chum, and the same fatigues beneath a sun nearly vertical, on our N.West coast, in the years 1818, 1819, & 1820 that cut him down also had their debilitating effects on me . . . How sadly am I now made to know and feel how a series of years intense

pursuit of Flora's charms in climates almost Tropical, will, in spite of one's every care, wear down a poor mortal's existence!!!

 . . . in all your Excursions among the natives, look to your necessary comforts & never 'rough it' excepting in cases of necessity.[51]

The advice about roughing it was sublimely ignored by Colenso, whose trips into the bush were uniformly marked by deprivation and physical hardship, but he gained an entrée into a wider circle of botanists and scientists around the world through Cunningham, and later Joseph Hooker. This provided the forum in which he developed his other professional self. His self-fashioning as a botanist was partly in compensation for his treatment at the missionary settlement at Paihia. Colenso and his travelling partner, William Wade, were both outsiders when they arrived in the Bay of Islands. Colenso, an 'orthodox Evangelical' (in A. L. Rowse's phrase) and Wade, a Baptist, did not feel included in the High Church Anglican community of Henry Williams and later Bishop Selwyn. After Wade had left for Sydney, he wrote to Colenso about the 'horribly cold state of the Mission' they had experienced.[52] Botany offered Colenso not just a new field of interest and a way to make his name, but a new social identity in class networks not unlike those from which he was effectively sidelined at Paihia.

Botanical discovery was fashionable and important, and consequently a highly competitive arena. It also depended on a print culture,[53] both to publish new discoveries and to provide the tools with which to make them. Botanical writing reflected the advance of Western epistemology and methodology as the botanist struggled through unfamiliar forests, his vasculum over his shoulder and a copy of Carl Linnaeus's *Systema Naturae* in his hand. Botanical reference works were both expensive and hard to obtain, though various bibles of classification were sent to Colenso by Cunningham or the Hookers. Colenso's letter of 1840 to 'My dear Sir William' thanks Hooker for a box of books, 'your own valuable copies of De Candolle and Don', and appends a list of his own botanical books. The Hookers were conscious of the difficulties Colenso faced in making botanical classifications without recent publications and did their best to keep up a supply, but it was irregular and infrequent. Colenso's letters are a stream of requests, comments and arguments about what is circulating in print. In 1840 his response to an enquiry from William Hooker suggests what is at stake in plant imperialism.

I dare say that what you saw 'in the papers', respecting the 'oil-producing seed', was from some person connected with the N.Z. Land Company; or some such association. I have, myself, seen astonishing things inserted in the papers respecting the productions of N.Z., even in those printed here, on the very spot! which I knew to be perfectly incorrect. I fear much of this is done in the present 'puffing age' in the way of an Enticing bait.[54]

Colenso took to heart Cunningham's enjoinder to him that botanising should be a vocation, and often referred to his work having been done 'con amore'. In a letter sent from the Bachelors' Lodgings, Pitt St, Sydney, on 11 April 1839, just a few months before he died, Cunningham urged Colenso to bear in mind

> this humble request of mine, viz. Not to lose sight of the vegetation of the Land you live in and not to scatter to the winds, that little you gathered regarding the peculiarities of those vegetables, when I was with you. Let these investigations be your recreation after the more important missny duties of the day are done. Thus in time you will acquire a mass of most valuable information, in regard to the Botany of Islands daily becoming more and more important in the Eyes of Europe, in this Age of Colonizn and immigration. Thus you will bring togr a body of statistical facts, in the way of vegetable product fitted for the purpose of commerce &c – a subject that the Idler, our friend the Resident, with his great leisure ought to pry into. Let me add, what you do, do well, with all your heart. Cherish a feeling for investigations of these kinds, that will urge you to go about them con amore – but enough.[55]

Colenso's activities outside the church and politics reflected this request for the rest of his long life, but he was also conscious that the field was not his alone. His letters to Hooker and to Cunningham reflect anxiety about the competition and reveal the force of his drive to make his name as a botanist. On 1 March 1839 he wrote to Cunningham:

> There are 2 or 3 Gents. now in the land styling themselves Botanists – one is at Tauranga and wishes to ascend Tongariro, the volcano, indeed, he is, I believe, already gone into the Interior on his way to the Crater. Do you know, by hearsay, a Mr Edgerly, living on the banks of the Hokianga? I understand he is employed by some noble or Gentle-man in England to dry and forward plants – A Dr Day (of the Coromandel) who pd me a visit the other day, said, that Edgerly had the Ferns I have & others also, and that he (E) had found Gleichenia flabellata 1/2 way up Maunga Taniwa (Mt. Camel) nr Kaitaia Station – I intend paying this gent. a visit, a-la-Paul Pry. Day had, also, a quantity for Engd. – I hope you will be so alert as not to be robbed of your lawful honours by any 'herb-gatherer' – no not even by the writer – I wd not give Day anything fearing what might ensue.[56]

Being robbed of lawful honours was much on Colenso's mind. He regularly wrote to William Hooker about the misattributions or appropriations he detected in journals or other people's books. In July 1846 he wrote to Hooker from Waitangi, near Cape Kidnappers:

> I Don't know how but I seem to be peculiarly unfortunate in many of my unquestionable discoveries – and that, too in those very plants on which I set the greater value. What toil I expended upon the different Fagi – and now I find I have not one to call my own! (yet,

if Mr. Bidwell ever saw F.Menziesii growing, he never saw it at 'Waikare Lake', a place unvisited by him.) . . . and then again my Myrsina . . . My Thuja (which cost me a world of diligent research, year after year), – my Calceolaria Sinclairii (discovered, vide 'Journal', while our friend Dr. S. was enjoying the otium cum dig. of the Bay of Islands). – But enough: poor Cunn. lamented in a similar strain.[57]

Attaching your name to a new plant species was an inscription of the specialist knowledge and labour of the discoverer on the landscape, and on the dissemination and reproduction of plants around the world and in botanical history. The provision of botanical specimens had become such an industry by the nineteenth century that questions arose about the protocols of the profession, including whose place it was to furnish names for new plants. In his early days as a botanist, writing to Allan Cunningham, Colenso asked:

Another thing I wish to know is, the best mode of taking plants to Engd; and what kinds are most prized there; what unknown (by sight) to Botanists, & c & c & c – I do not intend to become plant-Hawker, or Market gardr., but I may have to go to Engd & shod be glad to take home some plants from N. Zd.[58]

Being a professional botanist, a gentlemanly activity, had to be demarcated from having a short-term commercial interest in selling plants, and Colenso later comments to Hooker about plant naming:

By-the-by I will just give you a remark (while I have it floating before me) which a gentleman high in office made to me a short while ago. He said, 'I have one thing against you Botanists, and that is, your giving of Plants any one's name: let him be ever so immoral a Character or needy an adventurer, or, even a person who collects plants for sale, or hire! You name those plants after him; which to me appears monstrous'. Now, I think, this is, in some degree, correct. I think that all persons who do so collect for 'Sale or hire', certainly ought not to have a single plant named after them.[59]

Colenso sedulously monitors the progress of his consignments of specimens and his classifications in the European print media. He sent large boxes of specimens to William and later Joseph Hooker at Kew at irregular intervals well into the 1850s.

I have this day finished putting up another small case of specimens for you containing nearly 700 little numbered lots, some of which I know are novelties. I have worked very hard indeed to get this ready, and it will now leave by the first ship for ~ England . . . believe me I have done my best – con amore.[60]

But Colenso's laboriously collected cases were not uncritically received. Many of the specimens, gathered in bad weather or carried for too long in his shirt or his hat before being 'put up', deteriorated in quality, and there were often too many examples of the same thing. One of Colenso's letters to Joseph Hooker replies to a comment by Hooker that the 'miscellaneous scraps such as you sent and all so carefully numbered are not worth the time and trouble of looking over':

> Of course, having troubled you with such trash, must be set down to my ignorance; or, perhaps more correctly, to both that and my over-zealous efforts not to leave anything – even the minutest unknown to you. However, I shall not willingly offend again in this matter.[61]

The extent to which Colenso learned on the job can be gauged from some of his early specimen lists, sent to Allan Cunningham. This is a selection of entries.

Plants to Mr Cunningham
May /09 for Rev ? -Taylor

1. Buttoned-like thing – Mangungu
2. Fern from Station Mangungu
3. That spinous padded thing muddy mangungu (Indigenous?)
. . . .
10. That little thing road to Waiomio? out from sand hills
. . .
12. that pretty little mingi like little shrub from low sand hills
. . . .
32. little rounded thing like Drosera from bog Kaitaia[62]

Colenso's 'Bush Journal', Vol. 2, pp.45–46 (opposite page) and 'Memoranda of Journies', pp.58–59 (above). ATL 88-103-2/02-45

The manuscript collection of the Alexander Turnbull Library contains a series of brown paper-covered notebooks with the hand-lettered title 'Bush Journal'. When I opened one I found tucked between its pages fragments of dried fern and a feather. The pages are written in pencil, and contain lists of children, numbers of Maori present at prayer meetings, sketches of coastline and headlands, Maori vocabulary. The contents of the journal, jotted down as Colenso trudged on his way, speak of the process of gathering information and mark the waypoints of a journey through a landscape which also becomes a journey through an accumulation of different texts: from the perishable and portable handwritten notebook, bearing the traces of its passage through bush, to the formalised and copied journal pages sent to London and copied into the *Missionary Register*, and to the published text printed in the London *Journal of Botany*.

I thought on Humboldt

The anxiety expressed in many of Colenso's letters about competition, specimen cases, appropriation of his discoveries, and delays in reply from the Hookers, registers the pressure he felt himself to be under, both personally and in the professional world he was entering. The published accounts of his journeys negotiate diverse territories which are not only cultural but also professional and personal. As Colenso struggles through the weather and the bush, registering in his narrative the different modes in which he is operating – explorer,

European, botanist, ethnographer, Christian, stranger – he is also undertaking a literal journey of the book, distributing copies of his biblical texts, and a journey of faith, holding prayer meetings, preaching and countering the spread of Catholicism. These underpinnings of his journey appear only fragmentarily, but their inclusion suggests the extent to which botany is both a codification of the natural world and a code for Colenso's professional desire. The figure of the botanist takes precedence over the ambivalent circumstances and disappointment of the lay preacher, and each new case of specimens represents the advance of science, natural history, literacy, Christianity, colonisation, imperialism and Western civilisation. Colenso acts as an agent for forces and movements which will transform the world he encounters and is himself configured by the pressures and tensions driving his journeys.

He looks out over Hawke's Bay on 4 September 1850, and sees in the view before him images of the mythic narratives of Western expansion:

> . . . little wee things often lead one's mind to a most heterogeneous association of bulky ideas. I just now carefully looked out at my window, and, on beholding the snow still lying on the mountains, I thought on Humboldt on Chimboraze; while the keen 'southerly' which has been blowing all day, with its usual accompaniments of blackness and darkness and cold, immediately took me to Ross' huge Antarctic barrier of ice and the fearful collision of his two ships – a mental scene, at which my mind instinctively shudders.[63]

CHAPTER 3

Swells' sons run out: the travel writing of rovers, ramblers and adventurers

Imperial adventure stories were . . . collectively the story England told itself as it went to sleep at night – Martin Green[1]

The Martyr of Erromanga and the white savage

Shortly before his premature death in 1839, the botanist Allan Cunningham wrote to William Colenso about the Sydney visit of Rev. John Williams, author of the popular and widely circulated book about missionary activity in the Pacific, *A Narrative of Missionary Enterprises in the South Sea Islands* (1838).

> . . . the Rev John Williams, London Mssy Socy is here the 'Lion' at this time. All favourable to mssy labour have had him to their houses and his book of 'Enterprizes' is on every table . . . There is a fashion in all things and while it lasts all attention is given to it. The rage for publishing books of Enterprizes, Adventure, hairbreadth 'scapes, and the like is as rabid as ever, and whether these have a reference to a missionary, a mariner or a monarch, they are read with appetite greedily by the multitude, who have never had the shame of being thrown into such difficulties all their lives and therefore they read of them and then gaze on the simple unassuming man who has braved them with wonder and admiration. Mr W's society is courted by all. He is called to Public Meetings, is asked to take the Chair and speak perhaps of Enterprizes he has not yet printed. In fine his book has fixed him in public attention and not simply has it effected it by reason of the subject-matter, but also by the way in which the book has been got up, its vignettes and capital Portraits.[2]

The agencies and institutions of European expansion into the Pacific (including New Zealand) in the early part of the nineteenth century – evangelism, scientific expeditions, commercial interests and colonisation – produced a broad and various documentary record, which shifted over time from what Anthony Pagden has called the 'counter-histories of civility' of the eighteenth century to an archive rich in narratives of redemption, savagery and adventure.[3] The historical shifts in representations of the Pacific and its peoples have been brilliantly described by Rod Edmond, Vanessa Smith and Anthony Pagden, among others.[4] But the dynamic observed by Allan Cunningham, where missionaries were lionised for their books of 'enterprize', reveals both the market demand for certain kinds of stories and the difficulty of separating an interest in civilising missions from a rage for adventure in the minds of readers. Narratives of the Pacific inevitably registered the 'dangerously seductive and anarchic appeal of the South Sea islands' (in Rod Edmond's words),[5] and tales of mission work traded on the dramatic interest of the conditions in which it occurred. Missionaries were very aware of the volatile context in which they worked, both as evangelists and as writers, and of the mixed populations – readers, adventurers and 'unprincipled seamen' – who accompanied their labours.

John Williams, who became famous as Britain's second 'Pacific martyr-hero' (in Rod Edmond's phrase),[6] was one of the missionaries sent to Tahiti by the London Missionary Society in 1817. Williams began his evangelical work on the Leeward Islands but soon moved on to the Rarotongan group, where he worked for the best part of eighteen years. The preface to *A Narrative of Missionary Enterprises* (1838) emphasises both the duration and the extent of his labours, metonymically indicating the size of his spiritual task but also explicitly drawing attention to its scope, which is hard to compress into a 'continuous Narrative':

> Having travelled a hundred thousand miles, and spent eighteen years in promoting the spread of the Gospel, he has gathered a mass of materials, from which he could have composed many volumes with greater ease than one . . .

Within his grand narrative design to display 'the wisdom or goodness of the great and beneficent Creator', Williams's express authorial intent is to

> take his reader with him to each of the islands he has visited . . . make him familiar with their chiefs and people . . . show him what a Missionary life is; and to awaken in his mind emotions similar to those which successively filled his own.[7]

Rod Edmond has characterised *A Narrative of Missionary Enterprises* as variously a 'conquest narrative', a 'campaigning work', 'a kind of business report' and 'above all, a providential narrative',[8] but he observes that its popularity was due to the 'Robinsonnade' qualities of the narrative, in which, for example, Williams describes in great detail building a sixty-foot boat for travelling between islands.

Williams's own desires as a reader are articulated in terms which recognise the potential of the mission text as a work of travel writing:

> I have felt disappointed when reading the writings of Missionaries, at not finding a fuller account of the difficulties they have had to contend with, and the measures by which these were met. It appears to me that a work from the pen of a Missionary should not contain just what might be written by one who has never left his native country . . .[9]

In November 1839 Williams went ashore from the *Camden* at Erromanga with two other missionaries, Harris and Cunningham. They were attacked and, though Williams managed to make it to the water's edge, the beach was stony, he lost his footing and was clubbed to death. The public appetite for 'books of Enterprizes, Adventure, hairbreadth 'scapes, and the like' (in Allan Cunningham's phrase), compounded by the circumstances of Williams's dramatic death in the New Hebrides, ensured heavy and continuing demand for his book and his story. In England Williams became a cult figure, cheap editions of his book were produced, and his inscription as the 'martyr of Erromanga' by John Campbell's biography,[10] and by the best-selling author Samuel Smiles, founder of the Self-Help movement,[11] ensured the transmission of his story to succeeding generations of readers.

Just before Williams left England on his ill-fated return voyage to the Pacific, he was farewelled at Tabernacle House in London by a large congregation and various distinguished members of the London Missionary Society, among them Rev. William Ellis, author of *Polynesian Researches*, one of the most read and influential ethnographic books of the nineteenth century. The addresses, prayers and hymns were gathered into a small volume under the title *The Missionary's Farewell* and published in 1838, about eighteen months before Williams's murder. In his address, Ellis described the changes effected by Christianity on the 'vicious propensities' of the Tahitians, but acknowledged that various 'formidable difficulties' remained in the path of the missionaries. The worst of these

> has arisen from the unprincipled seamen, who, for the purpose of gratifying a depraved propensity, have left their vessels, settled among the natives, and created vast mischief. . . . One wicked man among a people like the South Sea islanders is capable of effecting immense mischief.[12]

Ellis's evocation of a fleet of British vessels, whose 'canvas has whitened the waters of every sea' and 'banners have floated on every breeze', met with the enthusiastic acclamation of his listeners in Tabernacle House,[13] but other audiences were more interested in the sensational possibilities of missionary experience. Williams's murder was part of the broader picture, in which exotic and violent experience

'Mitiaro.' An illustration from
*A Narrative of Missionary Enterprises in
the South Sea Islands* by John Williams,
1838, p.264. ATL B-K-505-264

was the fabric of Pacific stories, whether they were about a 'missionary, a mariner or a monarch'. On its intended second voyage to the Pacific, for instance, the missionary ship *Duff* was captured by a French corvette off Rio de Janeiro, her crew and passengers dispersed and cargo seized.[14] A number of missionaries, their wives and children died in the field or were forced to retreat by indigenous resistance. And around and beside the missionary presence flowed the backwash of Pacific sea trade, referred to by Ellis as 'unprincipled seamen', adventurers, drifters, runaway convicts, deserting sailors, mutineers, beachcombers and Pakeha-Maori, who spread across the ocean in ever-increasing numbers and produced their own versions of European expansion, a travel literature which contests tales of civilising missions and missionary field work.

There are two major characterisations of this mobile, volatile population. One is what Rod Edmond has referred to as the 'white savage', those people who had turned their back on civilisation and settled in primitive societies, famously typified by the *Bounty* mutineers[15] or in Herman Melville's novel *Typee*, which represents the life of an American sailor in a remote valley of the Marquesas as an 'indulgent captivity'.[16] The other is adventurers, 'rovers' and 'ramblers', looking for opportunities, variety or adventure, moving restlessly on to new coasts and horizons. Despite its more benign versions, white savagery was generally denounced, especially as it was often associated with lawlessness. Runaway convicts got a bad press and, as John Boultbee's accounts of sealing in Bass Strait suggest, abuse of indigenous populations by people who had washed up among them was common. New Zealand, and specifically Kororareka, was infamous for its white trash population, described by both Charles Darwin and Joseph Hooker.[17] In an 1837 leader the *Sydney Gazette* declared:

> it is quite time that the press generally call the notice of the local government to that savage land, where crime is fearfully making the most rapid strides – the most dreadful ravages, despite of the Missionaries – the British Resident, and the occasional visits of our men-of-war ...[18]

What kind of travel writing did these roving visitors to New Zealand produce?

A 'Journal of my chequered life'

'Rover' or 'rambler' is how a number of footloose male travellers of the early nineteenth century describe themselves. Their writing is typically introduced with a description by the author of the conditions which produced his book, and a claim to a transparent realism, an 'unvarnished' eyewitness reporting. Vanessa Smith notes that beachcomber texts emerged from 'the elusive context of oral narration to depict outlandish stories for a Western readership' and have a 'less confident relationship to textual authority'.[19] Like beachcomber texts, the journals and books of rovers and ramblers, with their descriptions of exotic practices, places and people, carry many traces of oral narration, and anticipate or try to pre-empt the reader's disbelief. Readers harbour a 'suspicion of narrative unreliability', Smith claims, 'whose foundation is primarily social' – that is, the education and social status of the author bring his narrative into question.[20] Sometimes the artefact itself, handmade and expedient, like John Boultbee's journal written on 'unusually rough, porous handmade paper ... joined to a cover made from a fragment of sailcloth'[21] and bearing smudges and inky thumbprints, speaks for the mobile makeshift life from which the text springs and which it claims to record.[22] John Rochfort's *Adventures of a Surveyor* (1853) is typical of such texts in making it seem as if the conditions in which the text was produced remain in its material form:

> it is but a journal, written in leisure moments, sometimes under a burning sun, and at others during a storm, with the waves running mountains high and the wind whistling through the rigging.[23]

Most rovers represent their writing as eloquent of an experience that is not 'literary', and as uncontaminated by literary qualities. Edward Lucett dedicated *Rovings in the Pacific from 1837–49* (1851) to Sir Edward Bulwer Lytton, whose 'varied works have yielded large stores of intellectual enjoyment to a rover in his wanderings o'er the deep', but declared in his preface that the

> author's days . . . have been passed, not in the idealities of life but in its downright rough realities . . . this simple record of his experience may stimulate many a youth . . . to seek, in the Isles of the Pacific, the home and the adventurous career which he is sure to find there . . . [24]

Barnet Burns, an Irishman who lived as a Pakeha-Maori in the 1830s and received a full facial and body moko, which made it 'impossible to walk the streets without exciting the curiosity of all who see me', earned his living for a time exhibiting himself in England. He described his pamphlet as a 'plain statement of facts . . . my object being only to detail the truth, without resorting to the aid of imagination'. Like most adventurer-writers making a claim for both the authenticity and plainness of their texts, Burns hopes 'some allowance will be made by my readers for all deficiency of style'.[25] Authors of 'plain unvarnished tales' claim factual transparency for their narratives, but George Bayly, whose *Sea-Life Sixty Years Ago* (1885) recounts his experiences as trading officer on the *St Patrick* under the command of Peter Dillon, declares he has 'relied on neither memory nor imagination'. He says his book 'is compiled entirely from letters and a journal written on the spot, and now brought to light again'.[26] Neither time nor fancy is permitted any effect on the transmission of events sixty years old.

Travel and lies

Stephen Greenblatt argues that the act of witnessing is the 'foundational rhetorical device which fabricates and accredits the travel text as a recorded understanding of otherness'.[27] But the problem for the eyewitness text is authentication, particularly when travel is generated by opportunity, need and chance, and when the author's self-representation puts him on the margins, only loosely tethered to European social norms. The long association of travel with lying and with sexual licence lies behind many admonitions to the reader that the narrative is faithfully recorded experience. F. E. Maning, the 'Pakeha Maori' of the title page of *Old New Zealand: a tale of the good old times* (1863), addresses his preface to 'the English reader, and to most of those who have arrived in New Zealand within the last thirty years'. To these people, Maning says, 'it may be necessary to state that the descriptions of Maori life and manners of past times found in these sketches owe nothing to fiction . . . all the persons described are real persons'.[28] At the same time

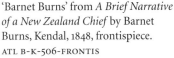

'Barnet Burns' from *A Brief Narrative of a New Zealand Chief* by Barnet Burns, Kendal, 1848, frontispiece.
ATL B-K-506-FRONTIS

such texts want to capitalise on the rover, the deserting or abandoned seaman, the beachcomber, as a figure of otherness and opportunity, romanticised as a survivor, demonised as a savage, and the powerful attraction of a story coming from the half-lit world of South Pacific islands.

John Martin's preface to his *Account of the Natives of the Tonga Islands* (1818), 'compiled and arranged' from William Mariner's 'extensive' oral 'communications', emphasises Mariner's memory (giving as proof of its accuracy examples of his ability to recount the same story a second time in identical terms) and his adoption into Tongan society as key authentications of his story. Mariner spent four years in Tonga after the privateer on which he was employed as captain's clerk, the *Port au Prince,* was captured in 1806. In the preface to the second edition Martin announces an 'additional weight of testimony in favour of the facts related' provided by Jeremiah Higgins, a young seaman who by means of 'assiduous' questioning corroborated, to Martin's satisfaction, 'the truth of the great outlines of the matter contained in the following sheets'. The conjunction of oral accounts by participants of different social standing (Mariner's greater education allowed him to move in and analyse Tongan political circles, whereas Higgins was the son of a hay-binder) allows Martin to make his confident editorial assertions of truth-telling. He provides an assurance of both mediation and cross-examination.

Stephen Greenblatt makes the point that, with very few exceptions, 'Europeans felt powerfully superior to virtually all of the peoples they encountered' and this conviction was bound up with the 'literal advantage' of writing.[29] Although Mariner handed over the work of authorship to John Martin because he felt that he would not be up to the job after 'several years out of the habit of either reading or writing', he was aware that his oral story had further possibilities in print. The 'foundational rhetorical device' – eyewitnessing – in books by adventurers typically seeks to dissociate itself from literary devices and stresses the use of unrevised journal entries, whose claim to have been composed on the spot seeks to recreate the (truthful) spontaneity and artlessness of an oral tale in written form. Edward Lucett, whose anonymous title page to *Rovings in the Pacific* identifies him only as 'a merchant, long resident at Tahiti', claims that the notes on which his journal account is based 'have undergone little alteration, addition or subtraction, and but few remarks have been interpolated. They are entirely without claim to literary merit.'[30] Lucett's linking of editorial practices with 'literary merit' reveals how he perceives his role as an author and the nature of his text: style is as much a distortion of fact as 'alteration'. Such authors claim a special transparency for their texts partly because of what Smith calls the 'suspicion of narrative unreliability' but also because they see themselves not as writers but as people with such interesting experience to relay that the medium in which it is conveyed has to be neutralised, stripped of its potential as an art form and an artifice, which might get in the way of what they wish to tell.

There are several examples of a good oral story passing through the hands of an editor who, like Martin, acts as guarantor for the truthfulness of the tale. Archibald Campbell's *A Voyage Round the World from 1806 to 1812* (1816) was edited by James Smith from the oral report of a journey made by a seaman on a Thames Indiaman. Smith's preface describes his role and the issues it raised. Campbell's narrative was produced mostly 'from the recital of the author', and so the editor aimed only for 'simplicity and perspicuity . . . the ornaments of style, which are generally misplaced in such relations, would have been peculiarly incongruous in the mouth of a common sailor'. Much of Smith's preface is taken up with arguments about the quality and status of the narrative, suggesting the ranking of different kinds of information and their potential marketability.

> In those parts of the work which relate to places already well known, the narrative is entirely confined to the personal adventures of the author; and had the editor been aware that so much had been recently written regarding Kamchatska and the Aleutian islands by

the Russian navigators, the description of those places would have been altogether omitted or much more condensed.[31]

According to Smith, Campbell's narrative is valuable for its portrait of 'Tamaah-maah', 'King' of the Sandwich Islands, some 'useful nautical information' about reefs and harbours, and its 'personal adventures'. Although it is published principally for the 'benefit of the poor fellow who is the subject of it' (Campbell had both feet amputated after severe frostbite and had to undergo subsequent amputation to the knee because of the poor quality of the first operation), the *Voyage* also 'rescue[s] much of what is true and extraordinary from the oblivion to which the obscure condition and limited powers of the narrator would have condemned it'.[32]

Smith's apologia is typical of claims made in most such journals and narratives which seek to protect the text from the criticism of obscurity its 'limited powers' might attract. At the same time, the limits of the text as a literary artefact, its claim to speak from the 'mouth of a common sailor', is an authentication of its truth-telling. The lack of ornament reflects both the conventions of the medium – the common mouth through which the story is told – and the deliberate avoidance of any textual dimension which might detract from the reader's perception of an unproblematically transferred reality. John Boultbee's *Journal of a Rambler*, recounting his experiences sealing and roaming around Australia and New Zealand in the 1820s, opens with a claim both to the material evidence of experience provided by his papers and to the personal authenticity of an oral narrative.

> In compliance with the wishes of a dear deceased Father, I have been in the habit of keeping a Journal of my checquered life; this I now have copied from my half worn out papers, and produce it as plain and unvarnished as if I was relating my adventures personally.[33]

The question of readership is also critical. Boultbee declares that he knows he is 'not laying myself open to criticism from the circumstance of writing more for the amusement of my relations and friends, than with a view to that of the Public'. In fact, Boultbee's journal remained in family circles until edited for publication by June Starke in 1986, but its preamble anticipates a wider audience: 'I said I wrote the Journal for the amusement of my friends, yet as probably others may by chance see it.' Boultbee's amplification of his narrative with an autobiographical sketch mapping his family history and social identity, and providing some contextual information (including that his interest in travel was sparked by 'reading some Voyages and travels'), suggests that he wished for a readership unfamiliar with the details of his life and times, but also that his perception of the kind of text he was writing had literary antecedents that needed to be acknowledged. Nothing has been added to, diminished or heightened in the history of his adventures, he claims, but his awareness of telling a certain kind of story, showing 'what a labyrinth of trouble I have entered into through thoughtlessness and want of stability', shapes both his text and his description of it. Boultbee's introduction to his journal negotiates the status of his personal and family narrative in the public and critical world. In making claims about what his text does not do he also makes strong claims about what it does do, attempting to establish its value and place in hierarchies of knowledge, experience and print.

Texts of motion

The texts of rambling journal-keepers like Boultbee, or rovers like Lucett, record a certain kind of knowledge, produced by what might be called counter-direction, a movement of opportunity, not intention, and of individuals, not agencies or institutions. The texts record movement, not stasis: the characteristic of experience is its onward motion. As J. G. A. Pocock has observed:

> the antithesis between the stationary and the mobile is central to the concept of the voyage and the encounter, central also to Enlightened accounts of the evolution of society and the morality of colonization.[34]

The adventurer's purpose is not to produce a stationary effect, like conversion to Christianity or a settled trading-post, but to allow circumstances to drive him forward – whether to combat monotony, like Edward Markham; or to pursue commercial opportunities, like Edward Lucett, or employment, like John Boultbee; or to see the world, like Augustus Earle; or, on the further edges of outward movement, to avoid punitive European systems and settlements, like the runaway convicts who ended up as Pakeha-Maori.[35] It is opportunist motion that differentiates the rover both from the institutions of his originating culture and from the 'stationary' and other cultures of encounter. Boultbee attributed his restless life to an 'innate foible . . . a fondness for change and roving about', but his desire to travel he identified as the result of reading voyages and travels: 'I became so bewitched with the descriptions given by their Authors, that nothing would serve me except I went myself to realize the pleasures I anticipated in exploring different countries, and in seeing different customs.'[36]

The primary mode of these travel narratives is picaresque. They tell a story of what occurs, a personal history of events and people and places; they are gossipy and there is a breathless quality and often an air of competition about them – to be among the first to arrive anywhere is part of their claim on history and the world. These texts and their authors inhabit a small social world, and many of them take the chance in print to dispute the correct version of events with each other, or to establish a set of distinctions that authorises some voices and not others. Distrust of people who live roving unsettled lives is widely voiced. *Omoo*, Herman Melville's fictionalised account of his roving in and around Tahiti, describes beachcombers as

> certain roving characters who, without attaching themselves permanently to any vessel, ship now and then for a short cruise in a whaler; but upon the condition only of being honourably discharged the very next time the anchor takes hold of the bottom; no matter where. They are, mostly, a reckless, rollicking set, wedded to the Pacific, and never dreaming of ever doubling Cape Horn again on a homeward-bound passage. Hence their reputation is a bad one.[37]

Edward Lucett, however, in *Rovings in the Pacific* denounces Melville as 'a most reckless loafer . . . His sketches are amusing and skilfully drawn but bear as much relation to truth as a farthing does in value to a sovereign.'[38] Lucett's simile draws attention to the connections linking different worlds and activities. Melville's skills as a writer do not compensate for loafing or being light on the truth, but are nevertheless connected to money. The market observed by Allan Cunningham for stories of hairbreadth 'scapes is powerfully present in Lucett's link between truth and value.

To be once more a rover

John Boultbee and Edward Markham, whose reasons for travelling are very different, display in their journals the quality of the 'restless rollicking set' Melville identifies. Boultbee set off on his first voyage at the age of seventeen, a 'wild fellow' who enjoyed Brazil 'exceedingly'. He then spent two years at home 'living a Gentleman's life, or in other words having nothing to do', which he found very irksome, so in 1818 he embarked for the West Indies on 'a boistrous passage', and after his return to England, the death of his father and financial difficulties in the family, he left with his brother for Hobart in 1823, 'with a light heart, good health and stout body to be once more a rover – that delightful character'. On his arrival in Hobart, Boultbee, who had no 'wish to settle', unlike his brother, who established himself with a land grant, 'wished to go and see some of the islands in the South Sea, but could find no opportunity of getting to them and at last desperately situated, went on board a miserable dirty Schooner . . . going on a sealing excursion'.[39] The boat was owned by a man described by Boultbee as a 'French adventurer' and identified by June Starke as Antoine Hervel, a Sydney merchant. On board he finds himself in the kind of company alleged by the *Sydney Gazette* to be the mainstay of sealing and whaling ships and responsible for populating New Zealand:

> The crew were in all about 10 men, and how shall I describe them? – they were the refuse of merchant ships, and some formerly convicts, thieves and scoundrels fit for no society, void of every good quality, and only one man on board had the principles of a man; he was fortunately the master of them all . . .[40]

Boultbee's account of sealing in Bass Strait is full of encounters with various 'half-barbarous looking' seal-boat crews, most of whom he believes are convicts. According to him, the abduction of Aboriginal women by the sealing crews is both commonplace and the origin of a number of hostile encounters with indigenous people. Boultbee, whose narrative is sprinkled with literary references, particularly to Shakespeare,[41] distances himself from the crews and their activities, and is also recognised as being from a different class. The sealers he meets in Kent's Bay on Cape Barren Island

> came to ask me if I was not a 'Swell's Son run out,' meaning a gentleman's son who had spent his fortune, but to their enquiries I answered with seeming indifference, some remarked I should cut a better figure amongst Swells than among the 'likes o' them' but they 'reckoned as I had played at bowls I must expect rubbers'.[42]

The hardships and privations endured by the sealers around Bass Strait, 'heightened by the disagreeable proceedings of the rascals on board', drove Boultbee to leave the ship at Phillip Island, where he existed on seals, parrot fish and shellfish for two months until, half-starved, he was rescued by a schooner trading in seal skins and returned to Hobart.

Boultbee's decision to ship for New Zealand arises from the same combination of circumstances and job opportunities that led to his experiences in Bass Strait. It is not his desired destination. 'My wages being paid, I cleared my debts and sought for an opportunity of getting to Otaheiti.' He declares that Tahiti is a place 'my fancy led me to select as a second Elysium',[43] but his lack of resources means he has to take the work offering each time his money gets low. Boultbee had read Cook's *Voyages* so it was probably not just his fancy but a received idea of Tahiti as an earthly paradise for Western men that led to his repeated wish to get there, and in the brutal environment of Tasmanian sealing, with its violence towards the indigenous population and desperate living conditions, Tahiti keeps surfacing as the desirable end-point of his journey. Both New Zealand and the way-stations around Bass Strait are diversions from this, but it is also clear that the life he experiences on sealing ships represents the degraded – in Boultbee's eyes – version of what he might expect in a 'second Elysium', where social

The handsewn sailcloth binding and cover of *Journal of a Rambler* by John Boultbee.
ATL QMS-0257

practices and distinctions allow for greater freedoms. The shifts between Boultbee's hope for a voluptuous sexuality and his experience of a violent and abusive licentiousness reveal a crucial difference between the role of fancy and imagination in travel texts and the actual cost of exploration and adventure.

Going on down to New Zealand

Edward Markham decides to go 'on down to New Zealand' in 1834 because the diversions offered by life in Van Diemen's Land (Tasmania) have become monotonous. Markham's circumstances differ greatly from Boultbee's in that he is a gentleman traveller who may have had some speculative motives for making his journey to the southern hemisphere. In his *New Zealand or Recollections of It*, Markham refers to 'mak[ing] good the Titles that I had had or was going to have Mortgages on but this is entre nous – well when all was compleat I went [?] to make up my mind for New Zealand',[44] but is otherwise self-sufficient and has no need to progress from one paid job to another. Markham and Boultbee are alike, however, in the loose knitting together of opportunities that results in a narrative of more or less unintentional travel, and their texts reflect a broad similarity of social, though not financial, status. This suggests not only the circumstances in which rovers produced written texts of their travels but why they did so. Despite the highly idiomatic, personalised and informal mode of their writing – Boultbee says his tale is as plain as if he was 'relating it personally' and Markham's diary jottings are full of asides and personal references – both men place their narratives in a print culture. Both had read Cook and refer to the *Voyages*. Markham had read Earle, Cruise and Yate, and Boultbee refers to a literary education – Shakespeare, Cowper, Sir Walter Scott. Recording their journeys was part of an acculturated response to experience and an awareness of a literate readership, even as the inflections and broken syntactical patterns of the spoken voice call vividly to mind the oral communities which both men represent.

Markham intended to stay at the Bay of Islands only three weeks, but the lack of a Sydney-bound ship meant he stayed for four months and travelled around. Markham's narrative of his activities in New Zealand, with his sexual experiences with Maori women, the drunkenness and brawling of the male community he inhabited, and the land dealing and commercial opportunities he pursued, represents the adventurous and unruly margins of social behaviour. His indulgence of various freedoms speaks for the permissive possibilities of travel, and his reported behaviour is a gentlemanly version of what missionaries and other visitors denounce in the Kororareka beach community.

Markham's two sexual partnerships with Maori women take place on the other side of the island from the mission station and he is careful to keep them concealed, deciding not to take 'Arungher Mar' with him to the Bay of Islands when he is going to visit the missionaries. Markham's amatory dalliances are a usual part of his travels. When he says goodbye to Arungher Mar, he gives her a garnet ring which he had 'intended for a Chere Amie in Hobart Town', evidently an extra-marital dalliance, as he notes that the ring 'might have caused Suspicion' so the Chere Amie 'refused to accept it'.[45] Arungher Mar, whom Markham distinguishes from the parade of his sexual encounters by saying, 'I do not know that I ever cried in parting from a Girl before except one in Paris', saved Markham's life when he was attacked by an enraged chief for mistaking the chief's nephew for a slave. The garnet ring was a reward for her bravery, and a farewell gift. The story of Markham's relationship with Arungher Mar is presented in mock-heroic mode:

> I made a conquest of a very superior Being to be known hereafter by the name of Arungher Mar or the Lady Arungher; she accepted my protection a week after and proved a very affectionate Creature and a Good Girl.[46]

But there is a clear demarcation, expressed in terms of class as well as race, that plays around Maori women generally in Markham's text, and is also implied by

'A dance called Karne Karne or Cune Cune.' Watercolour by Edward Markham from his manuscript journal 'New Zealand or recollections of it', 1834, pp.6–7.

his perhaps only half mock-courtly mode of referring to Arungher Mar. When he sees eighty women dancing at the hakari or feast given by Moetara, a feast described by many early writers, he comments: 'I never saw a finer set of Women or Girls in an Opera Ballet.' He asserts that

> the Ladies enjoy these Feasts, as they have glorious opportunities of Intrigue . . . [they] work each others passions up, as to the different abilities of their temporary [European] Husbands, all the Scandal of the different Parrs or Native Villages and of the Europeans up and down the country is recited . . .[47]

Markham's account evokes a world of complaisant and available sexual relationships with Maori women, though the story of his previous liaison has some uncomfortable aspects. Not long after he arrived, Markham reports a meeting upriver with one of the local chiefs in which he was asked 'if he had a wahine':

> No. Would I like one? Certainly. Then take my daughter, which I did in the New Zealand fashion. I took her out of his women's hut, She screaming till I put her into the Hut drest for me. The Row ceased and no further opposition was offered.[48]

Markham notes he had to 'pay for my Night's amusement' with a shirt to the father, 'lucifers' to the mother and a pocket handkerchief for the girl. Despite the disturbing features of this story, not least the status of Maori women under customary law, Markham's recounting of the details suggests a history of sexual encounter between European men and Maori women, with expectations of exchange and a *droit de seigneur* flavour. The following evening Markham notes: 'No noise this evening; like a good girl she was awaiting her Lord'.[49] He says there was a great laugh at his expense when he got back to camp as everybody up and down the river knew what he'd been up to.

One of the interesting aspects of Markham's descriptions of sexual encounters with Maori women, who represent the seductive 'wildness' attributed to Polynesian women since the eighteenth century, is the way he links his behaviour to a demi-mondaine European sexuality, and suggests that 'wildness' may also be transferred to European women associating with Maori men. When he recounts the story of Betty Guard, wife of the captain of the whaling brig *Harriet* wrecked on the Taranaki coast, who was abducted by local Maori along with her two children in 1834, he focuses on the appearance of Mrs Guard when she was eventually recovered by HMS *Alligator*, sent from Sydney to retrieve them. Mrs Guard was said to have become the property of a Maori chief. When she came on board the *Alligator*, Markham reports her as 'looking beautiful in the Native Cacahow and Hair loose, and a Wild look about her'.[50]

The male homosocial world reported by Markham is characterised by wildness too. One of the first Europeans he encounters on landing is 'Mr Chand', almost certainly the same Mr Shand who accompanied Augustus Earle across the Tasman, whom Markham describes as a

> Scotch man, well educated and doing the most menial Offices about the Establishment, as he would do anything for drink, and if Grog was to be had, he would have no scruples if he could but get it but a man who had been articled to the Cygnet in Edinburgh. Oh this is a Wicked World and Full of Drink!!![51]

Drunkenness and brawling are constant features of masculine life in the Hokianga. Markham has a low regard for his companions, especially Henry Oakes, whom he had met in Tasmania and travelled across the Tasman with, and whom he identifies as the brother of a Colonel Oakes he had known in Florence, and F. E. Maning, whose *Old New Zealand* is described by E. H. McCormick in his introduction to Markham's *Recollections* as a 'masterly if unscrupulous' version of 'some of the experiences so ineptly recorded by Markham'. In Markham's text, Maning is a 'low minded Savage', a 'dirty mean beast', a 'double faced sneaking Thief . . . who would have done honor to the back Woods in America'.[52] Despite Markham's condemnations, Maning surfaces repeatedly in his narrative as one of the central figures of a cohort connected by their drinking, fighting, trading and dealing. Like Boultbee, Markham is conscious of his own status in the social configurations around him. Mentioning a runaway convict named Brown, he observes 'most of my friends are of that Class', but also records a 'warm' dispute in which a person accused of encroaching on the property of the Wesleyan missionaries declares he does not 'care a Straw in disagreeing with all hands, but Mr Markham as he was a Gentleman above the Common'. The narrative is a litany of gentlemen's sons who have lost their fortunes in drink, like Mr Craigh, 'well educated from Haddington near Edinburgh', or the son of Major Doubleday, who had been trying to get his son home, saying 'he knew his failing Drink! and for that he gives up his Inheritance, to live this Wild kind of Life'.[53]

Markham's most usual mocking frame of reference for New Zealand is Paris or Italy. Tiring of his monotonous diet of fern root and potatoes, he records that fern root 'is not at all satisfactory after One has once known what it was to have been at Veray's or the Caffe de Paris or Caffe Hardy'. But his self-fashioning as a *bon vivant* and man of the world also claims for his narrative the authority of worldly but gentlemanly experience, an experience he is both frank and insistent about. In an aside described by Markham's editor, E. H. McCormick, as a 'fragment of gossip', he adds a note to a story about a young Christian Maori woman whose long-arranged marriage to a chief was interrupted by the missionaries. The intervention resulted in a brawl in which the young woman was seriously injured. Markham comments:

> They try to marry them Young. Because vy as Fanny Kemble says, They will not keep. Mrs Chaloner once said to me when talking about a Miss Brown succeeding her sister in Mr Turton's bed, 'I am afraid a Warm Climate is very bad for Morality'. Query how long it was since the Old Lady had the Bum fidgets, but to proceed. Marriage is Sacred here, as much so as elsewhere.[54]

The Turtons are referred to earlier in Markham's narrative as living in the Casa Filicaja, and McCormick suggests they may have been members of the English community resident in Florence. The associations in this little diversion suggest the various ways in which Markham is placing himself. Distanced from the missionaries, and also from Maori (whose customs he reports impersonally though sympathetically), he aligns himself with an upper middle-class, masculine, expatriate, sexually adventurous but explicitly English community, which suggests something about the normative sexual behaviour and licence of English men and women abroad.

Although Markham does not denounce the missionaries as Augustus Earle does, he represents them as holding a line he is happy to break. When he goes to the Wesleyan Mission church at Mangungu with Oakes (with whom he is at odds throughout his time in New Zealand), he thinks they are coldly received at first, 'but soon they took me on one side, and told me that they should be happy to show me any Civility in their power, but that I was in the company of a very Indiscreet man to give it the mildest term'.[55] Despite his constant denunciation of Oakes and Maning, Markham remains in their company. At Waitangi in July 1834, he describes the mission and the way of life, commenting that the missionaries hate the ships to come into the Bay of Islands, because '400 to 500 Sailors require as many Women'. Like Earle, Markham believes that the 'Sailors have done as much towards civilizing the Natives as the Missionaries have done', but where Earle's reason for thinking so was a reduction in infanticide, Markham's argument is concerned with mobility.

> . . . now a Man may go from one Village to another, and the Children do not hoot them as they did formerly, and such a number have been in Whalers, as each Ship takes eight or ten New Zealanders and the Seamen pick up the language from them and the same prevails from the Sanwich Islands to Taheite and Tonga and Feegies.[56]

McCormick observed of Markham's text that 'Few persons not actually illiterate could ever have been so poorly qualified for authorship . . . [but] What may have been no more than an unpublishable effusion in 1836 had within 70 years become an historic document . . . Markham remains an unreliable guide to facts and events, but he is a rare witness . . . a unique repository of gossip'.[57]

The informality of Markham's *Recollections* and the many traces of speech and oral accounts it contains are precisely what gives his narrative its air of transparency. The writing, with its headlong undiscriminating mix of reportage, invective, observation, gossip and opinion, suggests a scarcely mediated engagement with specific circumstances and events, saturated by a colourful and relatively unreflective personality. It is possible to read around Markham's text to other views of the relationships he describes, as McCormick does. But Markham's own window on New Zealand is narrow: he never looks closely at the physical landscape, for example, or the wider political field, and his information is highly personalised. All this, together with writing in a stream of consciousness, produces an impression of intense verisimilitude.

When he arrives at 'the Coco' [Kohukohu], for example, he begins by suggesting its physical appearance but is at once diverted to commercial, political and social entanglements:

> The Coco, is a beautiful spot well adapted for the River Trade. There was about three Acres cleared by Kelly before we arrived, and Potatoes in it and other things, but when Oakes got there he made Confusion rows and fights.[58]

Everything in Markham's text is entangled – personalities, observations, gossip, reactions – as if what is coming at him is so fast and furious he has no time to process it, only to scribble it down. His text works not to stabilise the mobile subject but to record its mobility, and the points at which he comes temporarily to rest – attending church services in the Bay of Islands, for example – remain unelaborated. Like his exclamations about the beauty of the country, he pauses briefly to record a response, before sweeping on in a flood of new events.

> There is something so beautiful in the Rivers in this Country. A Stillness, fine sky over head! no Noise![59]

The wandering artist

By contrast, Augustus Earle's *Narrative of a nine months' residence in New Zealand in 1827* (1832) is a very considered and reflective text by a self-described wanderer addressing himself to a literate readership. Markham had undoubtedly seen Earle's book, which was published two years before he went to New Zealand, as he frequently refers to Earle's drawings. The similarities between Markham and Earle lie not in the nature of their narratives – Earle's follows clear genre conventions, providing an historical frame for his arrival in a new land, and processing his own story through ethnographic and geographic observation – but in the status they claim for themselves and their texts, their lack of objectives in travelling, and how they align themselves in a complex set of relationships. Generally, these are the identifying characteristics of the travel writing produced by rovers. Herman Melville's Wellingborough Redburn opens his 'sailor-boy confessions and reminiscences' by describing how as a youth he

> frequently fell into long reveries about distant voyages and travels and thought how fine it would be to talk about remote and barbarous countries; with what reverence and wonder people would regard me, if I had just returned from the coast of Africa or New Zealand; how dark and romantic my sunburnt cheeks would look.[60]

The identification of the traveller with his text is made by both the reading public and the travellers themselves – they are the medium through which the exotic destination and experience of the journey is transmitted, and physically represent it. This is especially so with travellers whose journeys occur without fixed objectives or destinations, for whom the movement, the constantly changing scene, the novelty, is the point, because their story of contact and encounter is premised on an individual with unconventional cultural affiliations telling a circumstantial story of experience which reflects chance and opportunity, appetite and desire. It is a distribution of energies – high levels of adventure, novelty and exotica – which conflates the textual and the human product, and makes it both marketable and marked out. As Melville's Wellingborough Redburn observes:

I very well remember staring at a man myself, who was pointed out to me by my aunt
one Sunday in church, as the person who had been in Stony Arabia, and passed through
strange adventures there, all of which with my own eyes I had read in the book which he
wrote, an arid-looking book in a pale yellow cover.[61]

Augustus Earle first went to sea in 1815 from 'a love of roving and adventure',
according to the preface to the 1832 edition of *A Narrative of a nine months'*
residence in New Zealand in 1827, which opens without preamble in mid-motion,
a characteristic of the rover's text:

Having made up my mind to visit the island of New Zealand, and having persuaded my
friend Mr Shand to accompany me, we made an arrangement for the passage with Captain
Kent, of the brig 'Governor Macquarie', and bidding adieu to our friends at Sydney, in a
few hours (on October 20th, 1827) we were wafted into the Great Pacific Ocean.[62]

Earle is more concerned than Markham to differentiate himself from the wilder
groups of Europeans living in New Zealand in 1827. Praising the 'laborious and
useful' Scottish sawyers resident in the bay leads him to delineate 'another class
of Europeans . . . who are both useless and dangerous . . . These men are called
"Beach Rangers" most of whom have deserted from, or been turned out of
whalers for crimes, for which, had they been taken home and tried, they would
have been hanged.' Furthermore, there is 'still a third class of our countrymen
to be met with here, whose downcast and sneaking looks proclaim them to be
runaway convicts from New South Wales'.[63] Richard Helgerson has written
(about Elizabethan travel texts): 'Texts, nations, individual authors, particular
discursive communities – all are both produced and productive, productive of
that by which they are produced.'[64] Earle's narrative produces him as the objectivist truth-teller reporting on a foreign and exotic country and people, and on the
version of his own society he meets there. He establishes his credentials to be the
teller of these tales by carefully delineating his relation to the societies he finds
and by addressing a readership who travel with him, producing his journey in
their imaginations.

The arrival of the *Governor Macquarie* carrying Earle and his friend Mr Shand
in the Hokianga in 1827 is immediately the site of cultural exchange – quite
literally as canoes full of Maori come up to the ship, crowd the decks, board the
gangway and climb up the chains and bow – in a scene repeated each time a ship
appeared in a New Zealand harbour in the early years of contact. The first thing
that strikes Earle about the Maori boarding the ship, one of two things that strike
him 'forcibly' in his first days in New Zealand, is that they are all armed with a
'good' musket, an observation he at once universalises and impersonalises, marking both historical difference and the print culture his own narrative is part of:

... every person who has read Captain Cook's account of the natives of New Zealand would be astonished at the change which has taken place since his time when the firing of a single musket would have terrified a whole village.[65]

Earle draws the reader's gaze to the detail which demonstrates that Maori are savages and not to be taken lightly, detail which sensationalises his own position in the scene and adds weight to its truth-telling claims:

Let the reader picture to himself this savage group, handling every thing they saw, each one armed with a musket, loaded with ball, a cartouch-box buckled round his waist, and a stone patoo-patoo, or hatchet, in his hand, while human bones were hung round each neck by way of ornament; let the scene and situation be taken into consideration and he will acknowledge it was calculated to make the young traveller wish himself safe at home ...[66]

When the group of Maori had 'increased to such a degree, that we could hardly move' they performed a 'dance of welcome', a ceremony which at once accentuates cultural difference and literally divides the parties in two. The lady passengers are 'obliged' to leave, as when the dance begins each man proceeds to 'strip himself naked', which Earle recognises as a 'custom indispensable among themselves'.[67] The encounter of Maori custom with European custom reveals the conventions of both groups, and starts to suggest a reflexive recognition of the complex social behaviour of Maori ('savages') that is characteristic of Earle's

'A dance of New Zealanders.' Aquatint by Augustus Earle from *A Narrative of a nine months' residence in New Zealand in 1827*, London: Longman, 1832. ATL PUBL-0022-3

text. When the 'savage visiters', now clothed in their kakahu or flax cloaks, are joined by the ladies at supper, they are so polite and respectful that the ladies declare (a declaration Earle reports directly in speech marks) "'they would be really very handsome men if their faces were not tattooed'".[68] Throughout the transactions of arrival, cultural boundaries are marked by the response of the ladies, which is both a gender and a class response – their action and reaction maintain the world they have come from and their compliments hold out a future promise of polite society for savages.

Brian Musgrove has observed that, in travel, the 'territorial passage from one zone to another, the border crossing, represents a critical moment for the identity of the mobile subject. The territorial passage is accompanied by – or even metaphoric of – another movement; the shift from "seeing with one's own eyes" to discerning the meaning of what is seen.'[69] Earle's account of his time in New Zealand elaborates just this shift from witnessing to discerning meaning. Earle's more formal narrative moves more quickly to 'discerning the meaning of what is seen' than Markham's mix of notes, observation and gossip about the Hokianga, but they share a cluster of topics: description of the harbour, encounter with Maori, some contextualising of Maori and a focus on cannibalism. But where Markham's text reports unsorted detail – a flow of impressions, hearsay, noise, anecdote and sights – goes in multiple directions and positions him (with some inflections) as the medium through which the journey experience is passing, Earle's narrative moves deliberately from topic to topic and positions him as the holder of various kinds of expertise, able to apply knowledge and context to what he is experiencing and process its significance for the reader.

> I examined these savages . . . with the critical eye of an artist . . . I have known Indians in America from the north to the south. I am persuaded that these South Sea islanders . . . are not of the same race.[70]

In all its formal aspects Earle's narrative belongs to a convention of travel writing with more distinct protocols than Markham's. Earle moves through the New Zealand landscape with a magisterial eye, mixing ethnographic, aesthetic, historical and geographic information, and, for all his reputed inaccuracies, his text is confidently informative and referential. It is distinguished from other travel writing of the 1820s and 1830s by his attitude and relation to European society, particularly his criticisms of the missionaries, and by his distance both from the institutions and agencies that produced other travellers and travel texts (scientific expeditions, commercial interests, colonisation) and from the opportunist adventurers represented by Markham, Boultbee or Lucett. His narrative is produced by a journey that has no ostensible object and no overt agenda beyond writing about and picturing what he sees, but also relates, as Richard Helgerson has written, 'what world those happenings require and suppose: what structures of identity, what division of power, what representational practises'.[71]

The second thing to strike Earle 'forcibly' occurs the next day when, having taken the female passengers ashore to spend the day with Mrs Butler, wife of a local trader, Earle goes for a little ramble. Rambling, on both a large and a small scale, is the characteristic way in which knowledge is produced in the texts of adventurers. Events and information occur by chance, and it is the randomness of the way knowledge is produced that acts as a guarantee of its authenticity.

> I had not rambled far before I witnessed a scene which forcibly reminded me of the savage country in which I then was; and the great alteration of character and customs a few days sail will make.[72]

What Earle sees and describes, in the universal formula identified by Peter Hulme,[73] which is evident again and again in early New Zealand descriptive texts, is of course evidence of cannibalism, 'the remains of a human body which had been roasted'. Cannibalism is part of his foreknowledge of New Zealand, so he is 'more shocked than surprised' and, though 'sickened of rambling', hurries back 'eager to enquire into the particulars'. Again it is the presence of the ladies which marks out the boundaries:

> We took care not to shock the feelings of the females by letting them know the tragedy so lately acted in the village . . . It would have been difficult to have made them believe that such a noble looking and good-natured fellow had so lately imbrued his hands in the blood of a fellow creature![74]

Earle's use of the conditional distances even the possibility of such a conversation from the imagination of his reader. It suggests that he too has difficulty reconciling the different aspects of Maori he is encountering, circling around not just his preconceptions and experience of Maori but where to place himself, and how to discern the meaning of what he witnesses. The spatial journey of the rambler is not linear, it circles around, and neither is his epistemological journey: Earle's observations circle and retreat, modify and transform his opinions. When he is listening to 'George' (Te Aara), the chief implicated in the massacre of the *Boyd*, he transforms himself into the reader of a narrative like the one he is writing:

> George also related to me the dreadful tragedy of the ship 'Boyd': and horrible as these relations were, I felt a particular interest, almost amounting to pleasure, in hearing them related by an eye-witness; one who had been an actor in those bloody scenes which I had before read of: narratives which from my very childhood had always possessed particular charms for me.[75]

'Sauvages de la Nouvelle-Zélande.' Engraving by Emile Rouargue, published in Paris in 1859.
ATL PUBL-0040-01

Earle presents himself in the role of eyewitness many times in his narrative, in presenting both descriptive or ethnographic information ('I witnessed a specimen of their summary method of executing justice') and the more sensational events he encounters ('This was the second murder I was very nearly a witness to since my arrival'). He also suggests that the reading pleasure of 'bloody scenes' and horrible stories depends on their validation as historical events, authenticated by the eyewitness, but, as his acquaintance with and knowledge of Maori grows, his representation of their society becomes more complex and he is able to suggest a different way of thinking about the more violent episodes of contact.

In February 1827 HMS *Pandora* visited the Bay of Islands and George asks Earle and Shand to accompany him on a formal visit to the ship. Dressed in a 'splendid war-mat' and accompanied by his family 'dressed in equal magnificence', they are received in a 'rude and churlish manner' by the captain, treatment which humiliates George and causes Earle to reflect:

> Living entirely among these people so long as I had done, I felt the absurdity of such conduct and the folly of treating them so harshly. If ever individuals are so situated as to need either the esteem or the confidence of savages, they must bear with their prying and childish curiosity, and not be afraid of treating them too kindly; by this means they become the quietest and gentlest creatures in the world; but if treated with contumely, and their wives

and families repulsed from your ship, they become dangerous, vindictive and cruel neighbours, as many a dreadful deed which has taken place in this vicinity will fully prove.[76]

Earle's writing works constantly to understand what has happened, what border he has crossed, and what the meaning of his territorial journey is, and to negotiate his relation to the complex social structures he inhabits. His criticisms of the missionaries are based partly on the 'cold' reception he says they gave him, partly on his observation and assessment of the interaction of the various groups at the bay, and partly on his glimpses of a Maori otherness. Maori society is represented as just as complex, divided and partisan as the Europeans pursuing their sectarian and vested interests on and offshore. Although his apprehension of Maori as savage ('capricious and barbarous') dominates the frame, he presents a complex picture in noting that they 'blend' 'ferocity . . . with humanity', and he makes an effort to understand and interact with Maori politics and culture. Earle attributes the 'tolerable security' experienced by whalers refitting at the Bay of Islands during his sojourn there to the civilising effects of the behaviour of whaling crews: 'hundreds of natives are permitted to crowd on board each ship; and no accident has ever occurred from this mode of treatment'. The behaviour of ships of war is in stark contrast, armed 'to the rowguard with cutlasses and pistols . . . while the only enemy that exists is in their own imaginations'.[77] Earle's assessment of the missionaries' endeavours and their role in the Bay of Islands is even more unflattering:

> abstracted by their own gloomy reflections [they] look with contempt on all who are in pursuit of 'worldly wealth'; and regard the arrival of a whaler as an enemy coming to interfere with the spiritual interests of their 'flock' as they term the inhabitants; though I never yet saw one proselyte of their converting.[78]

When he comes to the end of his 'nine months' (really only six) in New Zealand, Earle acknowledges the changes his sojourn has worked on him. He farewells the 'natives' with a 'great deal of emotion on both sides' and reflects:

> I had arrived with feelings of fear and disgust; and was merely induced to take up a temporary residence amongst the natives, in hopes of finding something new for my pencil in their peculiar and picturesque way of life. I left them with opinions, in many respects, very favourable towards them.[79]

It is Earle's critical distance from the powerful agents of European expansion, and his lack of objectives as a traveller, that enables his rambling narrative to be relatively open-minded, so that Maori occupy a role that, though broadly and principally identified as 'savage', also connects with Earle's humanism, and displays their abilities, cultural attributes and social practices as part of a more complex picture. The cluster of negative terms which surround Maori in the text

– savage, barbarous, cunning, cruel – remain, but are amplified with kind-hearted, free, independent, intelligent and handsome. Earle's narrative shows him favourably revising his preconceptions, which would be shared by most of his readership and here are not so much given up as modified and made more complex. At the same time his narrative practices, especially processing and contextualising information about New Zealand and Maori for a European readership, connect his apparently aimless wanderings with a society intent on both territorial and epistemological mastery of new lands.

Earle's narrative represents the most gentlemanly and educated end of rambling travel texts. The debate about the role Britain should take in New Zealand is part of his reflections, and the reactions to his text from journals in England demonstrate the currency of this topic. When *Narrative of a residence in New Zealand* was published, it was immediately attacked by prominent journals in long review articles. The *Edinburgh Review*, characterising Earle as an 'extraordinary phenomenon as any which he describes . . . a wanderer over earth and sea', comments on his 'defective' and 'erroneous' account of the early discovery of New Zealand, his claim that the 'English crews' are responsible for a reduction in infanticide among Maori, and his criticism of the missionaries.[80] The *Quarterly Review* and the *Protestant Journal* both particularly attack his 'sweeping sarcasms' about the missionaries, and all the journals agree (with differing levels of intensity) that, despite his 'spirited performance' and 'authentic' and 'amusing' details about New Zealand (*Quarterly Review*), Earle's deficient research and 'contradictory accounts' (*Protestant Journal*) have resulted in a 'mischievous publication'.[81] It is however, just this non-aligned stance which positions Earle's narrative in the adventure story mode. Like Markham, he is not of the missionary party, nor is he part of the whaling and shipping population at Kororareka. His interest is in the passing parade of events and sights and characters that engage his attention as he is moving on, and the sense that he, a cultivated European humanist, can make of them.

The gentleman poop-ranger

Edward Lucett's *Rovings in the Pacific* is more frank about both the opportunism of his movements and the personal boundaries of the narrative:

> By going abroad, I had no particular part of the globe in view; all I desired was to escape from scenes and faces I had known under different circumstances; and I thought that in some far distant country, where I was unknown, I might probably win my way through life, without exposing myself to derisive scorn or sympathy.[82]

Lucett embarks as an articled seaman on a convict ship and is at once plunged into a volatile environment where he has to renegotiate his social and material world. Advised by a friend to 'doff the exterior garments of a gentleman, and to don vestments more assimilating to the garb of those who earn their bread upon the waters', he has to follow up his change of clothing by fighting for his food, his sleeping place and the conditions of his work from the moment he lugs his trunk on board and it is dumped in the third mate's mess. Fortunately, Lucett, known to the crew as a 'gentleman poop-ranger', is equipped to fight and out-smart his companions. His narrative of survival valorises his capacity to respond to circumstances and anatomises the conceptual and biographical character of a rover. Between classes, between worlds, between divisions of power, between decks, Lucett's ability to take control of his demanding environment without becoming affiliated to any one of the groups on the ship demonstrates the rover's typical location and motion. His text demonstrates the qualities of self-interest and detachment that govern his behaviour, not least in the aphorisms and analogies which make the point for the reader. Describing his strategies to make the food both palatable and sufficient, Lucett declares that he 'proved the value of the saying, that a light heart and a thin pair of breeches carry a man through the world'. He is able to 'extract both fun and information out of my novel situation'. He also makes a metaphorical self-identification that reveals the unheroic aspects of his situation:

> One fine Sunday afternoon when we were thousands of miles from land, a solitary fly of the bluebottle species made its appearance on the poop, buzzing in the sunshine. It is impossible to tell where the wanderer came from, and its position seemed so exactly to correspond with my own, that I could not but entertain a lively interest in its welfare.[83]

Lucett's identification with a bluebottle implies the transforming experience of his passage, which he acknowledges more directly in another context. When the convicts are brought on board, he expects 'to have encountered an ill-looking set of scoundrels, with ferocity depicted under every guise; but the motley group that scrambled up the sides were a hale, hearty, fresh-looking set of fellows, humble and submissive as lambs'. He amplifies the overthrow of his expectations by listing the convicts' occupations.

> We had mechanics of all trades, tailors, shoemakers, butchers, weavers, carpenters, black-smiths, whitesmiths, locksmiths, tinsmiths, cabinet-makers, workers in brass and golds, engravers, bakers, pastrycooks, farmers, miners, itinerant musicians, glee singers, strollers and gypseys; and with reluctance let it be spoken, in the list I must include two solicitors and two master mariners.[84]

By the time of his arrival in Sydney, Lucett's sketches of his relations with the rest of the crew emphasise the completion of his heroic self-fashioning as a rover in command of the situation:

Thus by assuming a tone of roughness and manners somewhat assimilating to their own, I tamed these bears to the docility of led apes.[85]

Lucett's stay in Sydney, although lasting two and a half years, occupies very little space in his text, probably because 'Sydney is in every respect so completely English, that having made up one's mind to become a foreigner, you are rather surprised to discover that you have travelled so many thousands of miles to no purpose, for it requires a considerable effort . . . to believe you are out of the mother country'.[86] When he 'determines on proceeding' to New Zealand (his syntax and choice of verb suggesting an incomplete journey, the process of travel which is the roving life), it is to 'try the unexplored resources of a new country'.[87]

So in February 1840 he ships goods and takes passage in a schooner for the Bay of Islands. The settlement he arrives in does not live up to expectations, however. The market is 'glutted with goods', 'auction bells are going all day long' and a 'monomaniacal' land fever infects the whole atmosphere.[88] Lucett cannot 'see how it is possible that commercial transactions to any extent can be conducted here', so he stores his goods and decides to go off with the schooner on a trading visit to East Cape, a speculative journey subject to chance and accident which produces the bulk of his narrative.

Arriving at Rangitukia, Lucett goes on shore for a walk. In a topographical gesture familiar from exploration narratives, and figuratively establishing the relationship of the European visitors to the landscape and its indigenous inhabitants, he and his companion, a fellow passenger from the ship, make for a hilltop he refers to as Mount Prospect, so they can obtain a 'bird's-eye-view' of the surrounding country. This unfolds before them in deep narrow gorges, a level valley 'through which we could discern the meandering course of two silver streams', and lofty ranges.[89] They take a roundabout route back and miss the schooner, which is already 'standing seaward with a spread of canvass'. He and his companion are forced to start overland for the schooner's next stop. On this arduous journey their bird's-eye view is transformed into a ground-level experience of considerable physical difficulty and intercultural negotiation. Dependent on their reluctant guide, Toma, and subject to the protocols of Maori life, Lucett travels through a very different landscape from the 'broken, bluff, repulsive, sterile' coastline he sees from the ship. Near Rangitukia every hill is under cultivation in greater or less degree, their route takes them through settlements and past whare, tapu sites, and to stopping places where they look for the iron pot customarily left for travellers. They find themselves negotiating over their assets (clothing, tobacco) with Toma and other Maori whose land they travel through and whose provision of food they depend on; in other words they travel through a landscape dense with cultural boundaries and social and commercial practices which have to be negotiated in a direct and complex way. Much of the journey takes place at night. It is so dark they have to feel their way. Just as the sun is setting, Toma motions to them to take off their hats, points to the sunset and

> sinking to his knees . . . poured out his evening orisons to the Almighty; he sang a hymn and offered several prayers. I was much affected as I looked at the wild tattooed savage . . . We did not scorn to follow the example set us by the converted heathen.[90]

Later in the journey Lucett and his companion join Toma and a local family in prayers at dawn. Their 'decent and respectful attitude' and the 'fervency' of their responses 'would put to the blush many of our more civilized congregations'.[91]

Lucett's narrative of what he has seen and experienced on foot around East Cape reveals a response to the journey and an acquisition of knowledge which modifies his perceptions. He and his companion are forced into a series of transactions which prevent them from remaining elevated and distanced from the landscape they surveyed. Lucett describes himself as walking in silence through the darkness buried in thought, and his account eventually gives voice to his thoughts about Maori, European immigration, land dealing and colonisation. His text swings between an experiential narrative characteristic of the roving text, processing that experience, and the hard-nosed assessment of New Zealand by a merchant. Lucett spent several months in New Zealand, travelling extensively in the Thames and Waikato districts, and made a second voyage at the end of the year. He continues to find the appearance of the coast 'sterile, savage' with 'repulsive cliffs . . . relieved by sandy wastes',[92] and dismisses the country as offering no commercial opportunity. But his descriptions of his encounters and dealings with Maori and his observations on what is happening to them foreground questions of appropriation and behaviour. Arriving tired and ahead of his party at Wakatiwai in the Waikato, he hurries past various parties he meets on the way, taking no notice of them: 'it was quite laughable to witness the curious expression of their faces at my dogged nonchalance'. In the next sentence, however, he switches into a retrospective reassessment of his behaviour:

> I have often reflected since at the cool impudence we English possess, and at the way we treat these poor fellows. Fancy one or two comparative pygmies traversing a country of savages, knowing nothing of the language, entering houses 'sans ceremonie', helping themselves to whatever might be in their way, the natives looking on with deferential awe, bullying chiefs upon their own land regardless of consequences – and yet this I have often done without a thought of my arrogant assumption.[93]

He 'almost wonders' why the natives submit to it, but concludes it is 'nothing but an intuitive perception of our intellectual superiority' which 'induces them to do so'. What happens to Lucett in New Zealand is that his close encounters

'Slaves preparing food'. Hand-coloured lithograph by Augustus Earle from 'Sketches illustrative of nature, inhabitants and islands of New Zealand', London: R. Martin, 1838. ATL PUBL-0015-03

with Maori society start to deconstruct the relationship between 'civilised' and 'savage' and produce the beginnings of a reciprocity. His monologic narrative opens to a dialogic possibility and, as with Markham or Earle, different points of view and other languages and attitudes are indicated. Although Lucett's constant preoccupation is evaluating the landscape for its commercial potential (which he does not rate highly), he is still able to respond to what is happening to Maori, noting that the 'invasion of their country by so many European immigrants had created a painful sort of consternation among the natives'.[94] Because Lucett, like all adventurers, asserts the primal role of the traveller as eyewitness, his declaration that 'I only vouch for what I see' becomes the foundation for an attack on the attitudes of colonisation. His later text incorporates the 'specious promises' and 'deluded beliefs' of Port Nicholson colonisers marked in italics as 'the exulting exclamations of those who wish to be deceived', and his mix of reported speech, pamphlets, letters and opinion produces a multi-voiced narrative of shady deals and 'fallacious flourishes'.[95] This stands in contrast to the eyewitness narrative which precedes it, a story showing not only that the land does not live up to the claims made for it, being mostly sandy wastes or tumultuous hills, but also that it is already and everywhere inhabited, and negotiating the cultural landscape is complex and exhausting.

Entertaining knowledge

In 1830 George Lillie Craik, who was a friend of Thomas Carlyle, published a compilation of writing about New Zealand, *The New Zealanders*, in the Library of Entertaining Knowledge (referred to by Markham as the 'Entertaining Library'). Mixing reports of voyages with descriptions and reflections on the Maori, this has as its central narrative the dictated account of John Rutherford's ten years living with Maori in New Zealand, which was widely read, as Markham's throwaway references to it imply.

In 1816 Rutherford was a seaman on the American brig *Agnes*, commanded by the unluckily named Captain Coffin, which was blown off course by a gale and forced to take shelter in Poverty Bay. After trading muskets and gun powder for water, the captain noticed a number of Maori mustering on the beach and decided to make sail. But before the ship could get under way the three hundred Maori Rutherford estimates were by then on board threw off their mats, began a haka, attacked and killed the captain and the cook, and took the ship. The rest of the crew, including a badly injured mate who died on the way, were taken ashore and tied to trees. The following morning, after a long discussion, five of the seamen, including Rutherford, were untied and led into the circle of Maori; the others were killed. Rutherford then describes in considerable detail the process by which the bodies of these men were prepared, cooked and eaten.[96]

Craik observes that Rutherford was illiterate and that his account, which Craik gives in direct speech marks, was dictated to a friend on his voyage home in 1828: 'making allowance for some grammatical solecisms, the story is told throughout with great clearness and sometimes with considerable spirit'.[97] It also displays the conventions of a written narrative, including direct address to the reader:

'Gentle reader,' continues Rutherford, 'we will now consider the sad situation we were in: our ship lost, three of our companions already killed, and the rest of us tied each to a tree, starving with hunger, wet and cold, and knowing that we were in the hands of cannibals'.[98]

Craik treats Rutherford's story with both the caution and the respect generated by an adventure narrative in the eyewitness mode. Textually it stands somewhere between an oral account and a written narrative anticipating a readership, a position whose difficulty is both amplified and addressed by the contextualising Craik is impelled to do. The value of Rutherford's story is clearly perceived by both Rutherford and Craik to lie in its descriptive confirmation of Maori cannibalism. Rutherford's involuntary journey and the knowledge it produces are both valuable and intrinsically suspect, like all adventuring narratives, and Craik takes on the burden of arguing its authenticity in the absence of an 'author' able to provide his own written assertions. Rutherford's detailed description of the cooking methods used by Maori is immediately followed by Craik's long historical survey of the evidence for cannibalism in New Zealand provided by other texts, especially those by voyagers and earlier travellers.

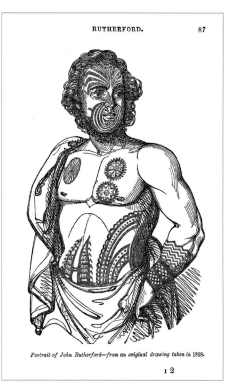

Portrait of John Rutherford—from an original drawing taken in 1828.

1 2

'Portrait of John Rutherford – from an original drawing taken in 1828.' Published in *The New Zealanders* by G. L. Craik, London, 1830, p.87. ATL B-K507-87

Anticipating his readers' response in exactly the same way as the prefaces of other roving narratives, Craik asserts authenticity by claiming the completeness of Rutherford's detail:

> The circumstances of this attack are all illustrative of the New Zealand character; and indeed the whole narrative is strikingly accordant with the accounts we have from other sources of the manner in which these savages are wont to act on such occasions – although there certainly never has before appeared so minute and complete a detail of any similar transaction.[99]

Regarding cannibalism and the various arguments about its extent and practice among Maori, Craik observes:

> Without attempting to theorise as to such a matter on the ground of such narrow views as *ordinary experience* would suggest, we may here state what the evidence is which we really have for the cannibalism of the New Zealanders.[100]

The claims Craik makes for Rutherford's story seek to address, in much the same way as John Martin on Mariner's Tonga, or James Smith on Archibald Campbell's epic voyage, the problematic status of a second-hand narrative with seductive attractions and accompanying anxieties. The eyewitness detail depicting often sensational and out-of-the-ordinary experience, the incidental movement of the narrative and the adventurer's characteristic distance from conventional behaviour and institutions make it attractively readable. Yet these qualities also open the possibility of untruth, or at least the suspicion of distortion or exaggeration. Adventurers and their editors make such insistent claims to truth-telling partly from a consciousness that the value, including the market value, of the material depends on its authenticity, and partly because the texts are produced by writers whose status in the world is itself fluid. Craik throws the weight of his scholarship and research behind Rutherford's narrative, while at the same time preserving its oral, eyewitness qualities. The narrative opens with an engraving of Rutherford naked to the waist to show off his moko, visible supporting evidence of both his transculturation and his narrative. When Craik describes Maori customs and practices, he uses Rutherford's narrative as the primary evidence, supported by extensive quotation from the authoritative published texts of Cook, Marsden, Cruise, Nicholas, Dillon and the *Missionary Register*. Rutherford's account of his experiences, enfolded in layers of supporting and verified texts (verified by the institutions associated with their production, readership and use), speaks for inside knowledge. From inside the tattooed body he speaks for the experience of being Maori; from a context of formal authenticated publication, his narrative speaks for informal, personal oral record, a primary act of witnessing foregrounding the witness and rhetorically marked by his voice. When Rutherford's story reaches the point at which he is living in the village where he stayed for the rest of his time in New Zealand, Craik puts him down, or aside, while he delivers another kind of information:

> we may consider him now as fairly domesticated among his new associates, and may therefore conveniently take the present opportunity of completing our general picture of the country and its inhabitants.[101]

The claims often made by writers of adventuring narratives for the transparency and immediacy of their texts are surpassed here by Craik's organisation of his own text around the events in Rutherford's, as though he has personally left him in a whare to bide his time while he catches up with 'a few matters which have not yet found a place in our narrative'. The continuing story of Rutherford's life in New Zealand provides the pegs on which Craik hangs ethnographic information and builds an authorising context of scientific, anthropological and exploration commentary. It also enables him to shape the reader's response to some of the events. When Rutherford's companion is killed, Craik interrupts the narrative to opine that 'exposed as he was every moment to the chance of . . . provoking their capricious cruelty, Rutherford it may be thought, must have felt his protracted detention every day more insupportable', before continuing with Rutherford's account of being made a chief and marrying the two eldest daughters of 'Aimy', the chief of his tribe.

After describing the battles and other tribal encounters he took part in, Rutherford's narrative finishes with an account of his escape from New Zealand which is interesting for the way it shifts through key points of reference. Craik reasserts that this part of the narrative is 'in his own words'. A ship is sighted off the coast and the local chiefs gather at Tokomaru with pigs and potatoes for trading. In the evening a basket of food is presented to Rutherford by a slave, 'saying it was a present from his master. I asked him what was in the basket, and he informed me it was part of a slave girl's thigh, that had been killed three days before. It was cooked he added, and was very nice'.[102] Rutherford makes a present of it to his companions. The chiefs decide that if the ship lands they will take it and murder the crew, and Rutherford promises to act as a decoy. His narrative then spends some time describing in detail what he wore.

> I was dressed in a feathered cloak, belt and turban, and armed with a battle axe, the head of which was formed of a stone which resembled green glass but was so hard as to turn the heaviest blow of the hardest steel. The handle was of hard black wood, handsomely carved and adorned with feathers.[103]

With one eye on an ethnographic reading and the other on the sensational aspects of New Zealand life, Rutherford's narrative ends on a finely balanced distribution of reader sympathy. On the one hand Rutherford betrays his Maori companions who have, after all, been his protective as well as threatening cohort for ten years, while on the other we are reminded of the unacceptable aspects of Maori life. In the middle, the value of Rutherford's eyewitnessing of Maori practices and artefacts is reasserted. In the absence of any more of Rutherford's words, Craik supplies a brief biography and a character assessment. Taken to Tahiti, Rutherford is married by one of the English missionaries to a 'chief woman', whom he leaves a year later for England, promising to return. Back in England he 'maintained himself by accompanying a travelling caravan of wonders, shewing his tattooing, and telling something of his extraordinary adventures'. Craik concludes with a kind of testimonial:

> The publisher of this volume had many conversations with him in January 1829 when he was exhibited in London. He was evidently a person of considerable quickness, and great powers of observation . . . his manners were mild and courteous . . . he was fond of children . . . and a man of very sober habits. He greatly disliked being shown for money, which he submitted to, principally that he might acquire a sum, in addition to what he received for his manuscript, to return to Otaheite. According to this account the attack

'Portrait of John Rutherford, the tattooed
Englishman' by George Scharf, ca 1829.
ATL A-090-028

made upon the Agnes would seem to have been altogether unprovoked by the conduct
either of the captain or any of the crew; but we must not, in matters of this kind, assume
that we are in possession of the whole truth, when we have heard the statement of only
one of the parties.[104]

The travel texts generated at the edges of European expansion into New
Zealand and the Pacific are shaped by itineracy, appetite, adventure and opportunity. The popularity of books about shipwreck and beachcombing, tales of
experiences among indigenous peoples and stories of roving shows the attract-
iveness of the exotic and marginal life to the stay-at-home reader, and suggests
the purposes of the authorial and editorial insistence on authentication. Pitched
at a reading market eager for excitement, the travel narrative is also dutiful
about the limits of representation and the boundaries of fact, betraying an
anxiety to be taken seriously while exploiting the 'rage' for books of enterprise
and adventure. As Dennis Porter has remarked, 'borders of all kinds are perceived as dangerous as well as exciting places':[105] the adventurer's travel text
insists on itself as truth-telling while it marks social freedom, documents varieties
of disorder and relates desire and transgression.

CHAPTER 4

Travel with interest

*. . . defined as the constant interchange of goods, words, ideas
and emotions, commerce presents the world perceived and the
mind perceiving as transactional, so that the knower apprehends
both the world and himself as they pass from one set of hands to
another. – J. G. A. Pocock*[1]

Many early travel books were written by people who came to New Zealand for
professional reasons as soldiers, businessmen or clergy, and their production of
books for a general readership reveals travel as a purposeful function of the state
and its interest groups. Travellers like Joel Samuel Polack, Ernst Dieffenbach,
John Carne Bidwill or Edward Jerningham Wakefield addressed their books to a
readership eager for stories of adventure and derring-do, but also keen to be
informed about new resources, markets and the possibilities of colonisation.
Such travel writing also underlines the connections between claims of 'civilising'
missions and the agencies of a forceful imperialism. A travel text by a soldier
requires the reader to make a connection between a military presence and travelling, and travel texts by missionaries pull into focus the relationship between
imperialism and religion, drawing attention to factional and territorial differences among Christians. A travel text is also a claim to authority and ownership.
The conceptual field represented in the terrain of the journey is described in a
range of professional knowledge – ethnography, geography, geology, natural
sciences – and the writer is displayed as an authority over the execution of the
journey, the knowledge-gathering process, and the people and events encountered en route. Travel writing by professional men can also be a political tool or a
professional showcase, and display the extra-professional interest of a polymath,
but it is always shaped by, and shapes, the assumptions, ambitions and ideologies of the institutions they represent.

THE CHURCH

William Wade's 'uncomfortable and unprofitable suspense'

William Wade arrived in New Zealand with William Colenso in 1834. He was sent by the Church Missionary Society (CMS) to superintend the printing press which Colenso was to operate, producing the books needed by the mission. When they arrived in the Bay of Islands, however, the press was put in Colenso's sole charge and Wade was given various other jobs by the missionaries at Paihia. Both Wade and Colenso were from a dissenting background and neither was ordained, which made their integration into the High Church Anglican community at Paihia difficult. Wade left in 1840 to join the Baptist Missionary Society, and was appointed as minister to Hobart. His *Journey in the Northern Island of New Zealand,* published in Hobart in 1842, is dedicated to Lady Franklin

> who has/taken a deep interest/in the country and the people/of/New Zealand/this volume is,/with her kind permission,/humbly and respectfully dedicated/by her lady-ship's obliged/and obedient servant,/The Author.

Lady Jane Franklin, the intrepid and adventurous wife of the Governor of Tasmania, Sir John Franklin, visited New Zealand in 1841 and was widely associated with botanical and scientific investigations (Colenso named a fern after her). Her patronage is further enumerated on the following page of Wade's book, at the head of the List of Subscribers, which puts her down for six copies. The list contains some 425 names, which seem to be mostly from Hobart, and in a note at the end additional orders from Longford and Launceston are mentioned, making the subscribed print-run well over 500 copies. Closing the subscription list, the author gratefully acknowledges 'the very flattering encouragement afforded him, by the many and highly respectable names with which he has been unexpectedly favoured'.[2]

In reconstructing the human and institutional interactions (to use D. F. McKenzie's terms)[3] of the production and publication of Wade's travel text, the title page, dedication and subscribers' list offer some metatextual information. Travel texts and accounts of New Zealand by missionaries in the early years of settlement are relatively unusual. Wade's *Journey,* Colenso's narratives of his exploratory and botanical journeys and William Yate's *An Account of New Zealand* (1835) form a small cluster of books produced by missionaries which are not scriptural. None of them was printed on a missionary press (though Yate's book was published by Seeley & Burnside, who published many missionary and religious texts). The great bulk of missionary writing took the form of reports sent to the CMS and recorded in the *Missionary Register,* while Colenso's

'View of the Missionary House, Waimate, New Zealand', 1830s or 1840s.
Watercolour by Thomas Gardiner. ATL A-049-020

travel narratives were first sent to England as extracts from his journal and transcribed into the *Register*. Why did missionaries choose to publish travel accounts at all?

Both Wade and Colenso were lay missionaries or catechists. Both desired to be ordained and both were blocked from ordination by the missionaries at Paihia because of their background. Wade's history of service in New Zealand for the CMS was not a happy one, and the appearance of his book about New Zealand in Hobart in 1842, at a time when he was establishing a new ministry in the Baptist Missionary Society, is revealing, both as a response to his experiences in New Zealand and as an expression of church politics. When the printing press at Paihia was put into the hands of Colenso alone, Wade, 'after waiting un-employed, except in picking up a little of the language', was sent to Tauranga to help establish a mission there. After a few months he was 'peremptorily' ordered by the CMS in England to go back to the Bay of Islands, where

> in short, my dear Sir, the Press became the subject of appeal and counter appeal. Orders from home of the most decided character were totally disregarded, or at best trifled with by the Missionary Committee here, and with a wife and family (I have now <u>three little ones</u>) have been living in a state of most uncomfortable and unprofitable suspense up to the present moment.[4]

In the context of his troubled relations with the mission at the Bay of Islands, Wade's subscription list and the dedication to Lady Franklin have a political air. Two years after his departure from the Bay of Islands, he has established a new community and powerful connections – he is encouraged, flattered and favoured. On the title page a descriptive sentence under the author's name sketches the identity politics of his publication: 'Minister of Harrington-Street Chapel, Hobart Town; Formerly a Resident Missionary in New Zealand'.

Wade's *Journey,* based on his diary of travels in 1838, is a conventional mix of ethnographic, social, botanical and geographical information, including some discussion of the Maori language and reporting of Maori traditions and legends. Peter Gibbons has noted that it is marked 'by suspicion of and contempt for the New Zealanders',[5] revealed by the way Maori appear in the text as well as descriptions of them. Few Maori are individualised, and when they are, as in 'David . . . formerly called Taiwanga', the first named Maori to appear on Wade's journey, the description of him stresses the sensational aspects of his previous history and dwells on his 'ornamental disfiguration' and 'disgusting filthiness'.[6] Wade's account opens with a description of the CMS station at Waimate, interesting for the way it sets in place the principal tensions of the text. It describes the establishment of the mission and maintains a running comparison between the 'indefatigable' missionaries and the recalcitrant Maori, who haggle and obstruct. Building Waimate mission, with its 'fifty thousand bricks', bridge and water mill, is represented as a labour accomplished by perseverance, faith and moral fibre in the face of great odds. As an emblem of civilisation, 'the most English-like spot in all New Zealand', Waimate is the point of origin for Wade's extended descriptive judgements about Maori.[7] The reason for his journey, Wade tells us, is 'purposing to collect . . . miscellaneous information relative to the country and the people', but the gulf between Wade's assumptions and premises and what he is witnessing is always apparent. Two examples follow.

Getting up early to leave for Mangakahia on the second day of his journey, he finds

> the two natives who had gone before with their back loads, and were staying at the pa, were not disposed to join us. At last they condescended to come down and tell us, that not a step would they stir unless there and then payment was given. To this they were incited by a native named Coleman. I could not but feel grieved as well as vexed, to find those who were making a profession of religion still full of their native covetousness.[8]

Although Wade expects Maori to be productive, work as hard and in the same way as Europeans, and adopt European practices and beliefs – he praises Maori who have established agricultural areas – they are not supposed to drive a hard bargain or be properly paid. He refers to 'fair compensation according to the usual rate of native labour',[9] which mostly means blankets, and, though he concedes that 'with regard to land, the natives of some parts were taking a lesson of their civilized neighbours', Maori demands are invariably 'exorbitant' and 'native covetousness' an 'old innate principle'.[10] Unlike Colenso, he shows no affection for the Maori he encounters and gets to know, and represents the consequences of contact and colonisation for Maori as following from moral failure on their part.

> The constitutional change effected in the people by a sudden transition of habits, – their universal carelessness with regard to health, with their stupid unwillingness to use proper means for maintaining it, – the covetousness and aversion to persevering labour which so generally mark their character, – and their reckless apathy as to a fair national advancement of themselves, – seem a few among the many indications, that the aboriginal race of New Zealanders will ultimately become extinct.[11]

Wade's loaded adjectives tell their own story.

The second example is an anecdote that bears witness to the role of books as currency for the missionaries. Wade presents it as a story about Maori preference for figurative language, but it also reveals Maori perceptions of the nature of the transaction between them and missionaries. At Taumatamu in the Maunga-tautari district, most of the village was away. Wade pitched his tent near the house of a young chief named Neke, and went to bed. He was roused by Neke's angry voice demanding food.

> His tone grew sharp and angry: – 'What business have you to come here, putting up your tent in my place? Is this the spot on which you were born? Get up immediately: light your candle, and give me some food.'[12]

After an argument in which Wade threatened to pack up and move on, Neke came to the side of the tent and

> in a softened voice asked me where I had left my books; whether I had not given them all to Ngatiruru . . . I said it was true that I had given most of my books to Ngatiruru, but that I had one in reserve for him. With this he seemed perfectly satisfied . . .[13]

In the morning Wade finds that the request for food was figurative and that Neke expected him to understand the request was for books, but he perceives this not as a comment on the nature of the bargain between Maori and missionary, but as an example of the troublesomeness of Maori rhetoric.

Wade's political troubles with the other missionaries at Waimate are never mentioned in *Journey in the Northern Island of New Zealand*, and seem to be divorced from his praise of the missionary labour in establishing the Waimate

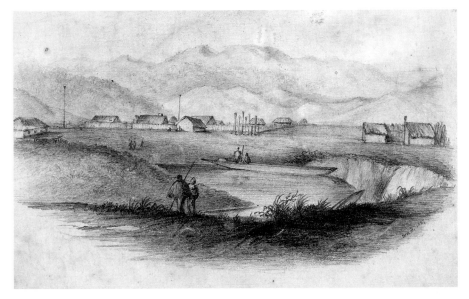

'Mission settlement – Puriri in May 1836. From the W.N.W./W.R.W. 1837.'
Drawing by W. R. Wade. ATL A-113-001

mission. Interestingly, though, this persevering and active group remain collectively undifferentiated, as the 'Missionaries', until well into Wade's account, in
sharp contrast to his later meetings with members of the various Wesleyan
missions he visits, who are named and whose hospitable and kindly qualities are
detailed and praised.[14] Wade's book, framed as it is by the material evidence of his
supporting subscribers, delicately insinuates some differences between mission
groups and represents him as an authority on the indigenous people of New
Zealand, a shift in emphasis away from his underemployed and unordained
status in the Bay of Islands. Some of the antagonisms present in the missionary
community are evident from Wade's unpublished review of William Yate's book
about New Zealand, which Wade sent to the CMS in 1837. Wade castigated Yate
for 'ignorance, exaggeration and high colouring' and asserted his own status as an
authority on New Zealand by observing that 'it is worthy of remark that the
Author, who seems to represent himself as a great traveller, never made more
than one journey to any distance from the Waimate'.[15]

A Journey in the Northern Island of New Zealand describes a trajectory which
is social and political as well as geographical and ethnographic. Because *Journey*
is also a tool of identity politics, Wade's comments on New Zealand and the
people he is observing raise complex questions about the motivation and voice of
travel writing. What authority is claimed by the cleric turned travel writer, and
who is he addressing? In Wade's case these questions have more than one answer.

The letter Y

William Yate's *An Account of New Zealand*[16] is the only published work on New Zealand by an ordained missionary not written from the 'retrospective view-point of old age'.[17] Produced from journals during Yate's voyage to England in 1834, it brought him a brief period of fame after publication in 1835,[18] when it went through two editions and he toured England on behalf of the CMS. In 1836, on his return journey to New Zealand, Yate stopped in Sydney to act as temporary chaplain at St James's Church and was accused, first, of a homosexual relationship with the third officer of the ship he had just travelled on, Edward Denison of the *Prince Regent*, and then of 'revolting' conduct with Maori in New Zealand.[19] The charges were never publicly substantiated but they ruined Yate's career and made his name notorious, to the point where his relative, the Reverend Benjamin Yate Ashwell, asked the Secretary of the CMS 'that the name of Yate & even the letter Y may be omitted & erased in all letters and packages sent to me by the Society, for it is a name justly abhorred in New Zealand'.[20]

Written while Yate was still in favour with the CMS and the mission at Paihia, *An Account of New Zealand* is intended to report the 'plans and operations of the Church Missionary Society'. What A. G. Bagnall calls the 'customary formal description' of New Zealand[21] is followed by an extended ethnographic description of the Maori and concludes triumphally with the establishment of the mission. As Peter Gibbons notes:

> What purports to be a realistic account is, in fact, carefully plotted to denigrate the New Zealanders in their natural state, to glorify the mission, and to amplify the success of evangelism.[22]

Although Yate appears in his narrative in the first person, and it is based on his journals, his presence as narrator is effaced. *An Account* is largely impersonal and descriptive, claiming an empirical authority more than the presence typical of an eyewitness. Embarking on a lengthy taxonomy of New Zealand's 'natural beauties', Yate sets himself as the point of transmission for a set of observations on 'everything which naturally strikes the eye as beautiful or sublime': he saw, he gazed and he was astonished by the 'solemn, silent majesty' of Hikurangi, the hills with their 'deep dark and frightful' caves, the lakes, the waterfalls, the ferns and forests. As a detail, Yate notes 'several dead bodies, deposited by the natives in some of these caves . . . in others . . . the remains of the bodies of murdered victims, carelessly rolled down here, to save the trouble of further interment'.[23] Yate's extensive catalogues of trees, birds, fish, reptiles, insects, shells and minerals, and his descriptions of the manners and customs of the people, their material culture and social practices, 'account' for New Zealand to an educated and European reading public.

Yate's self-characterisation as the dispassionate observer places the author and his text in a larger context than the country about which he is writing. Drawing on ethnography, geography, aesthetics and anthropology, he writes in a well-established set of genre conventions[24] for a conditioned and metropolitan readership whose connection with the place and people he describes is intellectual and ideological. As his account of New Zealand as a place 'reserved by Providence for the use of man'[25] builds to its climax with the gradual transformation of the savage and barbarous New Zealanders into an 'attentive and devout' congregation, there is an increase in authorial observation and response. This works both to mark points of extreme difference and to celebrate the progress of conversion and the promotion of Christian knowledge. The print culture that Yate's book contributes to and is shaped by is Christian, collective ('We notice', 'We at first begin'), scholarly, comparative and eurocentric. His observations anticipate a readership whose knowledge of the world is geographically wide[26] and textually deep, and whose beliefs correspond to those of an evangelical missionary, for whom the advent of a new country and people supplies a providential opportunity. His text displays the formal qualities he brings to his work – scholarly knowledge and practices, religious conviction – and as his authorial persona shifts from the magisterial, objectified traveller of the first section to the ethnographer and missionary, there emerge the passion and conviction of a religious man contemplating the scene before him as an exemplary text of faith.

> How many happy Sabbaths have I spent at the Waimate! And how has my inmost soul rejoiced, as I have seen the once-deluded people of this land listening with delight to the sound of the "church-going bell", and hastening with willing feet to the House of the Lord! There is something peculiarly pleasing in the sound of the bell amidst the wilds of New Zealand.[27]

If the missionaries' efforts in the field might be described as establishing a cult of the Book[28] by disseminating biblical texts as widely as possible (Yate describes the first shipment of printed translations of the liturgy and the Gospels as the 'most valuable cargo that ever reached the shores of New Zealand'), its corollary activity was the dissemination of books about the mission and its work to a supporting home readership. *An Account of New Zealand* takes advantage of the two largest sections of the British publishing market: the interest in works of geography, history and travel, and in religious works.[29] It is a familiar mix, used by most missionary accounts of the Pacific; William Ellis's *Polynesian Researches* (1829) is the most famous example.[30] Yate's working title for the manuscript he wrote on board ship and presented to the CMS on arrival in London was 'Researches in New Zealand', and at a meeting of the society in February 1835 it was reported that 'Researches in New Zealand' would make a companion volume to Hartley's *Researches in Greece and the Levant* (1833), also published by Seeley & Burnside. A thousand copies were printed 'at the same size paper and type' as Hartley's book. A copy was sent to the King and the CMS congratulated Yate on the publication of 'a permanent and instructive record of the first fruits gathered by the Missionary band in that field'.[31]

If Yate had not had the misfortune to become so notorious that even the first letter of his name was demonised and his book tainted by association (as in William Williams's annotation to his copy: 'no one has brought so much dishonour on the holy cause of Christ in this land as the wretched author of this book'), *An Account of New Zealand* might also have become a standard work of reference on New Zealand and on the work of the overseas missions. But Christian missions dependent on public support and their own promotional efforts could not afford any retrospective sensationalist readers, so Yate and his book disappeared into silence.

THE MILITARY

Blotted with blood: W. B. Marshall and HMS *Alligator*

Mary Louise Pratt has pointed out that bureaucracy and militarisation are the central instruments of empire.[32] A military presence had been well established in the Bay of Islands before 1840, partly in response to events like the *Boyd* episode, and partly as a natural extension of the British presence in Australia and the Pacific. Missionary reporting began the flow of official information that was to result in a British Resident in the Bay of Islands, and military travel writing grew more or less naturally from the bureaucratic requirements of ship documentation – logs, journals and despatches.

While travel writing characteristically mixes information and readerships, the New Zealand travel archive, especially in the years before the tourist boom of the 1870s and 1880s, includes several examples of writing that is in some sense trans-institutional or interdisciplinary: narratives like Wade's, which is both a missionary text and a narrative of personal experience, and William Barrett Marshall's *A Personal Narrative of Two Visits to New Zealand in His Majesty's Ship 'Alligator' A.D. 1834*.

Marshall was a ship's surgeon in the Royal Navy who wanted to be a missionary. His book carries a note announcing that profits from its sale

> will be handed over to the Church Missionary Society for the immediate extension of
> their mission in New Zealand to the three tribes at Cape Egmont, who were sufferers by
> the military proceedings detailed in the second part of the narrative.[33]

He explicitly sets out to contrast the effects of a 'Christian mission on the minds and morals of the natives' and of a military expedition 'on their welfare and prosperity', as he declares in the dedication to Lord Glenelg.[34] Hostility between missionary and military enterprises is his argument for

> the desirableness of an impartial Visitor, relating to the public ear that which he himself has seen, heard and known of the unobtrusive labours of men occupying so remote a portion of our Lord's vineyard.[35]

Marshall's diary-based narrative of the *Alligator's* first visit to New Zealand mixes familiar traveller's observations on Maori and their social practices – slavery, prostitution and infanticide, the 'restless and vagrant habits of the savage'[36] – with close attention to the missionaries and their work and long disquisitions on Christian virtues and the gospels. He writes with one eye on the armchair traveller eager for sensational detail and the other on someone he calls a 'Christian reader', to whom he delivers homilies and abundant exemplary tales of the changes effected in Maori behaviour by conversion. Marshall knew William Yate from Sydney and travelled in Northland with Yate and Baron von Hugel.[37] He wanted to be ordained at a new mission station to be established at New Plymouth, and his book is also a showcase for his piety and scriptural learning and his knowledge of contemporary debate and writing about New Zealand.[38] It is a set of interests with more than one agenda. Marshall's perception of the need to regulate relations with and treatment of Maori by the 'extension of the principles of international law'[39] is coloured by his self-interested advocacy of mission work, which depends on a running illustration of the savagery and degradation of Maori, and praise for the virtues of Englishness. When he is travelling to Waimate with a midshipman, they pass 'a couple of women boiling potatoes in an English swing pot of cast iron':

> the sight of which, however apparently little a kail pot may have to do with patriotism, was not void of interest to one, in whose breast that healthful feeling has not yet ceased to glow, which rejoices to meet with the arts and manufactures of his own beloved native land, in all nations and countries, even to the uttermost ends of the earth. And surely the love of one's country may be suffered to luxuriate in the pleasure afforded by so trifling an incident as that of beholding the lately savage inhabitants of a savage country, not only feeding upon a root for which they were first indebted to an Englishman, but also cooking it after the English fashion in a vessel of English manufacture.[40]

Marshall's rhetorical questions build up to the assertion that the 'peaceable extension of our comforts and customs ... is one of the best conquests achieved by us as a people', but there is no doubt that he is describing conquest, emotionally powered by its appeal to patriotism, nostalgia and domesticity. Redemption of the Maori from savagery is homologously figured as a redemption of the landscape, which is bleak and barren, 'leaving the soul unsatisfied' – what Marshall negatively imagines into place prefigures colonisation:

> the absence of inanimate beings, the absence of human forms and human dwellings, the absence of every thing which an Englishman is accustomed to look for when treading in the known track of human footsteps, renders scenery a mere blank to me.[41]

Although Marshall's text does not achieve the impartiality he claims, his desire to be a missionary and his pietism allow him a space and authority (God) for a critique of official policy and practices,[42] illustrated from the first visit in his description of the presentation of a 'national flag' to the New Zealanders. The *Alligator* had come prepared, with three different ensigns to choose from. The chiefs assembled in a tent at Waitangi and the British Resident, James Busby, read them a speech explaining 'the object proposed in offering them a flag, and of the advantages to accrue to them from possessing one'. Marshall notes that two of the chiefs declined to vote, 'apparently apprehensive lest under this ceremony lay hid some sinister design on our parts':

> had anything like freedom of debate been encouraged, instead of suppressed . . . I have little doubt but that the real sentiments of those present would have been elicited; and assuredly, an opportunity might have been afforded of answering any objections as they arose, and, in that way, more completely satisfying the minds of the people as to the objects contemplated by our Government.[43]

The occasion of the *Alligator*'s second visit to New Zealand in 1834 was to rescue nine sailors and the wife and children of Captain Guard of the *Harriet*, wrecked on the Taranaki coast in April, and held hostage by local Maori. Marshall's account of this visit is an impassioned protest against the way the Maori were treated, from John Guard's failure to keep his promises to the actions of the military. His carefully detailed account of events as they unfolded makes it clear how volatile and trigger-happy the responses of the soldiery to the situation were. The *Alligator*'s Captain, Robert Lambert, had promised that the captive 'O-o-hit' should be set free when Betty Guard was delivered to the ship, and he was returned to shore wearing a blanket, shirt, jacket and Scots cap, 'as proud of his new plumage as any beau just released from the more gentle hands of some fashionable tailor'.[44] The Maori came off to the ship to barter, but the 'harmless traffic' was prohibited. Later, the senior lieutenant again approached the shore and 'a ball whizzed over his head, discharged from the musket of someone in the Waimate Pa', which was 'deemed a signal of defiance'. The drum beat, the ship edged to shore and a 'furious cannonading took place'. When the firing began the Maori hoisted a white flag, lowered it and rehoisted it.

> It seemed as though a signal, sufficient when used in the warfare of civilized nations, to command instant respect, and an immediate cessation, however temporary of hostilities, was powerless when shown by a savage people . . . or as if when a civilized power conde-scends to make war upon savages, it is at liberty to throw off the constraints imposed by civilized nations upon nations as well as individuals.[45]

Marshall's recognition that military behaviour is conditioned by precon-ceptions about the status of the enemy is burned into him by these and subse-quent events on the Taranaki coast, and his distress at the behaviour of the British produces impassioned exhortations and references to biblical and Miltonic adjurations against war. The text evokes a community of Christian readers who will bring individual conscience to their reading, and a nearer Christian audience who will understand the self-interested implications of Marshall's argument about the needs of savages. On the one hand he condemns the excessively puni-tive treatment of Taranaki Maori, which violated the rules of fair play and pun-ished them after they had met agreed conditions, deconstructs an opposition between savage and civilised in describing the British action, and forcefully critiques British policy in handling the Guard affair from Sydney and not through the British Resident. On the other hand, his peroration represents Maori as the objectified and needy recipients of a European ontology, whose misery is caused not by the destruction of their pas and canoes and families by British warships, but by their lack of Christian instruction:

'H.M.S. Alligator's boats off the Wymattee pahs endeavouring to get Mrs. Guard and her children from the New Zealand savages, 30th Sept., 1833 [ie. 1834].'
Watercolour by Thomas Woore. ATL A-048-008

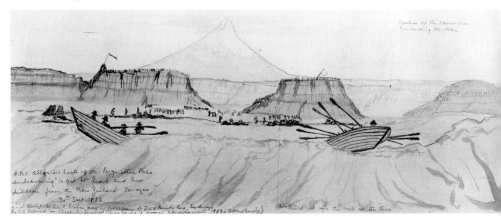

How devoutly is it to be wished that a Christian mission may be speedily established on this coast, along which, though there be few temptations to commerce, and no harbour to encourage the habitual resort of shipping, there is abundance of wood, plentiful supplies of water, a rich and productive soil; added to which, and above all which, there are many thousands of miserable savages, perishing for lack of knowledge, without God, and without hope in the world![46]

Despite Marshall's critique of British policy and the deployment of British force in New Zealand, the overtly proselytising religious discourse in which his critique is embedded leaves in place agendas of social change for the Maori which enable imperialist and colonial development. *A Personal Narrative of Two Visits to New Zealand* advances Marshall's own interests, while in both its content and its material form as a fundraiser it promotes the expansion and entrenchment of an institution and an ideology dedicated to the irrevocable alteration of Maori society. Marshall's social and religious conscience is the impetus for his efforts to expand the missions, and his personal ambition a driver for the production of his text.

The adoption of proper measures

Up to and including the New Zealand Wars of the 1860s, a number of travel accounts were written by military men, emphasising the function of the travel text as an act of graphic control, a double reconfiguration of space from occupied land to battle zone, and from battle zone to travel destination. In the same way, the naval log or military despatch is reconfigured into the travel narrative.

One of the earliest accounts of New Zealand was the journal of Richard Cruise, captain in the 84th Foot Regiment and in charge of the military detachment on the *Dromedary* in 1820. As Cruise explains in the preamble to his *Journal of a Ten Months' Residence in New Zealand* (1823), the *Dromedary* had been fitted up as a convict ship and, after delivering 369 male convicts to Port Jackson, proceeded to New Zealand with its detachments of soldiers from the 69th and 84th regiments to pick up a cargo of spars. The *Dromedary* spent ten months in the various bays of Northland and Cruise maintained a 'constant intercourse with the inhabitants' which he recorded in his journal, 'noted down while fresh in his memory'.[47]

Mary Louise Pratt notes that 'control over firearms [is] the single most decisive factor in Europe's subjection of others, right down to the present day'.[48] From first contact with Europeans firearms were used against the Maori,[49] who quickly sought to obtain their own supply. Guns became the prized currency and intense competition for them led to the Musket Wars of the 1820s and 1830s.[50] Cruise's first contact with Maori came on the Tasman crossing. When

'Tetoro, chief of New Zealand. Drawn by R. Read from life', 1820. Published in Richard Cruise, *Journal of a Ten Months' Residence in New Zealand*, London: Longman, 1823. ATL A-114-036

the *Dromedary* left Sydney on 15 February 1820, on board were the principal chaplain to the colony of New South Wales, Samuel Marsden, and nine Maori who had been living with him at Parramatta. Some had come for education and 'others had come to obtain muskets and gunpowder or merely to gratify their rambling disposition'.[51] Only two Maori are named in Cruise's account of the crossing: 'Repero, son of the chief Shungie'(Hongi) and 'Tetoro'(Titore), who is the 'most striking in appearance'. The frontispiece of the first edition of *Journal of a Ten Months' Residence* is a coloured engraving of a drawing by 'R. Read from Life 1820' of 'Tetoro, Chief of New Zealand'. He is standing on the beach with a seascape behind him, wearing a feather cloak which is open, showing finely woven mats and a tattoo on his thigh. He has a full facial moko, two huia feathers in his very curly hair, a full curly beard and is holding a taiaha. The frontispiece represents him as the principal figure in Cruise's text, an archetype of the Maori chief, recognisably non-European but constructed by a European aesthetic, and hints at his conversion into an object of scientific interest. Separated from his hapu or community, Titore stands by himself, not on ancestral lands, but on the no-man's-land of the littoral, the beach zone of contact, scene of encounter and contest, marked by his clothing and possession as 'native', an object of ethnographic interest, decorative rather than aggressive.

Cruise's attention remains fixed on Titore for the journey. However, all the shipboard episodes concerning Titore that Cruise describes involve guns or gunpowder. Most of the Maori on board had obtained 'firelocks' at Sydney and, when they saw the 'soldiers' arms, regularly ranged in arm-racks, they tied theirs in the part of the ship they occupied in a similar manner'. When a double-barrelled fowling piece belonging to one of the officers was handed to Titore

> he burst into the most enthusiastic expressions of delight, pressed it to his breast, said he would give thirty of his finest mats for it, and tying a thread pulled out of his Ka-ka-how or upper garment, round the guard of the trigger, said it was *tabbooed* and must be his when he got to New Zealand.[52]

On the grounds of prudence, it was decided to remove a quantity of gunpowder from him and lodge it in the magazine until the ship arrived at New Zealand. Titore fell into an 'agony of grief and despair', refusing to speak and rolling himself up in his mat until eventually the powder was returned to him. Cruise observes Titore exercising with his 'spear . . . on the poop with much agility, but terrible ferocity' and records him observing that the soldiers 'would not be acceptable guests at New Zealand; he seemed suspicious of the intentions of an armed force'.[53] On the Sunday before arriving at the Bay of Islands, the Maori attended a service performed by Marsden. They wore European clothes, which

> gave them quite a civilized look . . . Two of them had got soldiers' jackets and caps, of which they seemed extremely proud; and as they, in common with most of their countrymen, possessed the art of mimicry to a great extent, they amused themselves . . . in imitating the particular manner of walking or any singularity of attitude they had observed among the different persons on the ship.[54]

Cruise was a professional soldier but it is nevertheless striking how consistently he represents contact with Maori in the frame of warfare. His eye is always engaged by the Maori response to European weaponry, by the weapons they carry, by the accounts of battles and attacks on Europeans they gave him, by the consequences of intertribal warfare,[55] by their social practices resulting from intertribal warfare – slavery, preserving moko mokai. When he looks at the landscape, for example the pa at Whangaroa, he remarks 'its appearance was most imposing; and where firearms are little used, it ought to be in an impregnable position'; when he observes the people gathering to meet the boat, he sees the spears in their hands. He records the responses of a people encountering a superior military technology, responses which suggest a concerted attempt at mimicry and the anticipation of conflict, in the mode that Pratt has termed 'anti-conquest' – the 'strategies of representation whereby European bourgeois subjects seek to secure their innocence in the same moment as they assert European hegemony'.[56] Cruise's mode of reporting, which has been described as 'dispassionate',[57] observes an official, even anthropological, distance from its subject, never employing a singular personal pronoun, and preserving the form of a log with notes of weather, temperature and wind direction. His narrative identifies the principal Maori by name, describes Maori behaviour and custom and never expresses aggressive action or intent on the part of the *Dromedary*, but is constantly alert to the fighting strength of the Maori and continually reports threats made against the ship. The *Dromedary* frequently fires its big guns, an action Cruise represents as a salutation to the Maori. Ceremonial exchanges of fire occur repeatedly. Shooting parties go onshore after game, and there are repeated incidents of Maori showing 'the greatest reluctance to visit the *Dromedary*, declaring "that they were certain a plot was formed to hang them when they got on board"'.[58] On one occasion an officer goes ashore to retrieve a musket that had fallen overboard and been fished up by Maori. Learning that 'unpleasant steps would be taken for its recovery', the village produces all its muskets and 'Teperree' (Tepere) recounts the origin of each one. Cruise comments:

> This little incident will show how much the natives stood in awe of the numerical strength of the *Dromedary*, when an individual, alone, unarmed, and removed from the possibility of obtaining assistance, could, in the midst of a savage tribe, deliver to its chief so disagreeable a message without meeting with the slightest personal disrespect.[59]

The presence of sixty soldiers on the *Dromedary*, amplified by salutes from the big guns, is a message understood by Maori from their first appearance on board, as Titore's anxiety about the meaning of a military presence in New Zealand makes clear. The context for and the subtext of Cruise's judgment that 'mutual confidence was perfectly established' is a show of force. A running assessment of Maori strength is accompanied by continual reference to the military capacity of the ship, a dialogue perfectly understood by Maori, as the continual evaluation of the potential for conflict and Cruise's descriptions of their mimicry of British military behaviour show.

Journal of a Ten Months' Residence in New Zealand was rapidly circulated to a European readership. A second edition followed a year after the first in 1824, which notes Cruise's promotion to major. A long article in the *Quarterly Review* for December 1824 asserted that the *Journal* 'has a greater degree of accuracy and authenticity than the more pleasing form of a connected narrative', praised Cruise as a 'sensible' man but expressed reservations about his treatment of Maori cannibalism, accusing him of 'loose gossiping' on a subject on which the missionaries were silent. The function of the text as an act of graphic control is suggested in the *Quarterly Review*'s strictures about Cruise's 'loose' claim that 'anthropophagy exists among them and is practised, not only as a superstition, but as a sensual animal gratification'. Cannibalism in a 'spirit of revenge' is one thing, cannibalism for the pleasure of eating is another.[60] The *Quarterly Review*'s insistence on this point is supported by its observations on the beauty and utility of New Zealand's natural resources, its likeness to England and the 'immense importance to which New South Wales is rapidly advancing; and the intercourse, friendly or otherwise, which must take place between it and the New Zealand islands'. Although the *Review* reserves some of its strongest language for 'a swindling and unprincipled set of men in this country, who, under the pretence of making grants of land in New Zealand, are endeavouring to induce persons to emigrate thither', the article concludes with a description of New Zealand and optimism about the conversion of the Maori, which clearly points forward to the 'adoption of proper measures for extending the blessings of civilization to a people eminently gifted . . . and inhabiting one of the finest islands in the South Seas'.[61]

Cruise's journal, written as a shipboard log, is strategically positioned for the travel-writing readership. Mixing ethnographic information with personal witnessing, it downplays Cruise's profession as a soldier and represents him instead as the 'dispassionate' and 'sensible' observer his readers took him to be, attractively open to the Maori he encounters while maintaining a clear position on social practices distasteful – though interesting – to Europeans. The agency which enables his dispassionate and sensible observation, however, is never in doubt: the cultural field of a European traveller and writer is embedded in the force field of a soldier.

We all became warlike

During the 1840s the military presence in New Zealand was significantly strengthened as a result of the Flagstaff or Northern Wars against Hone Heke, Te Rauparaha's activities, and the resistance of Maori in the Hutt Valley to European settlers. In December 1845 Henry McKillop, a 22-year-old midshipman on HMS *Calliope*, arrived in the Bay of Islands prepared for battle. His *Reminiscences of twelve months' service in New Zealand* was published in 1849[62] and is dedicated to Rear Admiral Sir George Cockburn. His dedication is full of the language of persuasion. He was 'induced' to give 'such authentic information as I was able to gain', and to 'submit' his reminiscences, 'no one else having written on the subject'. McKillop's narrative is preceded by a 'slight sketch' of the growth of ill feeling between Maori and Europeans which includes all major instances of conflict since 1769, and portraits of the principal Maori protagonists – Hone Heke, Tamati Waka Nene, Te Rangihaeata ('a regular savage and glories in it') and Te Rauparaha, who was taken prisoner by McKillop himself and held on the *Calliope*. McKillop's little (17 cm) notebook-sized book is a combination of an eyewitness narrative of his own actions, including the taking of Te Rauparaha, physical conditions, accidents and social life, and accounts of the various battles quoted directly from despatches, brigade orders or newspaper accounts. Despite noting that land-jobbing and ill treatment of Maori by Europeans had caused the 'growth in ill feeling', McKillop's highly personalised narrative retains a simple division between the enemy and the gallant British soldier with a clear consciousness of what he represents – the scale of British imperialism. When Te Rauparaha was imprisoned on board the *Calliope*, McKillop believed one of the main benefits was

> in showing him how little we really thought of the importance of his country and its inhabitants, and what a very minor consideration they were in comparison with our Indian and other colonial subjects. The news of the war in the Sutlej reaching us during his captivity, he, observing the excitement, requested to be informed of the contents of the papers, and listened eagerly to every word as it was translated to him by the interpreter; the other prisoners also showing the same astonishment at the detail of such a war. The numbers engaged were beyond their comprehension; but they began to see their own insignificance, and to learn what our resources really were, on which point they had been very incredulous.[63]

McKillop's reminiscences have the flavour of a *Boys' Own* adventure story. There is no suggestion of political, ethical or moral ambiguity shadowing his accounts of military action: the Maori are 'malicious' or 'savage' or 'cruel', unless they are helping the British; British settlement is 'unoffending'; the country 'possesses everything to recommend it as a settlement', and the off-duty life of a young soldier is described with artless transparency. After a ball at Government House in Auckland, where the only deficiency was in ladies, there being 'an abundance of champagne', the young sailors took the flags of various nations off the walls and lay down on the floor to sleep.

> Happening to awake first, I was much amused with the ridiculous appearance the several sleepers presented in their various adopted banners: one of them had the lion of England grinning fiercely at his heels, which protruded from beneath the folds of the standard;

another having his head illuminated by the stars of America, the stripes of the free and enlightened nation giving him the appearance of a red-striped zebra.[64]

The life of a soldier is characterised by adventures, recounted with relish. When the *Calliope* arrived in the Bay of Islands on 31 December 1845 they were met at the entrance by 'a man of war's boat . . . who came to shew us the way in, and also to give the senior officer's orders, that on our arrival the marines and a party of blue-jackets were to be immediately disembarked and proceed to join the brigade'.[65] Everyone was 'anxious to be of the party'. However, McKillop was not allowed to join the fighting party but 'managed to get the captain to send me with the despatches for the Lieut.-Governor'. He took the six-oared whaleboat up the river to Pukututu's pa, where they stayed for several weeks while the fighting at Ruapekapeka continued. The principal event he participated in was carrying a heavy box of despatches across country on a very warm day. They couldn't find any water and two of the men, who had eaten nothing but raw salt pork, 'were completely knocked up and obliged to lie down on the road.' At last they came to a 'river in the valley, thickly wooded and beautifully cool', and after refreshing themselves decided to apply McKillop's sword to the padlock on the captain's tin box, and joyfully feasted on the cold fowl and port wine it contained. The next night he spent in the trenches but didn't 'satisfy the craving for fight', and on the return to Pukututu's pa managed to set the half-way camp and surrounding countryside on fire 'endeavouring to boil some water in a glass bottle to make coffee'.[66]

McKillop's boyish mix of mishap, adventure and patriotism produces a guileless narrative of deeply entrenched assumptions about the presence and appropriate behaviour of British soldiers in New Zealand, contextualised by a partisan documentary history of despatches,[67] letters and newspaper articles. The Maori as subaltern is explicit in his consideration of them, clustered around a set of tropes locating Maori as opponents, savages, or natives who can be assimilated:

As a proof of what may be done with them, I can safely say that the natives employed in the police force at Wellington and Auckland, in their neat green uniform, look as soldier-like and respectable as any of their comrades, their accoutrements always being well-cleaned and kept; and it is astonishing how well these men did their mixed duty of soldier and constable.[68]

McKillop's *Reminiscences* focus predominantly on his experiences as a young soldier with an air of *joie de vivre* and naivety, but finish with an unequivocal plug for New Zealand as an emigration colony. 'I cannot say too much in its favour', he declares, representing the immediate future as one of ably managing the 'praiseworthy undertaking of colonizing this extensive and unaccountably neglected country'. For most visitors who wrote travel accounts after 1840, questions about New Zealand's status as a colony were confined to issues of administration and governance. There was general agreement as to its suitability for British settlement: the 'comfortable and happy home of many thousands of our fellow-countrymen who are now wanting the common necessaries of life in England', as McKillop puts it.[69] Remaining difficulties with Maori are absorbed into an imperial adventure story, coloured by endearing pranks and youthful exuberance, the forerunner to a larger and more solemn story of colony and nation.

The work is intended to be a light work

One of the most accomplished and attractive soldier/writers to produce a travel account of Australia and New Zealand was Lieutenant-Colonel Godfrey Mundy, whose triple-decker *Our Antipodes*, illustrated with engravings of his sketches of Australia and New Zealand, appeared in 1852. *Our Antipodes* went into a second revised edition in the first year of publication and was published in third and fourth editions in one volume in 1855 and 1857. A German translation of the Australian material appeared in 1856, and was translated into Swedish the following year. Mundy's urbane, informed and convivial account of his 'residence and rambles' in Australasia sports a preface which establishes some subtle points about the reading public he is addressing. A book is a social transaction taking place within protocols of polite behaviour and between parties who understand the force of *politesse*:

> To publish a Book without a Preface, is like thrusting one's acquaintance, without the ceremony of introduction, upon some distinguished and formidable stranger.[70]

Mundy's book is based on diaries, and to that extent is a 'personal narrative', but is also and importantly the production of a public servant.

> The Author would have the Public bear in mind that, during the whole of his sojourn in Australia, he was their paid and of course hard-working servant. They will be pleased to contemplate him as part and parcel of his office-desk, plodding through returns and reports, records and regulations, warrants and other articles of war; exchanging an occasional dry word with his clerks perched on their long-legged stools, and enjoying only fugitive glimpses, over the rim of his spectacles, of more external and unprofessional affairs.[71]

The book's cover is engraved with an image of this reading and writing military man containing the world.

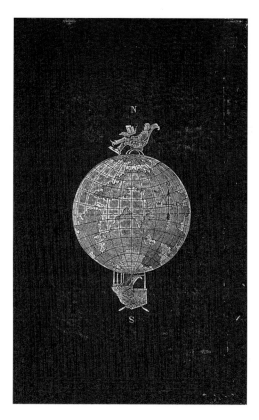

Front cover of *Our Antipodes* by
Lt. Colonel G. C. Mundy (1852) showing
the military man at his work.
ATL B-K-508-COVER

Godfrey Mundy came to New South Wales in June 1846 as Deputy Adjutant-General of the military establishment. He had served in India from 1825 to 1827, was present at the siege of Bharatpur, and in 1832 published *Pen and Pencil Sketches Being the Journal of a Tour in India*, which went at once into a second edition and was republished shortly before his death in 1860. Mundy's declared ambition for *Our Antipodes* is that it should be a 'light work' but 'useful as well as amusing'. He establishes boundaries for his authorship – the book is the 'recreation of his leisure hours, not the business of his days' – and he makes a strong claim for independent reporting, without 'pique, partiality nor prejudice'.[72]

Mundy's visit to New Zealand over the summer of 1847–48 included Auckland, the Bay of Islands and Wellington, and is described in his preface as being 'on particular service'. This meant an inspection of and report to London on New Zealand's military resources. The Northern Wars had recently been concluded and Grey was responding to the situation he had inherited from FitzRoy – a bankrupt administration, uproar over land and land titles, and a proposed constitution he disagreed with.[73] Mundy was in Grey's company most of the time, visiting military posts and battlefields, and notes in his preface, perhaps disingenuously, that 'a slight outline of the late Anglo-Maori war has, almost insensibly, linked itself with the personal narrative'. A long article in the *Quarterly Review* for June 1854, 'Christianity in Melanesia and New Zealand', treats Mundy as the authority on the Northern Wars, Maori leaders and the state of New Zealand politics, including lengthy extracts from the book and reporting his opinions and anecdotes.

For all Mundy's insistence that *Our Antipodes* is a 'light' work and the product of his recreation, and despite its comic burlesque mode, it circulates a set of assumptions which facilitate and develop what Mundy refers to as 'subjugation'; and for all that his attitudes are liberal, it is also very much the narrative of a soldier. Like McKillop, he has straightforward ideas about the relationship between British soldiers and their opponents. His time spent travelling across the Tasman in the sloop *Inflexible* is occupied with some of the print culture already generated about New Zealand – 'a small box of books, among which were sundry Parliamentary blue-books, one of which alone contains upwards of 1,100 pages, and weighs, as expressed on its cover, "under eight pounds!"' – and he uses it to provide an 'imperfect sketch' of New Zealand's history and to introduce his journal.[74] His historical sketch concludes with disappointment at the current tranquillity prevailing in New Zealand:

> I must confess a regret that up to this day the Maoris have never yet received what I verily believe would have been of infinite service to their particular complaint, namely – a good sound thrashing! such a one as has been frequently and salutarily administered by British blue jackets and red, upon troublesome people in well nigh every other quarter of the globe.[75]

As the *Inflexible* draws into Auckland Mundy switches into diary mode, noting features of the coastline, including Cape Rodney, 'a fine bluff' named by Cook after one of Mundy's ancestors, but generally he finds the landscape

> all alike in feature and expression. It was a very plain repulsive face indeed, with a dingy brown complexion, spotted over with extinct volcanoes – like irruptions on the human skin.[76]

The slippage from land to indigenous people enacted here reinforces Mundy's fundamental attitude to New Zealand and to Maori: the need for discipline, a discipline that he personally embodies, but is also evident in his narrative. Disciplined by his reading and supply of information, his professional conduct and objectives, and his skills as a writer, Mundy's narrative negotiates for the reader a comfortably jocular vantage-point from which to scan the history of the colony, the character of its indigenous people and its future prospects. Like McKillop's *Reminiscences*, *Our Antipodes* represents the life of a soldier as charmingly

'Middle Entrance Auckland Harbour, December 11, 1847.' Drawing by G. C. Mundy. ATL A-161-015

adventurous, sociable, jovial and energetic. Indeed, Mundy stresses his own physical fitness. When he visits Bishop Selwyn, who was famous for his physical exploits, Selwyn 'with rather a wicked smile on his lips' disappears into a 'deep, rough, ravine':

> Did I wrong him when I suspected that he had noticed my own long spurs and the light white ducks of my naval companion? Be it as it may, I hope I did not disgrace my Etonian training.[77]

Mundy uses various strategies to establish an identity with his reader. His characteristic mix of description, commentary, opinion and comic/dramatic scene-setting and tale-telling is well referenced – he refers to Angas, Wakefield, Bidwill, Polack and other well-known writers on New Zealand. He constantly instates himself as the representative of a professional and cultural elite, glossed as Etonian, who is able to enunciate an authority configured by class and nationality and modulated through a tone of agreeably reasonable good-sportmanship which does not, however, disguise its potency.

He also uses two main narrative strategies to position the reader. The first is that he establishes the relativity of his own, and by inference the reader's, relation to New Zealand and to the Maori by – sometimes comic – diminishment. Auckland houses are 'wretchedly small', Official Bay contains 'houses and gardens exiguous almost to the extremity of Dutch-toyism', military headquarters is located in a weatherboard building that was formerly a tavern and still sports a hand pointing 'to the Tap', with a roof so low the bear skin cap of the sentry reaches the eaves. Government House is a frame building sent out from England 'which looks as if it had been built in half an hour out of a dozen or two old packs of cards'. Mt Eden is a 'little Aetna'.[78] When Mundy visits Howick with Grey they are met by a police guard 'consisting of a little old English corporal and three strapping young Maoris', who, in Mundy's Indian frame, perfectly conform to the British imperial model:

> They were well looking, broad-shouldered, erect and smart young fellows – as a martinet would wish to see. I can imagine no race better adapted for the ranks. They would make excellent seapoys officered by English gentlemen.[79]

On a 'pleasant gallop' with Grey to Mt Halswell, Mundy notices 'evidence of a numerous and warlike population, now passed away'. Reflecting on the remains of fortifications he comes across, Mundy suggests a distant but vague past when the 'population in those days was undoubtedly tenfold more numerous than at present', a vagueness which significantly diminishes both Maori history and people, and is immediately succeeded by an image of European domination – 'from the crest of the mount we commanded a view of both the eastern and western oceans' – and a prospect of future utility – when the passage [of the Manukau harbour] shall have been correctly buoyed, it will probably turn out a good haven'.[80] While a process of distinction between superior Europeans and the inhabitants of the colony is continually taking place, it is coloured by Mundy's willingness to cast figures of authority, including himself, in a comic or ridiculous light, which humanises and naturalises the power they represent. Out riding with Grey they both experience mishaps and on their 'safe but soiled ascent' back to the road encounter

> The only carriage in Auckland, that of the officer commanding the 58th Regiment . . . conveying its owners to the viceregal dinner, as their host and myself, both looking as if we had been in a smart skirmish, entered the town.[81]

It is in his choice of descriptors for Maori, however, that Mundy most clearly displays the links between an English gentleman and a professional soldier in the service of Empire. The Maori is simultaneously Orientalised and Roman-ised, 'brave and warlike' but with 'something of the Lazzaroni about his nature'. His 'Brutus crop', 'toga of flax' and strapping physique, the 'naked philosopher' and 'noble savage', slides into the complexion of a 'Southern European' whose language 'resembles in character the "soft bastard Latin" as Byron calls it, of the modern Roman'.[82] This distinguishing metaphor, identifying Maori with an ancient civilisation now in cultural and racial decline, is kept firmly in place by

Mundy, even when he is at his most admiring. The description 'a good deal of Orientalism in the character of the Maori' comes as he remarks that he has 'rarely met a finer looking creature' than an unnamed Maori man who appears at Government House to observe the viceregal ball. Looking at the 58th Regiment drawn up as a guard of honour for Grey's inauguration – 'a scarlet wall coped with black' – he describes the Maori around them as being 'in strong contrast of posture – many in bare skins also' as they 'stood, squatted, and lounged in lazzaroni attitudes on the soft turf', enacting a familiar tableau of Europe's relationship to non-Western peoples.[83]

Even in their own cultural practice Maori can be outperformed. Watching 700 'native Christians' perform a haka, Mundy reflects on war dances he has heard of or seen. He finds the haka very disagreeable – savage, fiendish, diabolical – but with 'wonderfully correct measure'. He recalls 'the most animated Maori dance I ever witnessed', which took place in the Parramatta barracks where men of the 58th who had served a campaign in New Zealand, 'half naked and painted . . . sham-savages', performed a haka for the officers, in a de-authenticating counter-mimicry.[84]

Mundy's second major strategy for positioning the reader is to maintain a running awareness of what you might call the hard data. Anecdote, amusing incident and comic description aside, he provides a basic political and historical framework. He takes the time to recount the history of New Zealand as a colony, the Northern Wars and the Wairau incident, and gives the reader a bird's-eye view of the fortifications at Ruapekapeka, using events from the colony's history as powerfully emotive images of a confrontation between civilisation and savagery.

While he is in Auckland, Mundy attends the viceregal investigation into the murder of Lieutenant Snow and his family in the Bay of Plenty. The murder, as Mundy records it, was utu for Snow's having 'rudely ejected from his garden some natives'. Thinking about this, Mundy pictures the following scene:

> When the females of a family are seated in their verandah, or going about performing their household duties – the males being probably employed at a distance – the presence of half a dozen tattooed savages, rolled in their greasy blankets, and sitting with their fierce bloodshot eyes following every movement of the inmates, would not be an agreeable accessory to the privacy of an English lawn, nor be remarkably soothing to the nerves of an English lady – especially if she connect in her imagination the group of little fat flaxen cherubs playing around her, with the known 'fi-fo-fum' propensities of her visitors.[85]

Of course the reader's imagination is already engaged. The accused, Ngamuka, was subsequently shown to be innocent, but the proceedings involved long speeches by Te Wherowhero and Te Rauparaha, among others. In a smooth segue from the fat flaxen cherubs, Te Rauparaha's appearance signals the main focus. This 'hero of a hundred massacres and a hundred human-flesh feasts' is 'repulsive beyond description, and his long yellow teeth look as if they had torn many a butchered prisoner'.[86]

Mundy's reader is not only implied in his construction of a common frame of reference, but also figures as a present companion in the text. When he reaches the site of the first offensive of the Northern Wars, the sacking of Kororareka, he 'conduct[s] him also to the spot where the first blow was struck; and, having placed him by my side on the summit of the signal-hill, we will look forth over the scene of operations'.[87] The view is panoramic, seen from a 'narrow platform' of ground 'where a company of infantry could scarcely be paraded'. The point of focus is explicitly military and strategic, a survey of the battlefield, and with the aid of a 'glass' Mundy and his reader can even pick out the gunshot holes in the Anglican church. This is followed by a blow-by-blow account of the history of the war and an analysis of the British 'want of success' which concludes, in italics, that the 'main and true cause' is *the perilous habit of underrating our enemy*. To what is attributed the terrible and lamentable massacre of the Wairau, but to blind incaution and an arrogant assumption of superiority?'[88]

Learned, civilised and observant, tolerant, imaginative and good-humoured, Mundy's account is based on some unshakeable assumptions generated by his class, profession and nationality. His highly personal, rambling but purposeful text establishes its superiority more effectively by adopting a self-critical narratorial persona characterised by jocularity, fairness and a code of behaviour enshrined in the mythology of a narrow social class – the old Etonians whom Mundy both represents and draws attention to (especially Selwyn, hero of the playing fields of Eton), and the country they represent, playfully but powerfully figured as 'weedy seedy old England',[89] country of lawns and ladies and fat flaxen cherubs.

THE COMPANY MEN

Rambling with intent

Although John Carne Bidwill called his 'pamphlet' *Rambles in New Zealand* (1841),[90] he dedicated it to the Earl of Devon, Governor of the Plymouth New Zealand Company, and hoped that his book 'will add something to the little stock of information respecting the rising and important Colony of New Zealand'. Unlike the travels of Edward Markham or John Boultbee, Bidwill's rambles are purposive and explicitly framed by his commercial objectives. He comes to New Zealand 'rambling in search of information' so that time will not be wasted and unprofitable while he waits for the results of his application to buy Crown lands near Sydney, and from the beginning his observation of New

Zealand is commercially inflected. Considering the relative merits of Kororareka and Paihia as ports, Bidwill notes that Paihia, with 'considerable flat space at the mouth of a river . . . is a more fit emporium for the produce of the country'.[91] He is always on the alert for cultivable land, forestry and other crops, mineral resources and solutions to the various problems of access and transport.

Bidwill's rambles are notorious for his ascent of Tongariro. He had decided to 'penetrate to those high mountains', because he saw them on the maps and 'described in the book of the New Zealand Association'.[92] Bidwill's account of his journey from the southern shores of Lake Taupo to the 'much-dreaded place' is filled with accusations that the Maori had lost their way or were misdirecting him, until he emerges in sight of Ngauruhoe ('the cone') on 2 March 1839. Two Maori agreed to accompany him closer but refused to go nearer than a mile of the base, where they made a fire and waited, so Bidwill breached Maori tapu on his own. He had been told by the Maori that the mountain 'had been making a noise in the night', which at the time he thought 'only fancy', but as he was making his way to the peak he heard a noise and saw the mountain erupting. Undeterred, he reached the base of Ngauruhoe, 'a fitting scene for the wildest piece of diablerie that ever entered the brain of a German', and climbed 'heartily tired' to the top.[93]

> Had it not been for the idea of standing where no man had ever stood before, I should certainly have given up the undertaking.[94]

Another eruption and an earthquake occurred while Bidwill was on the mountain and, unsurprisingly, when he got back to camp he found a 'party of natives, consisting of three chiefs from Towpo' who had come to see 'how he was', prelude to a dressing-down given when he got back to Taupo.[95]

Bidwill's mix of motives in seeing the country – speculation, exploration and conquest – is facilitated by the tobacco and 'physick' he dispenses as he travels, and by his arrogant determination to get his way, which rides over both Maori customary law and protocols, presented as superstitious and quaintly primitive, and adverse conditions. Pocock's definition of commerce which opens this chapter expresses the wider dimensions of Bidwill's journey: his determination to climb Tongariro, and his effort to produce and transmit an account of what lay behind the known coastal areas of New Zealand back home, demonstrate the nature of the transaction between 'the world perceived and the mind perceiving', as knowledge of the world passes from one set of hands to another.

The Hebrew traveller

In a letter to William Colenso, the botanist Allan Cunningham copied by hand the main points of a review of J. S. Polack's *New Zealand* published in the *Atlas* of London on 11 August 1838. Referring to him to as 'our Hebrew traveller', the *Atlas*, and by association Cunningham, cast Polack in the ancient Shylockian figure of the grasping merchant.

> Our Jew auctioner's brother in 6 years travels over "<u>Every part</u>" of New Zealand; visits most of its native villages; transacts business (Jewlike) with all the chiefs from whom he could gain something; inspects their fortifications!; sails up & examines most of the rivers between N.Cape and Cook's Strait – and having ascertained in these more than ordinary movements the extent and Char[acter] of some districts that had not been closely exam[ine]d previously, he departs for England to give (or rather sell) to the world the results of the observations he had made during his sojourns in the land of Kauri trees.[96]

Neither Cunningham nor Colenso remark on the overt antisemitism of the reception of Polack's book. Hocken's and Bagnall's respective bibliographies note several reviews – in the *Eclectic*, the *New Monthly Magazine* and the *Journal of the Belles Lettres* – and Polack is frequently mentioned by other writers though not often favourably. Bagnall remarks 'he is a more useful early informant than the denigration of Colenso and others would imply'.[97] Polack's journeying in New Zealand is explicitly related to his trading activities, and as a result he advocated systematic colonisation to a House of Lords select committee. He

'Parramatta, Kororarika Bay, the residence and property of Mr. Polack, Bay of Islands, 1840.' Wood engraving by J. S. Polack. ATL PUBL-0064-2-TP

built a substantial house at Kororareka which was destroyed in the war of 1845 – the ruined site is one of those pointed out by Mundy to his hilltop reader.

In the Preface to *New Zealand* (1838),[98] Polack puts general principles of knowledge and civilisation ahead of commercial opportunity as the reasons for having written his book. As the idea of a 'new and unlimited mart for commercial enterprise' surfaces, however, so does a series of observations pointing to systematic colonisation and capitalism: a redundant population, adding to the riches of the mother country, affording an opportunity for the enterprise of her industrious citizens and initiating an 'interesting race of uncivilized man' into the 'habits and comforts of social life'. Polack's first enterprises – establishing a brewery and trading in flax, timber and general produce – show an acute grasp of both the market and the resources available, just as his advocacy of systematic colonisation shows his response to the political climate. In the same way, his book adapts the conventions of travel writing to present a trader/traveller who is both susceptible to the application of a racist stereotype and an acute projection of the self-interest and self-fashioning at the heart of the imperialist colonial project.

Polack's Jewishness is both figured and disguised in his narrative. He represents himself as a patriotic Englishman, renaming the South Island the 'Island of Victoria'

> with a presumption that may in some measure admit of an excuse, arising from dutiful feelings inseparable from a loyal subject, bestowed the appellation of VICTORIA, after her most gracious Majesty the Queen of these realms, on this largest island . . . with assured certainty, that no modern Cook, be he subject or foreigner, will feel disposed to deprive this extensive country of a name, additionally endeared to an Englishman abroad, without the pale of the protective laws of the dearly cherished country of his birth.[99]

Under the pressure of his claim to naming rights, Polack's customary prolixity becomes overblown and tends to point to the reverse of what he is arguing. His claim to be a loyal subject is framed by an excuse for presumption, and no sooner has he bestowed a name on the island than the figure of a 'modern Cook' arises, who, in a series of clauses which invoke what they seek to exclude, introduces the idea of the 'pale', a boundary designed to keep Jews out. Polack's contorted sentence attempts to keep him inside the 'pale' of a 'dearly cherished country' at the same time as the intensifying expressions of belonging suggest an anxiety about not being included in the phrase an 'Englishman abroad'. He is not a 'modern Cook', even as he asserts his Englishness as duty and loyalty.

Polack's Jewishness is also implied by his relative isolation from such communities as exist around him in New Zealand of the 1830s. L. M. Goldman in his *The History of the Jews in New Zealand* (1958) notes that 'Polack once stated that the only persons he associated with on the Bay of Islands were Mr Montefiore and a "Captain Powditch, a person equally respectable"'.[100] Polack's disagreements with Busby over the annexation and colonisation of New Zealand are well known. In a letter to his brother, Busby claimed that Polack 'is universally detested here. The other settlers know that he is as great a rogue as the worst of them, and he, forsooth, wants to play the gentleman among them.' Busby also referred to him as 'the Jew'.[101]

In his two-volume narrative Polack is invariably the sole European witness to the 'manners and customs' of the Maori he encounters.[102] He travels with a 'retinue' of Maori and there is little reference to other Europeans by name until towards the end of the second volume, when he is mustering arguments and support for his views on colonisation. Europe is seen as the historical and geographical point of origin for voyages and explorations of New Zealand, and Europeans are invoked as a collective noun represented by his presence and signified to Maori as enabling certain activities, transactions and ways of life. The first part of Polack's narrative describes journeys he 'performed . . . on a commercial speculation'. Well supplied with 'trifles', which are never specified but included jew's harps, he visits the tribes of the Hokianga, and in a series of reflexive mirrorings represents himself as the object of their gaze.

> In the morning I arose much refreshed; and, on waking, perceived the natives had formed a line, reaching some distance from my house, which was open to public inspection, and regarding what I was doing in silence.[103]

Attention is repeatedly drawn to the role of objects in Polack's transactions with Maori. He buys services with commodities, especially tobacco, and Maori responses to his toothbrush, shaving soap, comb, washing dish, towel and mirror are minutely described. In a scene familiar from much eighteenth-century African exploration writing,[104] Polack describes the people 'flocking' about him 'feeling my garments, others lifting up my trousers to examine my boots, and to determine their length. My jacket, waistcoat and hat, underwent the minutest regard; but few things gave more diversion than my pulling off an elderly pair of *ci-devant* black kid gloves.'[105] Missionary travel-writing never mentions Maori curiosity about their garments or persons, but Polack's narrative centres on the display of the person of the European traveller in his reception by Maori. He identifies himself as a '*Rangatira no Uropi* or gentleman of Europe, who was accounted a *rara avis in terris* in the settlements we proposed visiting'.[106] The effect of this is to assert Polack's nationality (and efface his ethnicity) and to seek to identify himself with the reader.

> Early in the morning I felt quite refreshed from the fatigue of the previous day, and, on opening my eyes, observed my cabin, which I stated was entirely open in front, crowded

'Maori bargaining with a pakeha, 1845 or 1846.' Drawing by John Williams. ATL A-079-017

with the inhabitants of the village, anxious to see me arise. My throat, which was uncovered, and was less bronzed by the sun than my face or hands, called forth universal remarks. The works of a Phidias or a Praxiteles could not have elicited from the most devoted lover of the art stronger terms of approbation. My readers will not, I hope, imagine I am indulging in silly vanity from the above expressions, made use of to express the surprise of the people which arose on beholding a complexion so dissimilar to what they had been accustomed to view.[107]

Polack's self-objectification here is quickly succeeded by anxiety, drawing attention to his apprehension about boundaries and protocols. Peter Gibbons has described Polack's style as 'overstated descriptions which . . . mock his hosts and travelling companions'.[108] They can also be read as expressions of anxiety about his own speaking position, which is overcompensated for by efforts at comedy and a florid vocabulary.[109]

Polack's triangulated gaze bounces from self to spectator to reader. It can also be read racially, from Jew to Maori to British reader; ethnographically, from European to native to Anglo-Europeans; geopolitically, from traveller to savage to metropolitan reader; and narratively, from author to character to reader. However, he provides a quality of observation about Maori even as he dramatises them as participants in a self-referential epic. Polack spoke Maori, the individuals and tribes he encountered are identified and named, he reports their speech and their reactions to his presence and propositions, he comments on their language and material culture. The overriding purpose of his narrative is always firmly in place. The mock heroic/comic descriptions of Maori establish a common relationship between the author and the reader to 'primitive' non-Western peoples, and the genres in which this can be elaborated. Though the narrative concludes with an enormous inventory of the natural productions of New Zealand and useful information about the country and its people, there is also a dramatisation of Maori society and people that registers them as subjects under a European gaze.

Company adventures

Works by people associated with the New Zealand Company are numerous – you start to wonder if there was an obligation on them to write a promotional book about New Zealand. Of course, interest in the colonisation of New Zealand picked up speed with the departure of the *Tory* and the establishment of settlements, and the Company explicitly engaged in 'puffery' to promote its wares. Artists like John Gully and William Fox were employed to give the best possible impressions of the new settlements, including adding more shops to the shoreline and ships to the harbour than were actually there, and the books were another marketing strategy. Books produced by associates of the New Zealand Company are, strictly speaking, narratives of settlement rather than travel, and they are more obviously directed to a professional and entrepreneurial readership, but they also cash in on the sizeable market for voyages and travel works which Simon Eliot has shown occupied about seventeen percent of the total book market in the first third of the nineteenth century.[110]

The draughtsman Charles Heaphy's *Narrative of a Residence in various parts of New Zealand* (1842) and the New Zealand Company naturalist Ernst Dieffenbach's *Travels in New Zealand* (1843) concentrate on providing the reader with diverse categories of information: the history of the various settlements and their prospects, geography, geology and botany, climate, birdlife and an anthropology and ethnography of Maori. Both explicitly address a reader whose attention is engaged by the 'regular settlement' of New Zealand and its prosperity, expressed by Dieffenbach as a question: Can the settlement produce all that it may require for internal consumption and will provisions be cheap as compared with the price of labour?[111] Both these books and Edward Jerningham Wakefield's *Adventure in New Zealand* (1845), whose title evokes the glamorous dimension of travel to New Zealand, were part of a publishing wave of works on emigration. In the advertising appendix to Heaphy's *Narrative*, eight books and nine 'views or plans' of settlements in New Zealand are listed. Once the annexation of New Zealand had been accomplished, it was immediately followed by an increase in publications designed to enhance and exploit the market for systematic colonisation. As Dieffenbach cogently put it:

to permit [the first settlers] to have an extensive choice, that they may select the good land in preference to the bad – to give them legal titles accordingly, and not to allow them to consume their capital after their arrival in the colony by a delay of the surveys – are the only means for securing prosperity to New Zealand.[112]

All these works are framed by the operations and ambitions of the New Zealand Company and supply the market for information which would persuade prospective colonists to make investment decisions. The question, why write a travel text? is less interesting to ask and easier to answer when the readership has clearly defined interests.[113] In the same year as Wakefield's *Adventure in New Zealand* was published, the *Publishers' Circular* for January to June lists numerous travel titles and several works directed at emigrants, including two further books associated with the New Zealand Company: Brodie's *Remarks on the Past and Present State of New Zealand* and Alexander Marjoribanks's *Travels in New Zealand*.

Marjoribanks' book has on its title page an epigraph from 'the evidence of Mr Montefiore before the House of Lords', not Polack's friend, but his distant relation Joseph Barrow Montefiore, the Jewish Sydney trader who first coined the phrase 'Britain of the South'.[114] Alexander Marjoribanks must have been the sort of settler the New Zealand Company hoped to attract, though he proved to be, unfortunately for them, a traveller not a settler. A well-to-do Scot 'of riper years', he arrived in Wellington in the *Bengal Merchant* in 1840 and moved on to Australia after a year. He also travelled to North and South America and after his return to Scotland published two books about his travels. *Travels in New Zealand* was published by Smith, Elder & Co in London and Edinburgh as a duodecimo cloth-covered volume on sale for 4s 6d. Marjoribanks distinguishes his book of travels, a 'short narrative', from the 'numerous works issuing from the press in regard to New Zealand' which are either too expensive or too 'tinged . . . with motives of self-interest, to exhibit a faithful and correct picture of that romantic country'.[115] Price and format also distinguished his book from Wakefield's *Adventure in New Zealand*, which was published two months later by John Murray in two octavo volumes for 28s. The *Illustrations to Adventure in New Zealand*, lithographed from 'original drawings taken on the spot' by seven artists in a 'magnificent'[116] descriptive letterpress folio, sold separately for three guineas, or even more expensively in a hand-coloured version.

Both *Adventure in New Zealand* and *Travels in New Zealand* were reviewed in 1845 by the New Zealand Company's *New Zealand Journal*, which ran from 1840 to 1852 and carried annals and proceedings of the Company, legislative reports, extensive correspondence, extracts from the British and New Zealand press and articles by members of the Wakefield family. The review of *Adventure in New Zealand* opens with a political sally.

It is a remarkable feature in the Colonial Administration of this country, that it does nothing towards communicating a knowledge of the scenery, natural history, or physical geography of the immense portion of the empire under its control. We learn everything from private sources and not from the Government.[117]

The production of knowledge was an important dimension to the New Zealand Company's claim to be the *de facto* authority on New Zealand affairs, which was promulgated through the steady stream of eyewitness narratives of settlement produced under its auspices in the 1840s.

Adventure in New Zealand, written by the son of the Company's founder, Edward Gibbon Wakefield, is presented as a documentary history of its author's 'adventure' and the adventure of the New Zealand Company's enterprises. Unusually among travel texts, *Adventure* opens without a preface or any kind of authorial framing device and truth claim. It is a suggestive absence. The narrative plunges into a 'statement of circumstances relating to New Zealand previous to the expedition' which skids over exploration voyages to concentrate on a propagandist and political history of annexation and of the New Zealand Association, pre-conditions for Jerningham Wakefield's departure on the *Tory* as an excited and observant nineteen-year-old member of a speculative voyage. The adventure is conducted within a very particular set of objectives (land purchases) but presented in the *New Zealand Journal* as a 'book . . . replete with sound colonial policy'. The reviewer criticises *Adventure* for falling into

> two distinct subjects which might have been written by two different writers . . . The first might have been entitled 'A History of Partizanship in the Colony of New Zealand by a Partizan'; and the second 'A History of the Practical Working of the Colony of New Zealand, by a Practical Colonist'. The first is a worthless subject . . . The second is a noble subject and, as such, has been well treated by Mr. Wakefield, in the very spirit of one who shared in the difficulties of a new colony.[118]

This distinction amounts to a pre-emptive strike. Dismissing the 'partisan' in favour of the 'practical colonist' allows the relation between the two to be dissolved in favour of a reading of *Adventure* as affirmation of the New Zealand Company's role and activities. The reviewer quotes long passages as evidence of the 'harmony which subsisted between the natives of Port Nicholson and their highly civilized visitors'.

As a promotional strategy, *Adventure in New Zealand* was very successful. The headlong youthfulness and what A. G. Bagnall called the 'springtime exuberance'[119] of the narrative represent its author's propagandist objectives as a transparently ingenuous dimension of the text, and Jerningham's self-representation as the lively 'young squire of New Zealand' (in Patricia Burns's words)[120] proved popular with readers, suggesting John Murray was right to market the book at an affluent readership. It did not go into a second edition and wasn't reprinted until 1908, suggesting that its readership was finely calculated and targeted. *Adventure* was reviewed twice in the *Morning Chronicle*, and given four pages in the *Times*, a paper unsympathetic to the New Zealand Company. It was extensively reviewed by provincial papers and copies were sent by the Company to the Secretary of State for the Colonies, Lord Stanley, and 'every important politician and official'.[121]

Marjoribanks's *Travels in New Zealand*, published in the same year as Wakefield's book, is jocular, opinionated and short. Marjoribanks's journey to Wellington with 'the first Scotch colony to New Zealand' had a grand send-off. The Lord Provost of Glasgow (a friend of Marjoribanks) with a large party and the band of the 1st Royals addressed the emigrants over a dinner with abundant champagne, telling them they were about to lay the foundation of a second Britain. Marjoribanks's text transforms the hopeful parting scenes immediately into disappointing arrival, built clause by clause into an eyewitness jeremiad – I saw, I heard, I witnessed – laced with quotations and the author's poems.

> Within a few short months I was doomed to witness those very beings who were cheering and shouting as they left the land of their nativity, cast as it were, upon a barren dreary and inhospitable shore.[122]

View on the Pelorus River. Drawn by C. Heaphy from a sketch by E. J. Wakefield. ATL A-145-007

The *New Zealand Journal* reviewed *Travels* in May 1845 and this phrase about the barren and inhospitable shore sparks a response.

> Fancy a band of emigrants, fresh from the 'porridge' and 'bean bannock' of the Highlands of Scotland, considering any shore between Spitzbergen and the Antarctic Continent 'barren, dreary and inhospitable', much less the shores of Wellington, which, at the period spoken of, were one dense mass of the most brilliant and gigantic vegetation.[123]

The review treads a cautious and revealing line between reprimanding Marjoribanks for putting off the casual reader, defending the New Zealand Company and its provisions ('every possible assistance and comfort') and suggesting the colonists were inadequate ('better have remained at home under the parental care of their mothers'), while conceding that his 'rough and ready' book 'generally speak[s] truth'.

> It is small, cheap and comprehensive and we must confess that we like it; not the less, perhaps, because it contains opinions, in some instances, very much at variance with our own. The emigrant to New Zealand or elsewhere, if he will be taught by its experience … will not regret the purchase of a book which, read rightly, will go far to make him half a colonist, before starting from his native country.[124]

The reviewer deploys various tactics to limit the potential damage to the New Zealand Company's market. Broad endorsement, with the significant reservation that the book is 'odd', 'sometimes indulging in fallacy', prods the reader into critique but stops short of an adversarial mode. The telling phrase 'read rightly' acknowledges the likely market for a 'small, cheap and comprehensive' book, but also the need to control its reception; it is a book which the reader who is (only) an emigrant must utilise to advance his transformation into an colonist. But *Travels* is broadly speaking in favour of the New Zealand Company's procedures and operations, and the personal narrative is framed by emigration debates, literature and policies. Its central narrative strategy is the distinction between a civilised New Zealand Company Scots emigrant and 'man in his savage state', embodied in the rhetoric of the text (which implies a cultivated, middle-class, gentleman (British) reader who can seize Marjoribanks's references and appreciate his oratorical style) as well as in its content. *Travels* concludes with a paragraph describing this savage man who is an object of horror and disgust but also part of the pastoral work of an aspiring colonist:

> The passion of fear alone keeps him in check, and when that is removed, the natural savage propensities of his nature come again into play, and he returns as the dog to his vomit, or as the sow that was washed, to her wallowing in the mire.[125]

Travels in New Zealand went into two editions and was followed by Marjori-banks's companion volumes, *Travels in New South Wales* (1847) and *Travels in South and North America* (1853), produced, according to the publishers' advertisement[126] at the end of the text, in three 'separate small volumes . . . within the reach of the whole of the reading community . . . forming in fact, a complete Colonial Library in themselves'. Both the publishers and the *New Zealand Journal* reviewer refer to the market for books of useful knowledge, a concept successfully developed by the Society for the Diffusion of Useful Knowledge, which had already produced some publications about New Zealand, including G. L. Craik's *The New Zealanders* in 1830. Aimed at the self-improvement of working-class people, and more contentiously seeking to replace politics with education, the Society for the Diffusion of Useful Knowledge published cheap books 'imparting useful information to all classes of the community' under its imprints, the Library of Useful Knowledge and the Library of Entertaining Knowledge.[127] Although *Travels in New Zealand* was not published by the society, the terms under which it was advertised and reviewed echo the society's goals as well as the objectives of its author, who, while asserting that he has written 'an impartial account of a singular country', also embarks on a lengthy defence of the principal rationale of the New Zealand Company's colonisation system, the concept of 'occupancy by labour'. The material form of Marjoribanks's book – its price, format and advertising – as well as its contents is aimed precisely at that 'labour' with which the New Zealand Company hoped to colonise New Zealand.

Transaction and perception

Travel books by military men, clergymen or advocates of colonisation worked to the same end. The transaction between the book-buyer and the bookseller in Edinburgh or London is only the last manifestation of a transaction beginning in John Carne Bidwill's determination to climb a forbidden mountain or Edward Jerningham Wakefield's ambition to have 'novelty and adventure'. The world perceived and the mind perceiving are materialised in the book, which, as it travelled out of manuscript and into print, directly illustrated the processes and technologies enabling people far away in an urban industrialised society to take possession of someone else's territory and rewrite it as their own. The book is the article of commerce which expresses and effects the central transaction of colonisation: the exchange of one culture and its ownership of territory for another.

CHAPTER 5

Empire travellers, 1: writers who travel

The travel boom

Exploding numbers of travellers are evident everywhere in the world in the second half of the nineteenth century. Technological advances to overcome distance, one of the key shifts towards modernity, made for the greater speed and comfort of steam ships[1] and produced a proliferating infrastructure: roads, networks of hotels, telegraph communications, regulated shipping routes and frequent connections. In New Zealand, the end of hostilities in the New Zealand Wars boosted development and saw a growing influx of travellers and settlers, the latter encouraged by the land made available through confiscations. Travellers also were encouraged by the personal example of the Duke of Edinburgh, who toured British colonies in the yacht *Galatea* in 1869 and was said by one traveller to have brought an elephant to New Zealand.[2] On his visit to Rotomahana, the Duke was one of the first people to write his name on the Pink and White Terraces, starting a trend deplored by later travellers who flocked in their hundreds to see the thermal wonders of New Zealand.

Who were these travellers? They fall into two main groups, which might be described as 'public' and 'private' travellers. Many of the famous visitors to New Zealand in the latter years of the nineteenth century came in a professional role with a proselytising task. Lord Lyttelton, Sir Charles Dilke, Anthony Trollope and James Anthony Froude came as historians, novelists, colonisers and imperialists, whose journeys to the other side of the world were made explicitly to gather information and inform public debate about the progress of colonisation and the resources, peoples and territories of empire. But, as travel became cheaper and easier, a great many steamer passengers simply came to see for themselves what the prospects were, what the empire was like, as well as to visit friends and family, and to go around the world because they could. Travellers increasingly arrived on organised tours and participated in the collective and pre-arranged experience of the tourist. Many of them wrote and published journals and diaries about their travels, belonging to a culture which valued the textual record (a record which also witnesses the developing importance of photography as the traveller's tool). The overwhelming majority, as the print record shows, were British, male and from a connected social world.

When it is projecting a collective and 'public' interest rather than the singular adventures of an individual, travel writing adopts various strategies to establish common ground with the reader, to shape an 'imagined community' (in Benedict Anderson's well-used phrase). It may call on literary techniques or historical knowledge, philosophical or religious beliefs about world order, cultural distinctions or ideologies. These strategies also demonstrate what Anderson has called the 'inner incompatibility of empire and nation'.[3] Empire, with its power structures disseminated from a distant centre, might have paid lip-service to the idea of nation, but in fact subjugated interests other than its own, as post-colonial history repeatedly demonstrates.

First-class travellers

When Lord Lyttelton gave two lectures about his trip to the Canterbury colony and the settlement which bore his name in 1867–68,[4] he listed the disagreeable features of the voyage out: sea-sickness, tedium, monotony of view, want of exercise, and so on. His list entailed fifteen footnotes in eight pages, and his range of reference extended from Stanley's lectures on the Jewish Church to Byron, Tennyson and Shelley. These references repeatedly connected his physical journey and his audience back to a shared, socially and geographically located culture. Lyttelton was a patron of the Canterbury Association and a supporter of Young Men's Christian Associations. His lectures on his visit to New Zealand were published without reference to the occasion on which they were given, but may have been delivered to the Amblecote Church of England Young Men's Association, like an earlier lecture on the religious aspect of the 'colonial empire'. When Lyttelton describes his journey in such a highly referenced way he gives his audience the means by which to deepen their connection with his journey and his destination. His account is one of many which 'organize the play of changing relationships between places and spaces', as Michel de Certeau puts it.[5] The distant space of New Zealand is converted into a meaningful place for the audience as Lyttelton fills distance with abundant references to his education and civilisation, references which make the link and organise the relationship between the beginning and end of his journey. The lectures are also a demonstration of Lyttelton's credentials and expertise as an author. The traveller, in Lyttelton's version of a defining journey, brings with him the intellectual, aesthetic and ideological tools to locate and interpret his experience, which delimit the community he represents and helps to create.

Lord Lyttelton is typical of a stream of travellers arriving in New Zealand after the wars of the 1860s who produce learned, cultivated, writerly texts of travel. They are writers who travel rather than travellers who write, and the claims their texts make on readers are to do with the way experience is processed: distance and difference are expressed in comparisons drawn from the author's geographical, cultural and historical knowledge, which enables the reader to share in an imagined community. When Lyttelton arrives in Wellington he finds it 'not very unlike the Lake of Lucerne', the town is 'not altogether unlike Ilfracombe' and the jetty has a 'very un-European look'.[6] Once he arrives at the house of Mr Justice Johnson, 'a kind of cottage one storey high', and goes inside, however, he finds it has 'a wholly English air, the rooms mostly small, so that one could just fancy oneself in an English parsonage or small country house'.[7] Lyttelton is making a report. He notes that the general look of Christchurch is 'somewhat slovenly and unkempt' and comments on the gas lights and macadamised roads, the state of the settlers, politics and the church. But the terms of his report, authorising the 'English' space of the New Zealand settlement, are unmistakable:

> Here you see a fac-simili, though on a small scale, of England as it is: there you see what England was ages ago, with similar vast powers of nature undeveloped and slumbering around, patiently abiding, as they have done for thousands of years, the informing hand of human skill and enterprise under Divine guidance to evoke them.[8]

In the 'Belgravia of colonies' Lyttelton is also interested in the reciprocal gaze of the colonist, but it is a gaze very much within the social paradigm enclosing him like a bubble as he moves across the world:

> What the people mostly thought of us . . . I never much learned, though I was very curious about it. Almost the only specific judgment I heard was that of a worthy trades-man, a market gardener, and Mayor of Christchurch, who thought me a respectable person, but that I leaned against walls in a way unbefitting an English Peer.[9]

The first 'tourist'

Charles Wentworth Dilke came to New Zealand when he was twenty-three years old as part of a world tour of 'English-speaking countries' in the spring of 1866. Geoffrey Blainey, editor of *Greater Britain: Charles Dilke visits her new lands 1866 & 1867*, has said that Dilke must 'have been one of the first people to go round the world as a tourist' because he used existing ship, coach and rail timetables rather than making his way independently across continents.[10] Dilke's preface to *Greater Britain*, however, describes his journey as an intellectual project to discover 'England':

> In 1866 and 1867 I followed England round the world: everywhere I was in English-
> speaking, or in English-governed lands. If I remarked that climate, soil, manners of life,
> that mixture with other peoples had modified the blood, I saw, too, that in essentials the
> race had remained the same. The idea which in all the length of my travels has been at
> once my fellow and my guide – a key wherewith to unlock the hidden things of strange
> new lands – is a conception, however imperfect, of the grandeur of our race, already
> girdling the earth, which it is destined, perhaps, eventually to overspread.

The hint of eugenics in the title of Dilke's 'record of travel' becomes more explicit as he expatiates on the idea which propelled him and which *Greater Britain* elaborates. Dilke's long career in politics – which ended in disgrace[11] – included other books,[12] but his best-known and most popular one remained his first, written with a triumphalist conception of British imperialism and celebrating a determinist view of nationality as race. This idea of nation as empire throws into clear focus the power relations of a Greater Britain.

The young Dilke announced his resolution to travel to New Zealand and Australia in a letter to his father from Kansas in 1866. As he travelled through North America he developed the beliefs about race and climate which overpower his otherwise Radical views (he was suspicious of existing institutions of government, in favour of democracy and female suffrage, and opposed to slavery). He held firm beliefs about the effects of a 'soft' climate supplying 'nourishment to an idle population' and represented the banana[13] as a climatological sign of lapsarian luxury and racial decline:

> The terrible results of the plentiful possession of this tree are seen in Ceylon, at Panama,
> in the coastlands of Mexico, at Auckland in New Zealand . . . The much-abused cocoa-
> nut cannot come near it as a devil's agent . . . The plantain grows as a weed, and hangs
> down its branches of ripe tempting fruit into your lap, as you lie in its cool shade. . . .[14]

Most of Dilke's description of New Zealand is viewed through the lens of the effect of climate on race, partly as a celebration of the qualities of Englishness which he believed contributed to a rightful domination of the globe, and partly as an explanation of Maori as a 'dying race'. The banana reappears in the context of cannibalism and New Zealand's 'terrible want of food for men': 'In New Zealand the windy cold of the winters causes a need for something of a tougher fibre than the banana or the fern-root.'[15]

If, as James Clifford has observed, '"travel" has an inextinguishable taint of location by class, gender, race and a certain literariness',[16] *Greater Britain* is a series of iterations of upper-class, white, male England and Englishness. As Dilke leaves America for Panama and the Pacific he pronounces, in a kind of reverse appropriation,

America is becoming, not English merely, but world-embracing in the variety of its type; and, as the English element has given language and history to that land, America offers the English race the moral directorship of the globe, by ruling mankind through Saxon institutions and the English tongue. Through America, England is speaking to the world.[17]

Twenty-nine days later he arrives in New Zealand, where his heroic description of arriving in Hokitika, with its famously dangerous harbour bar 'placed in the very track of storms and open to the sweep of rolling seas from every quarter'[18] is quickly succeeded by an encounter with a newspaper boy in which their shared game and vocabulary establish a number of recognisable features about where the heroic traveller has arrived:

> Instead of 'change', he cocked up his knee, slapt the shilling down on it, and said 'Cry!' I accordingly cried 'Woman!' and won, he loyally returning the coin, and walking off minus a paper.[19]

Fresh off the boat after a voyage across the largest ocean on the globe, Charles Dilke can engage with the local population as if he were on a London street corner, using a vocabulary and a set of relations that simultaneously establish social difference and a shared culture, in a region where the games and their codes are unproblematically transferable.

'Hokitika, 1869.' Chromolithograph by William Marshall Cooper. ATL A-104-025-9

Dilke's account of New Zealand swings briefly between descriptions of scenery and features of social life, including commodity prices and the use of convicts as road-builders, before giving way to colonial (speaking for England) politics. Crossing the Southern Alps with their 'one grand view' leads Dilke to reflect on the defects, political and administrative, of the provincial division of New Zealand. Considering this 'costly and inefficient' system of government leads him in turn to the 'difficulty . . . of a powerful and warlike native race'[20] reflecting Anderson's 'inner incompatibility of empire and nation'. The rest of his account of New Zealand is absorbed by his description – ethnological, climatological and political – of the Maori, whom he encounters at Parewanui and in the Manawatu. Very little of his narrative is concerned with the process of travelling or with situating himself as a traveller. After his dramatic arrival scene, and his immediate encounter with a society that simulates and projects England, Dilke's presence as a traveller and an Englishman abroad is established, and his narrative centres on the features of colonial administration which might have resonance in metropolitan political discourse, where the interests of empire and nation collide.

The two flies

Before visiting the great inter-tribal hui held at Parewanui over land grievances, Dilke gives an account of the origins and arrival of the Maori, comparing their physiology, language and traditions to Native Americans ('Red Indians'), 'Hindoos', Malays and South Americans ('Indians'), and concluding:

> The Maories without doubt, were originally Malays, emigrants from the winterless climate of the Malay peninsula and Polynesian archipelago; and, although the northernmost portions of New Zealand suited them not ill, the cold winters of the South Island prevented the spread of the bands they planted there. At all times it has been remarked by ethnologists and acclimatizers that it is easier by far to carry men and beasts from the poles to the tropics than from the tropics to the colder regions. The Malays, in coming to New Zealand, unknowingly broke one of Nature's laws, and their descendants are paying the penalty in extinction.[21]

Nature's laws not only offer a popular interpretation of British imperial ambition and success, but hold out the promise of an uncomplicated, guilt-free colonial inheritance, which reaches past the great hui at Parewanui, with its 'thousand kilted Maories', ceremonies, speeches and feasting, to a future when questions over the purchase and sale rights of land 'wanted by way of room for the flood of settlers' would have fallen into silence. As he drives away from the first day of the meeting, Dilke and his companions metaphorically consign the

Maori to a heroic past and a subject future: 'we talked over the close resemblance of the Maori runanga to the Homeric council'. Dilke bestows classical personae on the speakers at the hui, and concludes with examples of their 'noble eloquence and singular rhetoric art' in celebrating British sovereignty, building a picture of a noble but metaphorically defunct empire giving way to the next imperialists.[22]

Greater Britain's publication coincided with Dilke's election to the House of Commons and was written, from letters, during his election campaign. Well received by the press, it quickly ran through four editions and continued to be read for fifty years. Even twelve years after first publication it produced a substantial royalty of £8 12s. Pirated editions sold well in America and an abbreviated version was translated and published in Russia. Dilke's 200 author's copies were widely distributed. One was sent to J. S. Mill, who praised the author's 'advanced and enlightened views' while noting that he attributed 'too exclusive an influence upon national character to race and climate'.[23] Dilke's version of a determinist social Darwinism was consolidated, evidently to the satisfaction of the buying public, by the powerful textual strategy of moral parable. Having favourably compared the Maori with other indigenous subject peoples, he concludes his discussion with a notorious chapter entitled 'The Two Flies', which applies pseudo-science to imperialist objectives, proving them 'natural':

> The English fly is the best possible fly of the whole world, and will naturally beat down and exterminate, or else starve out, the merely provincial Maori fly . . . Natural selection is being conducted by nature in New Zealand on a grander scale than any we have contemplated, for the object of it here is man.[24]

Dilke's contribution to travel literature and to the debate about New Zealand is a magisterial defence of the progress of British imperialism, authorised by his own experience as an eyewitness, an Englishman and a politician, and relying on an identification of nation with race. His strategy of objectifying Maori through digressions into history, ethnology, anthropology, administration and racial theory aims to naturalise his profoundly class – and race-driven ideologies as knowledge, transmitted and maintained by the power relations implicit in his self-representation as a reflective 'scientific' observer reporting to a community of readers on Maori as objects of analysis. The popularity of *Greater Britain* suggests that Dilke's casting himself as the knowledgeable observer whose journey produces a meaningful Englishness in the world outside England was politically and culturally successful. The book projected a confident assessment of England's imperial power and potential into a future in which many things became more uncertain, including the moral character of the author.

Greater Britain and the literature of travel

Many of the travel books written about New Zealand and Australia in the 1870s and 1880s feature a clear line of descent from *Greater Britain*, including some direct descendants which recycle Dilke's title, like C. E. R. Schwartze's *Travels in Greater Britain*, published in 1885.[25] Most of them pronounce, with greater or lesser information, on the colonies' relation to the metropolitan world, picking up the idea of community implied in 'Greater Britain'.[26] The concept of the Maori as a 'dying race' is universally accepted, and the taxonomies and comparisons by which Dilke classifies non-Western peoples are adopted in some form by almost all observers. Dilke did not invent his methods or his attitudes, of course, but the popularity of *Greater Britain* helped establish it as a model travel text, and the role of the traveller as commentator, intellectual and cultural authority was mimicked by many writers in their own, much more personal and informal travel writing.

Dilke was one of the first of a stream of famous writer/travellers to visit New Zealand and Australia in the later decades of the nineteenth century, including Anthony Trollope, James Anthony Froude, Isabella Bird, George Augustus Sala, Constance Gordon Cumming, Mark Twain and Marianne North, whose books develop travel writing as the work of a professional writer or intellectual for an élite readership educated in the literature and language of the metropolis, though not necessarily resident there. *Greater Britain*, Trollope's *Australia and New Zealand* (1873) and Froude's *Oceana* (1886) established New Zealand's place both on the imperial traveller's itinerary and on the booklists of the metropolitan readership. These books helped to shape the preconceptions and expectations of boatloads of steamer tourists. Their express purpose was to evaluate the success of British imperial expansion, and their wider effect was to contribute to the development of print capitalism as a primary agency of imperialism. The idea of an unpeopled and 'unexhausted' world awaiting the boost of English settlement was perhaps particularly suited to New Zealand, which, as the last of the major emigration colonies, appeared to develop very quickly, and whose climate, island geography and settlement patterns allowed for numerous comparisons with Britain.

A famous novelist

Looking at the 'large, commodious and ornamental' public buildings in Dunedin, Anthony Trollope reflected:

> It strikes a visitor as absurd that there should be six capitals in New Zealand, a country which forty years ago was still cursed with cannibalism; – but it strikes him as forcibly with wonder that it should so quickly have possessed itself of many of the best fruits of

civilisation. This prosperity has come I think less from any special wisdom on the part of those who endeavoured to establish New Zealand colonies on this or another scheme than from the fact that in New Zealand British energies have found a country excellently well adapted for their development.[27]

When Trollope arrived at Bluff in the extreme south of New Zealand at the beginning of August 1872, he had already been to all the Australian colonies. But New Zealand had a different resonance for him.

I found myself struck, for a moment, with the peculiarity of being in New Zealand. To Australia generally I had easily reconciled myself, as being a part of the British Empire. Of New South Wales and Van Diemen's land I had heard so early in life as to have become quite used to them, – so that I did not think myself to be very far from home when I got there. But New Zealand had come up in my own days, and there still remained to me something of the feeling of awful distance with which at that time I regarded the young settlements at the Antipodes.[28]

Although Trollope was struck by this 'feeling of awful distance', when he reached Invercargill:

I felt exactly as I might have felt on getting out of a railway in some small English town, and by the time I had reached the inn, and gone through the customary battle as to bed-rooms, a tub of cold water, and supper, all the feeling of mystery was gone.[29]

It is notably the *domestic* arrangements of travel and particularly their familiar English inadequacy that make Trollope feel he is undesirably at home. New Zealand's perceived and promoted similarity to England, one of the great attractions for colonisers and settlers and remarked on by numerous writers, can be a counter-attraction for travellers, who are more inclined towards what J. Ernest Tinne called the 'powerful charm of novelty'.[30]

Opening his account of New Zealand, Trollope notes that more than 400 publications about the country had appeared before 1860, a figure he clearly finds surprising and makes him 'almost' reconsider his own project: 'In the face of this immense bulk of literature about New Zealand, I am almost bound to feel that more writing would be superfluous.'[31] In fact Trollope, who went to Australia 'chiefly to see my son among his sheep', had already seized the commercial opportunity offered by the sizeable market for travel books, and had an agreement with Chapman and Hall to write a book about Australia and New Zealand for £1,250.

In the introduction to his two-volume *Australia and New Zealand* he puts forward a suggestively Virgilian metaphor about the relation of colonies to Britain: 'Our people are going out from us as bees do, – not that the old hive is

Anthony Trollope from
An Autobiography, London,
1946. ATL B-K-509-FRONTIS

deserted, but that new hives are wanted for new swarms.'[32] Colonies are an illustration of the power of Great Britain 'to provide for her children homes in these lands' (specifically the 'emigration' colonies of Canada, South Africa, Australia and New Zealand). Trollope's organic and 'family' view of the mother nation and her 'natural' colonies had wide currency by the 1870s and determines his narrative. *Australia and New Zealand* has its eye firmly on the emigrant reader, who is told that if Trollope were to 'pitch his tent' he would pitch it in Tasmania.

Nevertheless he found being away from home onerous and the book difficult to write. He wrote to George Lewes and George Eliot: 'I am struggling to make a good book, but I feel it will not be good. It will be desultory and inaccurate; – perhaps dull, & where shall I be then?'[33] As a travel book Trollope's narrative sits between a dutiful reportage of useful information and a limitedly personal though sometimes lively account of his experiences and impressions – limited because, although he travelled with his wife Rose and went to visit his son Fred's sheep station, these members of his family barely appear in his book and Fred is disguised as 'my friend'. Even more than *Greater Britain, Australia and New Zealand* projects a view of the traveller as the provider of authoritative and comprehensive information. Trollope had already produced two other travel books, *The West Indies and the Spanish Main* and *North America*, and the dogged tour of his subject was a well-established model, to be repeated in his final travel book, *South Africa*, praised by the *Times* for having 'not a page uninstructive or dull'.[34] He also produced two colonial novels from his Australasian tour, one of which, *Harry Heathcote of Gangoil*, based on his son Fred, first came out in serial form to a wide readership in the *Graphic*. The reception of *Australia and New Zealand* was mixed, the *Times* finding it 'agreeable, just and acute' but the *Athenæum* and the *Saturday Review* declared the two volumes as 'dull as they are big'.[35]

Trollope came to New Zealand to 'see scenery' but what he saw made him conclude that 'in New Zealand everything is English. The scenery, the colour and general appearance of the waters and the shape of the hills, are very like to that with which we are familiar.'[36] Meaghan Morris has commented on the morbidity of description that afflicts travel writing, calling it 'a vast descriptive regime for destroying (and for Baudrillard replacing) reality'.[37] Trollope's sense of his task of description and evaluation is repeatedly suggested in sentences beginning 'I feel it incumbent on me to write a chapter on', 'I can understand', 'I am sorry to say', 'I may say', 'I am however able to say', 'I do not believe', and in paragraphs scattered with numbers and names. General description gives way to a racing flow of events only when the author is plunged into dramatic physical experience. Travelling overland from Queenstown to Dunedin, a trip of three days was lengthened to six by a snowstorm. Although the 'scenery was grand', it is his reaction to the 'tedium', the inns and the snow which dramatically locates the novelist-traveller in his body, on the road and in the landscape, responding to the conditions, reporting fragments of speech, interacting with other people. But generally Trollope's consciousness of his role as an authority on his subject, his readers' need for instruction and his own objective of a saleable book take precedence over the energy of a narrative. *Australia and New Zealand* is not an episodic window on New Zealand as the travelling novelist has experienced it, but an account of the process of reflection, analysis and information-gathering which has occurred in a particular place, formulated according to Trollope's racist and imperialist beliefs. He begins with the observation that 'in New Zealand everything is English', and the rest of his account describes places and people in order to determine their relationships across geographical distance but within a shared culture. He continually pronounces on the transmutations, opportunities or improvements effected by the shifting of English systems and social behaviour to the colonies, authoritatively judging their climate, housing, landscape, transport, economic prospects, and social and financial conditions. As a reviewer in the *Argus* noted:

[the author] manifestly entertains the highest respect for Mr. Anthony Trollope. He looks up to him as an authority . . . extremely safe and decidedly weighty, on the wide range of questions touched on in this big book. When our travelled Ulysses, who has done America and has done the West Indies, honours Australia and New Zealand by doing them, he evidently considers that his dictum on every possible subject in relation thereto will be accepted as final and decisive.[38]

Melting away

It is Trollope's comments on Maori, like his comments on Aboriginal people in Australia,[39] that most sharply define his views on colonial policy, politics and colonisation as controlled by race, producing 'empire' not 'nation'. He begins his tour of New Zealand in Southland, so Maori do not feature until he reaches the Canterbury Museum, where it occurs to him that 'Next to the Maoris, who are not as yet quite extinct, the moas, which are, must be regarded as the most wonderful productions of New Zealand.'[40] Moving on to the Wairau 'massacre', Trollope writes a history of encounter in a chapter entitled 'The Maoris', in which he explains he feels it 'incumbent' on him to write of the Maori because 'at home, we take more heed of the Maoris and of their battles than any of other details concerning the colony'.[41] In describing Gate Pa and Rotomahana, he develops the theme of extinction. Despite his recognition of a 'gallant people, whose early feelings towards us were those of kindness and hospitality', his discussion of Maori and their relations with Europeans is based on a premise from which his rhetoric of disappearance springs: 'I acknowledge that they have nearly had the gifts which would have enabled us to mix with them on equal terms.'[42] The force of that 'nearly' becomes explicit as Trollope repeatedly resorts to a vocabulary of violence: the Maori must be stamped out, kept down and 'melted away'.

Australia and New Zealand frames indigenous peoples as a necessary but temporary historical inconvenience to colonisation. Trollope's vocabulary suggests some unease about what he takes to be an inevitable disappearance – the idea of Maori 'melting' is reiterated to the point where it has the force of a wish, a hope, for a guiltless and graceful evaporation, occurring without blame or responsibility like a force of nature – but it is also clear that until this vanishing does occur the imagined community of the nation cannot come into being. 'Nation' requires a likeness, or as Anderson puts it a 'deep horizontal comradeship',[43] which in Trollope's terms cannot be achieved between races. As most of his narrative is determinedly factual and he barely allows himself to break into an adjective (the Pink and White Terraces are an exception but his description is, by contemporary standards, restrained), the terms in which Trollope discusses Maori and projects their future suggest the dangerous and unstable terrain lying outside and underneath the house of British imperialism, inside which most of his account of New Zealand occurs.

Travel and print capitalism

When Anthony Trollope embarked for Australia in 1871 he was still considered by many to be the foremost living English novelist, and was feted everywhere he went in Australia and New Zealand. In his 1883 autobiography he described his professionalism. He wrote for money and in an extremely disciplined way, counting the number of words on the page and writing for three hours each day with a watch in front of him. On the boat to Melbourne he wrote a novel, *Lady Anna*, at the rate of sixty-six pages of manuscript a week. *Australia and New Zealand* is a particularly good example of his research skills, his dogged writing and his sense of the market for informative travel narratives. Although the book frequently stalls in descriptive detail and contains indigestible wodges of dated information, he assessed the market accurately enough for the book to be run serially in the *Australasian* after its original publication in England in 1873, brought out in parts by George Robertson of Melbourne from March 1873 until the complete 'New Work on Australia and New Zealand' was advertised in June, and then issued in four sections by Chapman and Hall in August 1874 with another edition in two volumes in 1876.[44]

Trollope's observation that, until he thought of travelling to New Zealand, he had never opened a book about it makes the general point that reading for information has a narrower set of objectives than reading for pleasure, but it is the marketable combination of the novelty or entertainment of travel with professional commentary, education and information that shapes his text. Unlike fiction, travel writing must not be a waste of time. Trollope's readers receive very little personal information about him or his activities. Quick glimpses of him lying in bed listening to the landlord's conversation in a corrugated iron 'inn' in Otago or offering money to a young servant whose washing he had knocked into the mud in Christchurch are scattered sparingly through a text that presents the author as professional and reliably knowledgeable, a guide to the world outside Europe for European eyes and sensibilities.

Colonial readerships also were hungry for the incorporation of their nascent society in mainstream metropolitan print culture, and especially for a favourable evaluation by famous writers. The *Daily Southern Cross* of 2 October 1872 hoped that in his book 'Mr Trollope will not assign to New Zealand the lowest position in the galaxy of nations which is springing up around us'.[45] The booksellers in Auckland sold out of his novels while he was in New Zealand and, at the Young Men's Christian Association and Mechanics' Institute libraries, his works were 'engaged three deep'. At his farewell banquet Trollope reciprocated this attention to his work by complimenting New Zealanders on their superior reading habits. In an observation widely reported in the press, he noted that 'in every house in New Zealand he had been in he not only found some of his own works but many of the works of Thackeray, Dickens and other authors of eminence in all walks of literature'. [46]

The famous historian and *Oceana*

James Anthony Froude's 1885 visit to New Zealand was confined to Auckland, the island of Kawau, where he spent a considerable time staying with Sir George Grey, and the thermal region. He did not travel further south than Rotorua, and this in itself caused discontent. The *Edinburgh Review* thought that visiting Canterbury would have modified Froude's opinions generally, and that 'Canterbury is to Australia as much a foreign country as Massachusetts.' [47] His travelling companions were his son and his friend, Lord Elphinstone. Froude was sixty-six years old when he arrived in Australia, and a famous and controversial intellectual and scholar – famous as an historian of sixteenth-century England, controversial for his books about religious belief and his recently published life of Thomas Carlyle. As he travelled, a crisis developed over Afghanistan and for some weeks it looked as if England and Russia would go to war. As Froude was taking tickets through to London via New Zealand, 'English travellers, officers on leave, militia captains, colonels, &c., were streaming homewards from all quarters, like flights of rooks to their roosting-trees at evening'.[48] The prospect of war defines both the imperial centre and who belongs to it, and the direction of movement towards London makes the dynamics of imperial power very clear. Froude waits anxiously for the latest news from the telegraph wire, news which is mixed in with his conversations, observations and experience of Australia and New Zealand. A public figure, he travelled as a guest of the public. Staying with the governors of the various colonies he visited, he was accommodated in large baronial establishments and issued with free railway passes. Everywhere he went Froude was besieged by journalists. His opinion was widely solicited and reported on everything from the state of international politics and Britain's relation with the colonies to the quality of Australian wine, and his physical movement was facilitated and managed within narrow boundaries of comfort and social exposure.

His book *Oceana, or England and Her Colonies* is the product of both Froude's work as an historian, intellectual and commentator and the protected social environment in which he travelled. Froude's narrative constantly figures him as a man whose identity and primary occupations are intellectual, high cultural and European, and whose readership shares his values and range of reference. He represents and addresses a firmly bounded imagined community identified with

James Anthony Froude. From *Letters to Living Authors* by John A. Stewart, London: Sampson Low, Marston & Co, 1892, p.85. ATL B-K-515-85

and developed by a print-based culture and print capitalism. When he leaves the Cape Colony, where he believed British governments had 'aggravated every evil', he resorts to his portable classical library:

> As a book for the occasion as a spiritual bath after the squalor of Cape politics, I read Pindar, the purest of all the Greek poets, of the same order with Phidias and Praxiteles, and as perfect an artist in words as they in marble. Hard he is, as the quartz rock in which the gold is embedded; but when you can force your way into his meaning, it is like glowing fire.[49]

Both Froude's book and his range of experience suggest that the meaning of travel is found within British imperialism as a political and historical force, managed by an intellectual élite for the good of the whole community, and empowered by a tradition of Western liberal humanism and control of the oceans. *Oceana*'s title and opening paragraphs explicitly frame Froude's travels in Sir James Harrington's idea of a commonwealth based on control of the sea,[50] representing the colonies he moves through as an historically imagined political and cultural community. As a traveller Froude is both an exemplar (as product and practitioner) of an intellectual history and a sensitive barometer of what he calls 'the full sunshine of modern ideas', ideas that are tested by encounters with white colonials but do not disturb the boundary of empire and nation represented by race. When he meets two or three Australian tourists at Ohinemutu, Froude describes them in terms that differentiate them from but still count them as 'English':

> They were English-born and English in character, and spoke very sensibly about many things. They confirmed . . . that young Australians, growing in the full sunshine of modern ideas, were less absolutely benefited by those ideas than true believers in them could desire.[51]

But watching Maori in the village he finds that 'at every turn there was something peculiar'.[52] Maori and their customs are curiosities, and Froude's descriptions of individual Maori and of their landscape and behaviour continually reassert power relations, by either diminishing Maori or writing them out of the picture. Maori do not have to be taken seriously because their assets have already been appropriated.

> Here will be the chief sanitary station of the future for the South Sea English. The fame of it will spread, and as transit grows more easy, invalids will find their way there from all parts of the world. This desert promontory, with its sad green lake and Maori huts and distant smoke-columns, will hereafter be an enormous cockney watering place; and here it will be that in some sanitarian salon Macaulay's New Zealander, returning from his travels, will exhibit his sketch of the ruins of St. Paul's to groups of admiring young ladies.[53]

So does the nation imagine itself crossing the world. When Froude goes to the Pink and White Terraces, he meets a 'Maori on horseback [who] gave himself the airs of a lord of the soil'[54] and Kate, who is to be their guide, is a 'big, half-caste, bony woman of forty, with a form like an Amazon's, features like a prizefighter's and an arm that would fell an ox'.[55] Both are in sharp contrast to the tourists Froude and his companions watch disembarking from a five-oared boat, who are 'pretty figures in the general picture'.[56] The 'dreary impression' Maori generally make on Froude – landing on Mokoia island he finds them 'identical' to the Irish, a telling boundary – he puts down to the bad effects of European influence, but this explanation allows him to naturalise and codify the power relations between indigenous and European peoples.

> It is with the wild races of human beings as with wild animals, and birds and trees and plants. Those only will survive who can domesticate themselves into servants of the modern forms of social development . . . The negro submits to the conditions, becomes useful and rises to a higher level. The Red Indian and the Maori pine away as in a cage, sink first into apathy and moral degradation, and then vanish.[57]

The fuss about *Oceana*

The reception of *Oceana* by one of its readers gives shape to the cultural community imagined into being by the dissemination of an extensive metropolitan print culture to distant parts of the world. As Benedict Anderson has pointed out: 'It became conceivable to dwell on the Peruvian altiplano, on the Pampas of Argentina, or the harbours of "New" England, and yet feel connected to certain regions or communities, thousands of miles away, in England.'[58] A few months after *Oceana* appeared in 1886, Edward Wakefield, a prominent New Zealand politician and nephew of Edward Gibbon Wakefield, published a famously critical review in *Nineteenth Century* (August 1886).[59] Wakefield's comments on the colonial readership's relation to books about New Zealand show the developing hierarchies and distinctions of a colonial print culture and the complex dependence of colonial readerships on mainstream literatures for the production of meaning, always nuanced by the anxiety of separation and distance. According to Wakefield, no people in the world are so sensitive to what is written about them as British colonists, and this is because

> the people of these young countries, where the process of civilization which occupied twelve centuries in England has been completely achieved in fifty years, are self conscious just as boys and girls are in whom the mental and physical powers are prematurely and exceptionally developed.[60]

When these precocious colonists heard that historian James Anthony Froude, that 'sovereign prince of literature', was coming to visit them, they said: 'Now at last we shall have a work on the colonies which will be neither a dismal bluebook nor a mass of slipslop. Now at last a place in history will be given to the colonies by one who has the ordering of those things.' But in Wakefield's opinion *Oceana* turned out to be 'certainly the worst book that has ever been written on these colonies'.[61]

The specific charges that Wakefield levelled at Froude's book – that it spends too long on trivia, is banal, wooden and inaccurate – are less germane to his own cultural politics than his preamble about British colonists and what they want. In his edition of *Oceana* (1985) Geoffrey Blainey lists the points on which Wakefield accuses Froude of inaccuracy and adjudicates between them, two to seven in Froude's favour,[62] but it is clear from Wakefield's review that he is arguing not just for a text with no errors but for a textual and cultural endorsement of New Zealand by a metropolitan authority. As Wakefield notes, by 1886 there was no shortage of books about New Zealand, and colonists 'have been made to see themselves through the eyes of famous writers of all sorts and sizes; and we have come to be very callous to the opinions of any of them'.[63] Froude, however, is in a class of his own. His work and reputation precedes him and 'if the Delphic Oracle in person had made a tour of the Greek colonies in the Mediterranean, the honours that were paid to Froude in Australasia could hardly have been exceeded'. [64]

The only part of *Oceana* Wakefield likes is the first chapter, where Froude brings the weight of liberal humanist scholarship to bear on British colonial expansion, naturalising it in organic metaphors and historicising it within Elizabethan and classical imperialism while using Harrington's *The Commonwealth of Oceana* to appeal to patriotic pride and a textual culture. His opening evocation of 'other Englands' where there are 'unexhausted soil' and merry English children is imbricated in a print culture marked with significant waypoints: Plato, Horace, Sir James Harrington. But Froude's actual and recorded progress through Australia and New Zealand is fractured with his political and domestic concerns and takes place over long sea voyages and in cramped coaches and dirty steamers, and it is his account of these conditions that Wakefield objects to. In rounding on Froude for his 'most trivial narrative of everyday occurrences on steamers, the sort of stuff that a hobbledehoy who has never been abroad before would write home to his little sisters', [65] Wakefield's objection and objectives are entirely clear. Froude's task was to *redeem* New Zealand not just from the everyday preoccupations of material life and travel in the colony but from their textual reflection, by giving New Zealand a textual presence in English metropolitan print culture, as in Froude's impeccable if controversial contributions to it – his *Life of Carlyle, History of England, The Nemesis of Faith*, all his high Victorian, high church, high cultural output.

Wakefield's attack contributed to the controversy over Froude's biography of Thomas Carlyle, [66] but that did not prevent *Oceana* from being very widely read. Even more than Dilke's *Greater Britain* or Trollope's *Australia and New Zealand*, and despite Wakefield's condemnation, it became the text against which travellers measured the New Zealand they encountered. In the first six months of publication *Oceana* sold 75,000 copies, was issued in a popular half crown edition and released in New York. [67] It was still selling well enough to be reprinted in 1894, when Froude died. In 1892 John MacGregor, surgeon-major in the British Army in Bombay, could refer in his account of his travels around the world, *Toil and Travel*, to episodes or people in *Oceana* with perfect confidence that his readers needed no further information. When he was disappointed at not finding kauri trees where Froude had said they were, he asks plaintively, 'Was it in vain that I had so diligently read my *Oceana*?' [68] William Westgarth, travelling to Australia in 1888, considered *Oceana* a 'delightful' work, with its 'vigour and high literary style' which he could 'read to all full enjoyment during the leisure and quiet of the voyage'. [69] C. R. Sail, who is described on the title page to *Farthest East, and South and West* (1892) as 'an Anglo-Indian Globetrotter', spends a good deal of his final chapter processing his comments on Australia through the filter of *Oceana*, while

James Lawrence Lambe, leaving New Zealand in October 1887, agrees with Wakefield: 'If I had an opinion of the book before I visited the colonies, I now look on it as the worst mixture of rudeness, inaccuracy, folly and conceit ever committed to print by a man in Froude's position.'[70]

The floating literature of London: 1

Staying with Sir George Grey on Kawau, Froude goes exploring in the interior of the island and comes across a place arched over by 'four or five gigantic Pokutukama [*sic*] trees', with roots like a 'nest of knotted pythons'. In an extended rhetorical description he outlines the 'history' of this place, including a sketch he made of it entitled 'A Maori Banquet Hall'. It is a story of slain prisoners, bloody axes, slicing and cutting, spits and cauldrons: 'I could fancy that I saw the smoking fires, the hideous preparations, the dusky groups of savage warriors.'[71]

The island is now the property of Sir George Grey, a 'perfect host', and most of Froude's account of it is a description – biographical, political, intellectual and personal – of its owner, a 'singular man' whose garden, house and library all bear witness to his 'wealth of varied knowledge' and the personal qualities which make him 'among the best that [England] ever had'.[72] As Froude describes him, Grey and his island exemplify in miniature what he refers to as 'the "Oceanic" planets which still revolve around the English primary': 'Everything we

'Sir George Grey's house, New Zealand', from *Oceana* by J. A. Froude, London, 1886, p.252. ATL B-K-510-252

saw was his own creation, conceived by himself, and executed under his own eye by his own feudatories.'[73]

In the library of this cultivated and self-fashioned man, lined with bookcases and cabinets, oil paintings, Maori axes and 'Caffre shields and assegais all prettily arranged', is a table with

> Quarterlies, Edinburghs, magazines, weeklies – all the floating literature of London, only a month or two behindhand. Every important movement in domestic, foreign, or colonial politics could be studied as exhaustively at Kawau as in the reading room at the Athenaeum.[74]

The floating literature of London follows the 'Maori Banquet Hall' with the reading room at the Athenaeum, and thus transforms the Maori banquet hall into a textual artefact, imagined for the reader in a way that demonstrates both the remoteness of pre-European history in colonial New Zealand and the agency by which the community of the colony and nation is brought into being. The important thing about *Oceana* is not that it was received critically, but that it was received so widely, and that colonists and travellers felt impelled to record their responses to it, to engage in the *Oceana* debate. The sense of community created by shared texts not only naturalises the colonial presence, bringing the empire home and making a home in the empire, but also sets the terms by which the empire is known and understood. When Thomas Babington Macaulay, president of the Committee of Public Instruction in Bengal in 1834, declared that a single shelf of a good European library is worth the whole native literature of India and Arabia, he described not only the prejudices of an Englishman abroad but the essential tool for travellers in creating knowledge, meaning, readerships and colonies.

CHAPTER 6

Empire travellers, 2: travellers who write

Travelling for 'pleasure'

In 1883 J.H. Kerry-Nicholls, a gentleman explorer, travelled into the King Country, an area of the central North Island ruled over by the Maori King, or, as Kerry-Nicholls puts it:

> an *imperium in imperio*, situated in the heart of an important British colony, a *terra incognita inhabited* exclusively by a warlike race of savages, ruled over by an absolute monarch, who defied our laws, ignored our institutions, and in whose territory the rebel, the murderer, and the outcast took refuge with impunity . . . This fine country, embracing nearly one half of the most fertile portion of the North island . . . was as strictly tabooed to the European as a Mohammedan mosque.[1]

In the orientalist tradition of the eighteenth-century hero–traveller, Kerry-Nicholls set out into this politically sensitive and hostile terrain, armed with an introduction to Tawhiao, the Maori King, from former Governor Grey, with an interpreter and a head full of the myths and conventions of Euro-imperialism. After slogging his way through dense forest in the Whanganui river valley, where 'colossal trees rose like spectres around us, the enormous vines that twisted and twirled about them like coils of vipers, covered with grey moss like enormous spider webs',[2] he arrives at a Hau Hau village and presents himself to the hostile chief.

> When Te Pareoterangi came up, he squatted down with a sullen air, without going through any form of salutation, and then, after a pause, asked us what we had come for, and upon Turner telling him that he had brought the *pakeha* who was travelling for pleasure, a titter ran round the circle, for, if we did not look it, we felt half starved, we were drenched to the skin, and covered from head to foot with mud, and the chief,

evidently realising all the unpleasant features of our position, naively remarked, 'How can the *pakeha* travel for pleasure through such a forest as you have come?'[3]

Te Pareoterangi's question, seen by Kerry-Nicholls as naive, seems in the twenty-first century rather acute. It draws attention to the fact that Kerry-Nicholls is patently not travelling for pleasure, a *flâneur* on the hillsides of Taranaki, but engaged in a heroic imperialist enterprise. His narrative is charged with the language of domination: he penetrates the forest, discovers rivers and streams, ascends mountains and has successfully broken through into the tabooed mosque. The landscape he encounters enables him to display the heroic qualities which validate imperialism, and every action distinguishes him from the 'diminutive stature and ungainly appearance' of the Maori in the village.

But Te Pareoterangi's question also draws attention to the highly acculturated *activity* of travelling for pleasure, by siting it in a landscape so patently unpleasurable. What can it mean, travelling for *pleasure*? Te Pareoterangi's question illuminates the cultural weight banked up behind the nineteenth-century European traveller, a glimpse of how foreign the traveller looks to the people at home in a travelled land. When Miss Muller, author of *Notes of a Tour Through Various Parts of New Zealand . . . by a German Lady* (1877), was being canoed to the Pink and White Terraces in 1877, her party passed a 'native whare' where the family had 'gathered on the shore to see us pass':

> A lively conversation then began with the crew of the two canoes, my guide translated part of it to me. . . . My crew asked the guide to enquire of me why I had come so far to see the hot lakes, surely the world was full of Rotomahanas and Terraces everywhere?[4]

The tourist boom

By 1885, when James Anthony Froude came to New Zealand on the *City of Sydney* with its crowded saloon, 'American' fashion of dining (which he described as a 'multitude of small, ill-dressed dishes huddled around one's plate') and Chinese crew ('little creatures' whom Froude could not distinguish from one another),[5] a steady stream of tourists were crossing the Tasman to Auckland. When Froude and his party landed, the quay was thronged with a crowd 'collected to stare at the steamer and passengers'.[6] *Oceana* refers to 'swarms' of tourists at Cambridge, a '*table d'hote*' laid out there for forty people at least',[7] and at Ohinemutu tourists were 'lounging about by dozens': 'Parties were arriving hourly from Cambridge by the route which we had taken, from Tauranga on the sea or overland from Wellington. The carriages which brought the new arrivals returned with a back load of those who had exhausted the wonders'.[8]

THE KING COUNTRY;

OR,

EXPLORATIONS IN NEW ZEALAND.

A NARRATIVE OF 600 MILES OF TRAVEL THROUGH MAORILAND.

BY

J. H. KERRY-NICHOLLS.

THE AUTHOR.

WITH NUMEROUS ILLUSTRATIONS AND A MAP.

London:
SAMPSON LOW, MARSTON, SEARLE, & RIVINGTON,
CROWN BUILDINGS, 188, FLEET STREET.
1884.

Title page of *The King Country or Explorations in New Zealand* by J. H. Kerry-Nicholls, London, 1884.
ATL B-K-62-TITLE

Many, perhaps most, of these tourists recorded their travel in letters, diaries, journals and 'notes', and a surprisingly large number of them published their private texts. The tourists of the 1870s and 1880s travelled for 'pleasure', and travelling for pleasure brought its own set of obligations, attitudes and cultural disjunctions. Writing letters or keeping a journal is a print-acculturated response to experience, and the material culture of books, newspapers, journals and letters is both part of the equipment of travel and the intellectual agency for fixing the meaning of travel: travellers process their journeys through texts. It is as if the journey is not complete until it is received as a text.

Most writers are conscious of the characteristic modes of the genre. John Lawrence Lambe's *Twelve Months of Travel* (1888) is a typical and lively example of a privately published, journal-based travel narrative with no larger objective than to record the author's experiences and impressions. His comments about the road from Springfield to Bealey are placed in a context which shows his ironic awareness of the genre he is contributing to.

Tues 30th August 1887

Left Christchurch this morning by 8-10 train for Springfield. Then on in a stage coach forty-five miles to Bealey, through wild and desolate mountain scenery. It was the brightest moonlight long before I got here, and the last nine miles were gloriously beautiful, beyond all words. As for the road! I have never seen anything like so dangerous before, but if my friends wish to read of hairbreadth escapes and startling adventures I can only recommend them to the thousand and one books of the thousand and one travellers who describe such things. Only, I must disclaim the sentiments of these worthy people, which are usually more terrific than anything I can conjure up on the spur of the moment.[9]

Part of the experience of travelling was to read about it, and travellers moved in a tide of printed material, from shipping brochures to the ship's newspapers and libraries, the books they read to prepare them for the places they visited, and the letters and journals they kept. Froude himself reflected on *City of Sydney*'s offering:

A library is always part of the stock of a modern ocean steamer. There are religious books – some people read nothing else – there are books of travels for those who want to be entertained without feeling they are wasting their time.[10]

For the London illustrated papers and magazines, travel was a staple offering that reflected the activities of their metropolitan readers. Publishers' circulars featured a constant supply of travel books, and travellers represented a growing market for reading material: the 'armies of commercial and uncommercial travellers with spare half-hours', as an advertisement for Routledge's World Library put it.

The abundance of travel writing produced a need for travellers to distinguish themselves. Miss Muller begins with the announcement:

I am fully aware that upwards of forty books have been written on New Zealand – some by an able pen, learned and scientific descriptions that enter into statistics and politics. My notes lay claim to nothing of the kind – they merely tell what I have seen in New Zealand and how I fared among its inhabitants.[11]

Almost everyone offers some explanation for appearing in print, or for having embarked on the labour and presumption of a book in the first place. Alice Frere opens *The Antipodes and Round the World* (1870) with a question about travellers and their books:

'A 'spose whun ye gut hom', *like all foolish people*, y'intend t'write a buke?' was the half questioning remark made to me in Pekin by a young man fresh from the wilds of Scotland. At the time I had no intention of classing myself among that vast multitude . . . [but] On returning to England I was . . . persuaded to do so by the advice of friends.[12]

LIST OF BOOKS.

Many of the following works, and others, are named in the text. A selection will be found in the ship's LIBRARY, which is open to passengers in the First and Second Saloons. The rest are recommended for the reading of those who wish for further information.

AUSTRALIA.

Early Voyages to Terra Australia. Edited by R. H. Major, Hakluyt Soc. Pub., vol xxv. 1859.
Geological Observations together with Notices on the Geology of Australia, by C. Darwin. 1844.
The Geography of Mammals, by W. L. Sclater, M.A., and Philip Lutley Sclater, F.R.S. 1899.
Catalogue of Australian Mammals, by D. Ogilvie. 1892.
Catalogue of Marsupialia, by Oldfield Thomas. 1888.
Parrots in Captivity, by W. T. Greene. 3 vols. 1887.
Catalogue of Parrots in the British Museum, by Count Salvadori. 1891.
South Australia, its History, Resources, and Productions, by W. Harcus. 1876.
Australian Aborigines, Language, &c., by J. Dawson. 1881.
Australian Graziers' Guide, Silver's. 1879 and 1881.
Official History of New South Wales. 1883.
Australian Handbook, by Messrs. Gordon & Gotch   Yearly.
Australasia, by A. R. Wallace, with Ethnological Appendix by A. H. Keane. (4th Edition.) 1884.
Advance Australia, by Hon. Harold Finch-Hatton. 1885.
Official Year Book and Directory of Australia. Edited by Edward Greville. Yearly, from 1884.
Statesman's Year Book.
Australasia, Atlas, by Bartholomew.
Gold Metallurgy, by M. Eissler. 1891.
Rural Economy and Agriculture of Australia and New Zealand, by Robert Wallace. 1891.
Colonial Year Book. Yearly.
The Long White Cloud, by the Hon. W. Pember Reeves. 1898.
Old New Zealand, by a Pakeha Maori. 1887.
Captain Cook's Three Voyages round the World. Edited by Lieut. C. R. Low. 1892.
New Zealand Guide, by Sweetser. 1891.

CEYLON.

Murray's Handbook, India and Ceylon.
Tennant's Natural History. 1861.
Baker's Eight Years in Ceylon. 1884.
(Other books named in Chapter VI.)

List of Books published in the *Orient-Pacific Line Guide*, W. J. Loftie, 6th Edition, London, 1908, p.xxxv. ATL B-K 402-35

The insistence or encouragement of friends is the most common justification put forward by privately published writers for the existence of their books. James Edge Partington printed his journal to 'fill in the blank' left by his absence from his friends for three years,[13] and the notes of 'vacation tours' made by James Coutts, a Sydney barrister who died not long after they appeared in the *Town and Country Journal*, were collected and republished by 'many friends anxious to have some permanent memento of the author'.[14] Because so many travellers embarked on a long sea voyage and visited the hot springs of New Zealand for health reasons, a number of collections of family letters and journals were published as memorials after the death of the author. Frank Henley's *Bright Memories* opens with a memorial sketch describing his 'conversion' and his illness. He died at Sandhurst, less than eighteen months after he left on a voyage to restore his health.[15]

Perhaps the most common contributing reason for writing about travel was the boredom of the long voyage. Annie R. Butler, travelling as a missionary in the mid-1880s, referred to 'that great ship institution "my diary"',[16] and numerous travellers acknowledge diary and letter writing as occupational therapy. Mrs Muter was an officer's wife who travelled to New Zealand in the early 1860s, one of a number of journeys she made with her husband after experiencing and surviving the Indian Mutiny in Meerut, where 'the very air of India was charged with horrors'. On the long voyage from China to England the 'composition of a book' filled her time, but she steps back from claiming solo authorship, constrained both by social codes that meant relatively few women published travel books in the nineteenth century, and by the nature of her husband's input. Notes from her journal

> furnished the matter, my husband dictating while I wrote. Thus the contents came to be coloured by the peculiar character of his mind. Professional subjects are touched on, which many of my readers will see could not have emanated from me. Lieutenant-Colonel Muter used the opportunity of stating opinions he strongly held, and which he thought might be useful; but he would be sorry they should be published under the shelter of a lady's name.[17]

Claudia Knapman has observed that travel writing is a particularly literary genre: 'It is not an outpouring of observations and experiences by unreflective, passive and neutral observers'.[18] Her comment is a cautionary note to the 'realist' reading of nineteenth-century travel writing by women: 'travel writing, whether authored by men or women, cannot be read in the late twentieth century as if it consists of unmediated descriptions of "real" events and places'.[19] Many travel texts, however, do make precisely this claim, stressing their origins in journals, letters or 'notes', disclaiming any 'definite intention' of having their 'notes of a Journey Home' printed and published (as C. R. Sail puts it), and identifying subjectivity – 'my own impressions' – with truth. In the preface to his 1892 *Farthest East, and South and West*, Sail presents a series of disclaimers that shows the spectrum of travel writing and attaches significant qualities – intimacy, frankness, accuracy – to his own work, addressed to the reader-as-friend:

> What I have set down is just my own impressions of countries and climates, men and manners, as I have seen them; and I have not devoted myself to transcribing from Cyclo-paedias and Year Books and Compendia of Useful Knowledge facts and figures which those who yearn for may seek and find in books of that class. For these reasons, persons who require their mental provender to be set before them elegantly, in a pure and polished literary style, are respectfully warned off, equally with those whose delight is in statistics and historical disquisitions and political perpendings – in the Serious and Solid. For here is but a careless style, with no more merit in its matter than accuracy and absence of exaggeration so far as these may be attained by mortal pen, and a frankness of expression such as a man may use in writing to his friends.[20]

Sail's distinctions, which imply a difference between 'real' personalised travel writing, born of experience, and an officious and impersonal delivery of 'public' information, are repeated by Edward Payton, the artist and author of *Round About New Zealand* (1888). He dismisses 'that meddling and iniquitous being – the scribbling Globe trotter – who after spending a fortnight or so in the colony forthwith presents to the public a treatise on the political history, manners and customs, geology and every other feature of the land he has "rushed"'.[21]

The travel writing of ordinary steamer passengers may claim to be personal, unliterary and anecdotal but represents what Stephen Greenblatt calls the 'European dream of possession'. He talks of the 'primal act of witnessing around which virtually the entire discourse of travel is constructed. Everything in the European dream of possession rests on witnessing understood as a form of significant and representative seeing'.[22] Behind the nineteenth-century traveller's textual response to the world lies a sense of personal and cultural duty to share the sights and experiences of abroad, as well as knowledge and reflections about them, with people not present. If individually this represents a mode of ownership, collectively it gathers the world into European experience and epistemology.

Travel writing is also an act of control. By writing about their travels, tourists transformed them into a meaningful narrative and placed themselves at the centre of meaning. The traveller's conception of the heroic dimensions of a journey to New Zealand is reflected in the multitude of titles emphasising a global circuit: 'Round the World', 'Over the World', 'The Earth Girdled', 'Farthest East, South and West', 'A Boy's Voyage Round the World' and so on. This suggests that another motivation for publishing such a record was to lay claim to the figure of the traveller as adventurer, explorer and hero and to fix the travel experience in a printed text available not just to a readership wider than the recipients of a family letter, but to history. Most privately printed travel texts explicitly insist on their difference from a 'literary' book such as Froude's or Trollope's, and claim that their entries are unedited, unaltered and transmit an unmediated experience. Such a claim seeks to define the reader's relation to the text ('not to criticise too severely') as well as to indicate who the readership might be. Bertram Barton's preface to *Far from the Old Folks at Home*, privately printed in 1884, is typical:

> The following pages have no pretensions to being a carefully compiled book of travel or adventure. They are simply and solely the reproduction of my journal never intended for publication, and only passed through the printers' hands so as to be circulated more easily among friends.[23]

Like many journal-keepers, William Towers Brown in *Notes of Travel 1879–1881*, printed for private circulation in 1882, adds a material dimension to his claim of offering 'an accurate impression of things and people'. He asks his reader to bear in mind that the circumstances under which I wrote were often far from favourable: viz., after long days of travelling by rail, by coach, on horseback, or on foot; on board ship, in rough seas; in Japanese tea-houses, where the writing table was on one's knees, or in Chinese inns, in the midst of dust and dirt.[24]

John Lawrence Lambe travelled around the world in 1886–87 as a young man recently graduated from Cambridge. He published his journal about Australia and New Zealand in 1888, but notes at the end that the American part of his journey was recorded by a friend, who kept an 'elaborate journal which alas! he had not yet completed last time I ventured to mention the matter to him'. Lambe clearly perceives this as a deficiency he needs to explain to his readers, and to make up for it he appends a skeleton itinerary of their American journey, as if that part of their travels will not have happened unless there is a textual artefact of it.[25]

Who were the travellers?

James Clifford has observed that the 'long history of travel is predominantly Western-dominated, strongly male, and upper-middle class'.[26] Edward Payton commented that some of the 'so-called' guidebooks published by emigration agents and shipping companies 'try to impress upon one that the colony is composed almost altogether of people who have received the very best education . . . that every third person one meets is an Oxford man'.[27] While Payton ironically dismisses this claim – 'I don't think they could have been at home while I was in their adopted country' – many tourists identify themselves as Oxford and Cambridge men, often as a credential on the title page. J. Ernest Tinne MA, in his 1873 book *The Wonderland of the Antipodes*, which found a wide readership and was noticed in the *Illustrated London News*, described himself at length on the title page as 'editor and originator of the Eton College Chronicle and Oxford Undergraduate's Journal'.[28] C. E. R. Schwartze in *Travels in Greater Britain* (1885) refers to his recent Oxford degree on the title page, and Lambe notes the presence of 'Eton and Cambridge men' at various points on his travels in New Zealand, including on his ship as they arrive in New Zealand and while touring Auckland with the Earl of Shaftesbury and his party.

Tinne describes a visit to Napier in which he 'suddenly felt a tap on the shoulder and heard a "how d'ye do?" from a nice looking young fellow . . . It was N—, a pupil of the same tutor as myself at Eton.'[29] The same encounter is told from the point of view of N—, or H. W. Nesfield, in his book *A Chequered Career* (1881), confirming Clifford's point. The overwhelming majority of 'private' travel narratives of the 1870s and 1880s were written by young, upper-middle-class, educated and leisured Western males. In New Zealand's case they were predominantly British, drawn from such a narrow social spectrum they were likely to know one another. Nesfield was unusual in that he worked his way around Australia and New Zealand, and when Tinne meets Nesfield working as a cabby in Napier he is anxious about how to respond to Nesfield's situation, which he describes as a social anomaly that 'one can look at sometimes from a ludicrous as well as a distressing point of view'.[30] Tinne chooses to find it ludicrous and to make his point tells a tale about a Colonel Russell who hired a hansom cab to take him to a ball. After dropping off the colonel, Nesfield took the carriage down the road, tethered the horse, changed into evening dress and went back to the ball. At the end of the evening the colonel was found leaning against a wall looking fed up and waiting for his cabby, who was engaged for three more dances.[31]

Many of these young men were casting an eye over the new colony to see if it would meet their requirements for a cultivated and prosperous life. Tinne notes, talking about prospects in sheep farming:

> ... if I were asked about the pleasures of such a life I should tell anyone that, with a good horse, comfortable house and food, and all the latest English magazines and papers and such society as Canterbury Province affords (where every second man is from a first-class English school or University) he must be very exigent if he were not pleased. A man can have no fairer sketch of both sides of the question than you find in Lady Barker's *Station Life in New Zealand*.[32]

But such a view depended on the picture of New Zealand as an empty land, such as Tinne projects when he calls Kawau 'this little Paradise, a type of what New Zealand will become in future years when her lifeless plains are peopled, her willing soil is planted and her forests of endless green diversified with the bright colouring of English flowers'.[33] As Mrs Howard Vincent, author of *Forty Thousand Miles* (1885), commented, it was a view propagated by colonists. She speaks of their 'keen longing and anxiety that England should know and realize how prosperous, how civilized, how replete in comfort and luxury her colonies are'.[34]

Such diversity as there was in the travelling population – Froude talks of 'Australians with long purses and easy temper' who spoil the market for less 'amply provided' travellers[35] and there are accounts of visits to New Zealand by French and German tourists as well as other, mostly European, nationalities – displayed very little variation in class.[36] Tourists, and by extension travel writers, were people of means, unlike the waves of emigrants who travelled to New Zealand in the years before the New Zealand Wars and who often staked their material future on a ticket to the colony. Women travellers were still relatively unusual, and women travelling comment on their role and position. Annie R. Butler observed that 'ladies travel very little in this country; there were rarely

'Louis Vuitton: Travelling
Requisites.' An advertisement
from the *Orient-Pacific Line
Guide*, W. J. Loftie, 6th Edition,
1908, p.iv. ATL B-K-402-6A

ever any besides ourselves in the conveyances or at the boarding houses which
we chanced to stop at',[37] and Mrs Howard Vincent found herself the 'the only
lady amongst some twenty men' at dinner at the Criterion Hotel, Napier, in
October 1884.[38] Miss Muller declares that one of the purposes of publishing her
notes on New Zealand is to 'show how a lady may perfectly well travel by herself,
provided she be healthy, strong, good-tempered, and ready to put up with some
hardships'.[39]

There is some record of commercial travellers, whose books reveal, unsurprisingly, a different landscape from the leisure traveller or tourist, delineating the
networks of business interests rapidly developing across the empire. W. Little's
Round the World; notes by the way (c.1875) was published anonymously, identifying its author only as a 'Commercial'. Little's firm sold agricultural products
for sheep, and he recounts meeting both local businessmen and other 'commer-
cials' hawking their products and setting up business orders around the colonies.

His book, described as a 'Collection of Notes of Impressions at the time of writing', is clearly written as a personal diary for a familiar readership. It names acquaintances made on his journey, reports his conversations, describes his excursions and impressions (he refers to sightseeing as an 'errand') and notes his business appointments and business rivals. Much of his time in New Zealand is spent travelling between small farming towns and farms, where he was usually received by the manager and sometimes shown scant hospitality ('a shakedown with the men'), but the nature of his business is assumed and lies underneath his narrative as the explanation for his contingent social relations, his observations and his mobility. Little found that in New Zealand 'drunkenness prevailed in all directions',[40] an observation echoed by Isabella Bird.[41]

Henry Selden Young's *Diary of a Voyage to Australia and New Zealand* (1885, but not published until 1999)[42] records a journey made primarily for health reasons. But Young was the son of a well-known Birmingham bookseller, who was responsible for the White Star Line's ships' libraries, and he pays attention to the book trade in Australia and New Zealand, describing among other things the methods of a Canadian book salesman he ran into in Tasmania.[43] Like Little, Young gives an idea of the number of travellers engaged on business in Australia and New Zealand and, also like Little, is very impressed with the level of advertising and advertisements he sees. Young comments frequently on the level of education of the people he meets, what he is reading and how well read others are, though his opinion of New Zealand was generally unfavourable and he reported a view held by a clerk in the City Council Office that the Parliamentary Library in Wellington must hardly be used, 'so illiterate are most of its members'.[44]

Rest and roads

What James Clifford has called the 'materiality of travel'[45] is a staple and sometimes dominant element of travel texts. Paul Carter has pointed out the 'double aspect of travelling – an experience that . . . required places to rest as much as roads'.[46] The irritations of inconvenient accommodation, bad food, an uncomfortable coach or dirty steamer flavoured most travellers' sense of moving through a new and exciting environment. At the same they reveal the cultural inflections always present in travelling and in writing about it – the volatility of the idea of travelling for pleasure. Regardless of their authors' ethnicity, gender, class or profession, travel accounts of the 1870s and 1880s routinely share the preoccupations of any traveller with the conditions of travelling – which, as Carter notes, are also the conditions of knowledge, the familiarity through which a perception of novelty is intermittently achieved, which is tied to preconceptions of the role of the traveller and the world they bring with them. It

THE GRAND HOTEL, DUNEDIN.

The Grand Hotel, Dunedin. An advertisement published in *Maoriland; an illustrated handbook to New Zealand*, 1884, p.xxii. ATL B-K 510-22

Admitted by all Tourists to be the best Hotel in Australasia.

has been argued that travel writing by women is more likely to be self-reflexive and provide 'subtle but persistent subthemes that were a critique of Western lifestyles',[47] but in most travel texts domestic and personal conditions provoke conventional responses.

European tourists were delivered to New Zealand by a society organised on principles of minutely differentiated distinctions replicated in every physical detail of their circumstances, from the class of cabin they occupied to the menus they were offered, the books they read, and their social and political activities. Their response to the world they encountered reflected, and was processed through, a complex of socially generated expectations and attitudes and material circumstances. Isabella Bird, the famous Victorian travel-writer, went on a trip to Australia and New Zealand for her health in 1869. She left for Honolulu very unimpressed with what she had seen, complaining that Australia combined the worst of Britain with a fretful climate and in New Zealand everyone was drunk. Fellow travellers, costs, accommodation, food and transport constitute the 'worldly, contingent, relations of travel'[48] and the shared field in which travel writing is done. Travel writing is highly self-conscious. The traveller is always hyperaware of their own responses and sensations in a strange land, and of being in the unsettling and often anxious condition of travelling. When the painter and botanist Marianne North visited New Zealand in early 1881, she found it very cold and uncomfortable. Travelling from Dunedin to Christchurch

> the railway carriages were crammed with the most objectionable children. The views I had heard so much of I never saw, though I incessantly looked, and I was half-dead and starved when we reached Christchurch and its well-regulated and extra-English hotel. The next day was Sunday, and it was marked by all the meals being crammed together, 10am, 1, and 5pm, leaving sixteen hours to fast before another came; I was upset internally, and was very wretched for a week afterwards. My box, which I had left at the station of Invercargill to be forwarded on the day I landed, had never turned up or left Invercargill, and I was sick of everything belonging to that cold, heartless, stony island.[49]

The inventory of possession, the narrative of action

Nineteenth-century travel writing makes a giant inventory of colonial possession, ranked by utility. The sea routes, ships, hotels, menus and sights are all assessed and rated for a chauvinist public. Richard Tangye found the Yankee steamer *Mariposa*, which he took for the crossing to Auckland in April 1886, 'furnishes an excellent means of comparison between the much-vaunted Yankee superiority in everything mechanical over England'. 'Abominable' ventilation and facilities were compounded by 'shamefully close and few' lavatories, 'placed as to be common to first and second-class passengers'.[50] C. R. Sail offered his readers a day-by-day commentary on his accommodation, transport, dinners and sights, with comments on the accuracy of 'the guide-book' and Froude's *Oceana*. John MacGregor, whose 1892 *Toil and Travel* records his journey from 'the moment of starting from the Desert of Gharmsala till that of standing by the grave of Rob Roy', more practically advised his readers that

> advertisements about places are very misleading. They tend to make every particular scene the very best in the best of all possible worlds, and consequently but little real information can be got out of them. Even guide-books err in this way . . . So . . . you must value things at your own estimation.[51]

Most travel writers have a low opinion of other tourists. Count Fritz von Hochberg, travelling through New Zealand in 1907, finds everyone exceptionally vulgar, especially the tourists he shares coaches with, and thought New Zealand was the 'worst country for travelling'. Arriving in Waiouru, von Hochberg fulminates that the 'worst shed I've ever been in pompously calls itself an hotel'.[52] Miss Muller describes the offensive and penny-pinching behaviour of a Mr Jones at Rotomahana, whom she 'detected in sniffing his nose with his fingers', a socially defining act which contracted his name to 'Jones'.[53] Jones's behaviour, including that to Maori, preoccupied her partly because she was humiliated to be associated with him as a foreigner.

The Kennedys, a Scottish family who toured extensively in Australia, New Zealand and North America from 1872 to 1876, 'singing the songs of Scotland around the world', recorded every part of their journey with minute attention to the detail of coach travel, accidents, river crossings, food and accommodation. Every destination is reached with exacting physical effort. The landscape they move through is dense with obstacles – flooded rivers, trees across the road, clapped-out horses, roads so rough their heads bang incessantly against the roof of the coach – and crowded with activity. The Kennedys' progress continually reasserts their capacity as travellers: '"Thank your stars you're over that!" said the captain – "often and often have tourists wanted to turn back here".'[54]

What occupies travellers' attention, and energises their narratives, is the *action* they are engaged on, the business of getting themselves about, the physical effort it takes, how they are fed and sheltered, the surrounding detail of their physical existence. All of this may be new and unique to the individual traveller, but is an overused and much recycled descriptive field in travel writing generally, as well as to colonists. Edward Wakefield, in his review of Froude's *Oceana*, commented furiously that

> one fourth of *Oceana* is occupied by the most trivial narrative of everyday occurrences on steamers. . . . Mr Froude tells us about his own state of health and his son's . . . the passenger accommodation, the doctor and his pretty newly-married wife, the cook, the breakfasts, dinners, luncheons, the bread, the porridge . . . and so on and so on . . . he seems never to have noticed any of the wonders of the deep but to have given his attention wholly to the most commonplace human incidents . . .[55]

The floating literature of London: 2

When Lord Lyttelton visited Canterbury in 1867 he found that the pleasant and comfortable houses of the settlers 'invariably' had a 'quantity of modern English books, which come out from England in every ship'.[56] Seeing familiar publications gave many travellers a frisson of the familiar made strange that they remarked on in their texts. Mrs Vincent commented on her arrival in Auckland in the middle of a September night in 1884 that 'it gave me quite an "eerie" feeling to see on the tables around in this far-off land of the Maoris the cata-logue of this year's Academy'.[57] Many travellers remark also on the availability of the English illustrated papers. David Kennedy noted the variety of papers provided in Mechanics' Institutes: 'Every month fresh literary blood is infused into the community, and on the arrival of the Home Mail, people crowd the reading room to see the latest magazines and newspapers.'[58] Travellers also comment on the widespread use of illustrations from the English papers as wallpaper. Mrs Vincent records having luncheon at

> Griffith's 'Stables' in a one-roomed hut, that was entirely papered with pictures from the *Illustrated* and the *Graphic*. It formed a most interesting and thrilling wall paper, choos-ing, as had been done, all the most telling events of the years '81 to '83.[59]

Mrs Vincent's narrative, like J. Ernest Tinne's and many others, frequently refers to the growing body of travel writing about New Zealand – Dilke, Lady Barker, Trollope, Kerry-Nicholls, Constance Gordon Cumming. The attention travellers paid to the print culture which accompanies and precedes them marks its centrality, but also shows a hermeneutic instability produced by new, and not always knowable, contexts.

William Towers Brown, on his way to the thermal region in February 1880, stayed in a whare with a local Maori family where two of the three rooms were let to visitors. He wrote to his family: 'On the wall of the second was that large

'The Zulu War – battle of Ulundi. Final rush of the Zulus with the British Square in the distance.' Published in the *Illustrated London News*, 6 September 1879. ATL C-23598-1/2

picture that appeared in the *Illustrated London News* some months ago: "Battle of Ulundi – Final rush of the Zulus upon the British". This picture, marking the end of the Zulu wars, is a poster-sized engraving foregrounding Zulu warriors and showing the British army square drawn up in the far distance. Towers Brown comments in his journal:

> Below was written in Maori the interpretation of this heading. Just to think of its finding its way to a Maori hut in the wilds of New Zealand. The illustration must come home to the war-loving hearts of the Maoris. I wonder with which side they feel most sympathy. They are friendly enough with us, but still the Zulus are more a people after themselves.[60]

The battle of Ulundi, according to Jeff Guy, was represented by the British as a major military victory because they had already decided to withdraw from the struggle over the annexation of Zululand, and the propagandist view of the battle circulated in the British press deflected attention from what was in fact a repulse.[61] The interpretive possibilities for this poster seem endless, especially as the iwi or tribe whose village it was were Te Arawa, who were loyal to Britain during the New Zealand Wars. The presence of this picture in remote New Zealand bush, at home with Maori, illustrates the extent to which powerful imperial imagery circulated, and the fluid relational meaning produced by the print culture as it travelled across the world.

If the pages of the *Graphic*, the *Illustrated London News* or the *Leisure Hour* brought images of imperialism into the stables and huts of New Zealand, they also normalised and articulated the world of the imperial traveller in the compilation of news, fiction, travel narratives and politics they offered. In their regular reporting on the Victorian court and Westminster, the illustrated metropolitan papers map the pressures of the culture which spread out from London to the world. Regular information on the colonies sits side by side with the Irish troubles or the state of British poor. Illustrations of the evils of reading fiction are next to long-running serials; military and diplomatic negotiations sit beside sensational natural events like the eruption of Mt Tarawera in New Zealand or earthquakes in Japan. Displaying the anxiety and the glamour of expansionism, the energy and mobility of imperialism, these papers mediate the empire to a readership that is politically conservative but spatially adventurous. In writing their own accounts of what they see and do in the world outside Europe, these readers bring the Empire home.

CHAPTER 7

The business of travel

The Cook's tourist

By the late 1880s Thomas Cook and Son were providing the 'complete arrange-ments' and 'all necessary tickets for a Tour through New Zealand'. Cook's was represented in Auckland by an agent from 1880, but established a local presence in 1888 after the grandson of the firm's founder reported that in New Zealand 'there are more interesting sights to be found within a limited area than in any other country'. The expansion of international tourism agents into New Zealand brought a corresponding development of infrastructure and standardisation of services. Thomas Cook and Son established a system with three coaching firms for their 'mutual interests' and 'for the division of the road . . . Fixed prices were agreed upon . . . and Cook's confined its bookings to the three firms.' When rail links were established between Auckland and Rotorua, travellers could get rail concessions by booking with Cook's overseas, and 'the ever-increasing number of branch offices all over the world . . . were supplied with full information concerning the Dominion, and in a position to induce travellers to include New Zealand in their itineraries'.[1]

The *New Zealand Herald* welcomed the arrival of Cook's in a series of articles that reveal travellers' desires, the monolithic spread of tourism, and the develop-ment of systems to minimise expense and difficulty. Cook's offered sites and routes that combined exotic adventure with aesthetic sightseeing, but without inconvenience, discomfort or the fear of extortion. The *Herald* eulogised the

> wonderful achievements of this firm from the conveyance of an army up the Nile, or a caravan of Moslem pilgrims to Mecca, or of Christian pilgrims a thousand strong to the Holy Places, to the conducting of a solitary traveller to almost any spot on earth, with all his wants anticipated, and himself protected from the wolves in men's clothing baying at him in a hundred strange tongues and seeking to devour him and all his substance.[2]

Cook's Tours, title page of the New Zealand
pocket pamphlet, 1890. ATL B-K-516-TITLE

The job of the 'travellers' friend' was to turn travel into tourism, a 'practice de-fined as incapable of producing serious knowledge', as James Clifford has said,[3] with the tourist insulated from local cultures, conditions and costs, instructed in the production and acquisition of knowledge (what to see, where to go, what to think about it) and made to 'feel at home in thousands of spots scattered over the map'.[4] As the systems were streamlined and travel became populist and commo-dified, Cook's promotional literature characterised the tourist as a freewheeling individual receiving personally customised services, but the marked tendency of travel texts to recycle itineraries and descriptions of travel sights imposes a mass travel culture on the perceptions and choices of individual tourists.

A reaction against Cook's tours and tourists is found in the texts of other travellers, whose authors have already subscribed to a concept of authorship in which their travel narrative is individualised, producing meaning and expressing difference. One classic example, Thorpe Talbot's 1882 *New Guide to the Lakes and Hot Springs*, is discussed below, but Count Fritz von Hochberg's 1910 *An Eastern*

Voyage is perhaps the supreme example, delivering an energetic account of his experience through the intensely colouring filter of his opinions, snobbery, prejudices, character sketches and idiosyncratic observations. His reaction to the Cook's agent in Dunedin expresses a powerful social boundary:

> He told me I would do best to come round to his office there and then and he would provide me with all the tickets. I told him I shouldn't dream of doing such a thing. I never wanted to have anything to do with Cook, and I am quite capable of looking after myself.[5]

The business of guidebooks

Travel as business, as a source of commercial possibilities, was never far from the nineteenth-century traveller's mind. One of the significant topics repeated in travel books about New Zealand from the end of the 1860s was the size of the public debt. James Anthony Froude's comment in *Oceana* that New Zealand was likely to repudiate the national debt was a focus of the response to his book, including formal rebuttal. Brodie Hoare, who represented the Bank of New Zealand in London, was invited to Canterbury to address a local audience on the question of colonial investment, and subtitled a pamphlet of his impressions of New Zealand an 'antidote to Mr Froude'.[6] The well-known traveller–artist Constance Gordon Cumming exclaimed in 1881: 'Imagine this young colony having already contracted a national debt of upwards of twenty millions!'[7] William Towers Brown in the following year reports that the 'rate of interest in the colonies is very much higher than at home, and capital can be safely invested to bring in a return of 8 or 9 per cent'.[8] So many tourists comment on the size of New Zealand's public debt as they set off for the natural wonders that it blurs the boundary between a pleasure-seeking tourist and a colonial investor.

The shadowy area between business and pleasure, evident as the tourist gaze shifts between mountain peaks and valleys ripe for cultivation or forests full of suitable trees for logging, is also evident in the range of guidebooks as they position themselves between value for money and cultural value. Guidebooks, while signposting the tourist landscape, also occupy what John Frow has called 'an accessory . . . metaspace where the business of tourism is conducted'.[9] The ships, coaches and roads that transport the tourist and generate an economy based on mobility are themselves detailed sources of information about tourist markets and cultures. But they are differentiated from the travel destination by the work of the guidebook, which may provide practical information but also sets out to educate tourists in ways that allow them to look at an unfamiliar landscape and see there a 'place', marked by signs of cultural and aesthetic value. The 'business of tourism' includes the production and sale of books to accompany or facilitate travel. The character of the travel text, negotiating the cultures of home and abroad, sensibility and functionality, aesthetic satisfaction and disappointment, and the quotidian annoyances supplied by fellow travellers, inadequate services or insufficient adventure, is to some extent generated by the work of the guide-book in shaping the traveller's expectations and creating what Frow has called the 'structural role of disappointment' in travel.[10] Can any landscape, however replete with natural wonders, whose access is arduous, lengthy and expensive, support the aesthetic freight of promotion as the 'most wonderful Scenic Para-dise in the World'?[11]

The history of New Zealand as a destination for migrants is synchronous with its development as a tourist location, and the first guidebook to New Zealand, G. T. Chapman's *Traveller's Guide Through New Zealand* (1872), sites its origin in the fiscal contact zone between immigration, investment capital and tourism.

> During the past few years New Zealand affairs have been in a transition state, for immedi-ately Great Britain severed the leading strings, the colony determined to get into debt by borrowing *millions*, for what previously *thousands* would have been found sufficient. This borrowing propensity has aroused the curiosity of business and moneyed men in Europe and America; the result is that 'many are running to and fro' in the land, but knowledge is deficient, as in almost every book printed and published out of New Zealand, referring to this colony, there are no end of blunders.[12]

Chapman's guide is a blend of factual information about the colony on the Royal Geographical Society's model, as set out in Colonel Jackson's *What to Observe; or, The Traveller's Remembrancer* (1861),[13] and a personalised anecdotal narrative which enables the traveller to identify the important sights. In the absence of 'history' (the book opens with the statement '[T]he History of New Zealand has yet to be written'), Chapman's guide offers descriptive geography, topographical description, tables of statistics illustrating the 'progress of settlement', travel advice and short discussions of each major settlement, with maps and pencil sketches in cheap purple reproductions. The guide is pocket sized with paper covers, aiming at the portable and disposable end of the travel-guide market, and addresses all readers as male British tourists.

Published only a few years after the end of armed confrontation, Chapman's guide negotiates the difficult field of the New Zealand Wars by focusing on the transformation of the recent military past into an historical landscape. At Tauranga the 'open and wide' face of the country is dotted with comfortable homesteads and cottages, and the tourist will find 'rifle pits, ditches and embankments still testifying to the struggle with the Maori'. At Gate Pa the 'Maori displayed the most undaunted courage, and the chivalry of a warlike race'. At New Plymouth the tourist can 'take the stage coach to Whanganui and Wellington, crossing the line of country for ten years the theatre of war, and

THE GRAPHIC

'With the Australian Squadron in New Zealand Waters' from the *Graphic*, 5 February 1887, p. 136. A little later than Chapman, this sketch reinforces images of a happily subjugated people. N-P 547-136

which has not inappropriately been termed "the garden of New Zealand"'.[14] Visiting Napier, the tourist is told the barracks are worth a call as a 'relic of Imperial rule' from which an 'extensive prospect may be had'. The other place worthy of notice is the 'experimental school at Pakowhai', the 'first school in New Zealand, started by a native chief to teach native children in the English language'. Chapman is unequivocally approving:

> What a lesson is this to us, that we should have been trying in vain for 58 years (over half a century) to teach the Maori the Christian religion in their native tongue; – actually inventing a language and literature to keep them in barbarism.[15]

The impression of a land of peaceful developing communities and potential prosperity is implicitly aimed at immigrants. Warlike attributes of the Maori are relegated to a heroic past which has been overtaken by a bucolic present. Maori living in Hawke's Bay are said to be 'in easy circumstances' with 'rentals [that] amount to about £30,000 a year'. When he describes visiting the school and settlement at Pakowhai, Chapman gives the impression that Maori culture has been forgotten and is an object of ethnographic interest even to Maori:

> the ridge pole and side posts [of their 'place of worship'] are elaborately carved, and on the top, in front, a representation of some unknown creeping animal (quite different from the Taniwha) about four feet long and eighteen inches broad. We asked a native the name of the monster, but he only shook his head. Its name and nature were alike unknown to him.[16]

The conflict over land which resulted in the New Zealand Wars appears in Chapman's version to have been settled at Napier in favour of Maori, who are said to have 'reserved some fine land on the Plain for themselves, on which they live very comfortably'.[17] The next generation are being transformed into English speakers at the initiative of their own chiefs.

Chapman's advice to travellers is generated both from other textual sources – he cites a number of well-known books on New Zealand, including Charles Dilke's *Greater Britain* and Edward Jerningham Wakefield's *Adventure in New Zealand* – and from personal travel experience. The reader/tourist accompanies him on a comfortably informed and familiar journey through both islands, pausing to look at delightful panoramas, consider the facilities available in each settlement and listen to tales of early life. Population figures, export revenues, the status and availability of land and the number and tonnage of steamers are reinforced by a convivial and collegial tone, anticipating and stimulating the tourist's journey as being made with and among friends, and presenting New Zealand as an extension of networks and opportunities available to 'moneyed men'.

Guides to 'Boiling Water Land'

Other early guidebooks to New Zealand specialised in promoting the primary, already established tourist attraction of the thermal region of the North Island, the 'hot lakes' around Rotorua. Charles Morton Ollivier's account of a trip there, published as a slim 38-page paper-covered booklet in 1871,[18] led the way for a flurry of similar guidebooks about 'Boiling Water Land' (in George Sala's phrase) in the later 1870s and 1880s, described in the next chapter. For Ollivier, Tauranga was the starting-point for the lakes, and Gate Pa, where 'the natives made their most determined, plucky and well-fought stand',[19] is an historic site. Most travel texts follow this route and repeat many of Ollivier's observations. Through lapidary accumulation Gate Pa, constructed as the site of heroic but defunct Maori, functions as a preliminary after which the actual encounter with Maori at Rotomahana becomes anti-heroic and disappointing, demonstrating what John Frow has called the 'vanishing horizon of authenticity'.[20]

Ollivier's brief account of his journey was quickly followed by a more structured and informative guide produced by the enterprising publishers of the *Bay of Plenty Times* and intended to capitalise on the growing tourist market arriving in Tauranga.[21] Widening their target readership, Langbridge and Edgecumbe declare their handbook is designed to meet a 'want felt by the inhabitants of both islands, by the tourist and invalid from Australia and Europe and . . . even the residents in the Bay of Plenty'.[22] The handbook aims to 'assist the tourist' in the exploration of the lake country and to promote knowledge of the 'resources and advantages' of the Bay of Plenty for settlers. It conducts its reader on a carefully mapped and scripted journey, noting the distances between stopping points, varying its typefaces for emphasis, and employing descriptions of the Pink and White Terraces from other travellers and writers, including Ollivier and Robert Browning's friend Alfred Domett, whose romantic epic *Ranolf and Amohia* supplies the descriptive force lacking in Ollivier's text.[23] As a further, and metropolitan, validation of Rotorua's claims as a tourist destination, they reprint an article from the *Illustrated London News* on 'the Tauranga and Hot Springs District', highlighting in italics the article's references to the success of the thermal waters in curing rheumatism and skin disease, the accessibility of the lakes and regularity of the coach service.

In 1882 Thorpe Talbot, author of three novels, produced *The New Guide to the Lakes and Hot Springs*. Published by an Auckland printing firm, Wilson and Horton, it was aimed at what is now known as the 'freedom' traveller, rather than what Talbot called 'general globe-trotting humanity'. The lucrative travel market brought 'keen' competition among coaching services and hotels, and *The New Guide*'s discussion of estimated costs for a four-day excursion from Auckland to Rotomahana develops a well-established, class-based distinction between the resourceful and independent hero/traveller and the infantilised, undiscriminating organised tourist, always represented as a faceless crowd:

> There is a system of travelling with 'through tickets' at present very popular; but I would not recommend it. It is much better to make the tour independently – without being hurried through on a routine plan and compelled by agents to press on regardless of weather and one's own health and inclinations. Moreover it is quite easy to make the trip at as low rates as those incurred by the 'through ticket'. And to show how this may be satisfactorily done is the present and pleasant duty of this little Guide.[24]

The reader of *The New Guide* is presented with an alternative model of travel to the group tour. Taking her time, Talbot sprinkles her narrative with accounts of amusing or colourful incidents, names and characterises the Maori and Europeans she meets, describes Maori society and culture, and intersperses her account of the wonders with anecdotes, poetry and legends. Her journey describes both the geophysical and cultural authenticities of the landscape and the distinctive experience of the individual traveller, which adds meaning and interest. What Judith Adler has called the 'problem of attaining and authoritatively representing knowledge' Talbot resolves by layering different kinds of texts – newspaper articles, poems, analysis of the mineral waters, reported speech from named speakers – in a narrative expressing a 'subjectivity anchored in wilfully independent vision'.[25] *The New Guide* makes no attempt at objectivity. The information it delivers is personal and idiosyncratic, the experience of a traveller who chooses 'independent vision' over mass tourism. In this mode the traveller's perception of the sights remains within established aesthetic codes, but the procedures of travel are accidental and individual.

Three years later, *The Newest Guide to the Hot Lakes by a Man Constantly in Hot Water*, a 'little handbook' by 'T.T.H.', offers 'a digest of the many handbooks that have gone before, giving facts and figures, the different routes, distances, cost etc'.[26] Eighteen pages long, *The Newest Guide* addresses itself to every choice a traveller may have to make on the way to Rotomahana – 'Which route shall I take? Where shall I put up?' – and delivers a verdict. Unlike Talbot, T.T.H. recommends the 'through ticket system', which relieves the tourist of all trouble, and does not attempt to describe

> any of the objects of interest in this 'Wonderland'; I have simply tried in an unpretentious way to furnish a vague idea of the different places and things that *ought* to be seen, the distances, and what is of great importance to many, the cost.[27]

The Newest Guide is aimed at tourists with limited time and means, who want to register the sights in three days of travel. The natural wonders at the centre of the journey are treated as already known: the tourist will 'believe all that he has read in the "Arabian Nights" Entertainment', but description of the actual sites is withheld and their beauties remain as the implied substance of the guide's promotion. Although it claims to be a digest, the names of Kelly's Coaches and the Palace Hotel, owned by Mr Kelly, appear in uppercase in the text, and the Palace Hotel in an illustrated advertisement on the back cover. T.T.H., evidently a local man, is 'unhesitating' in his recommendations of the hotel, the coaching services and Kelly's driver. He knows about local land history, is critical of the government's failures to keep promises to Maori, and recounts the story of Gate Pa as an example of outstanding chivalry, but mixes in derogatory attitudes towards Maori as a commonplace tourist response.

> I never saw a Maori yet, who would not spin you any amount of 'cuffers' for a glass of grog and some tobacco, and then putting their tongue in their cheek, do, as Mark Twain said of the Red Indian, 'Retire into the primeval forest to conceal their emotion'.[28]

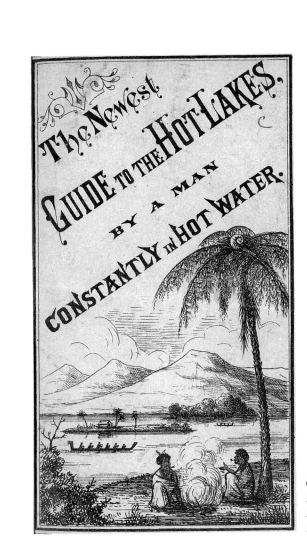

Cover of *The Newest Guide to the
Hot Lakes by a Man Constantly in
Hot Water*, circa 1885.
ATL B-K-511-COVER

Stupendous grandeur and rubbishy books

The shift of focus from independent travellers to bulk tourists, generated and
facilitated by the development of mass travel systems and infrastructures, is
reflected in the production and marketing of guidebooks generally. The Union
Steam Ship Company published two guidebooks at the end of the 1870s:
J. Chantrey Harris's *The Southern Guide to the Hot Lake District of the North
Island of New Zealand* (1878) and Thomas Bracken's *The New Zealand Tourist*
(1879) 'circulated at Sydney within a month of the opening of the Exhibition'.
The Southern Guide declared that its purpose was to 'smooth the way for
tourists' by providing advice based on the 'personal experience and observation'
of a special commissioner sent to the lake district to 'compile a concise work on
the route'.[29] It must have been a successful publication for the Union Steam Ship

Company, as it was followed by Bracken's *The New Zealand Tourist* the next year. It is an indication of the company's perception of the market that they began with a guide specifically about the thermal region and followed it with one aiming to convey to the reader a 'general idea of the whole country'. Bracken's preface, weighed down with adjectives ('peerless land', 'marvellous magnificence'), apologises to his reader/tourist for the absence of gilded domes and marble palaces, and figures the traveller as coming from a Grand Tour, familiar with European cultural monuments like the 'white palaces of Genoa'. He offers them a land 'fresh from the hand of its Maker': a 'land of stupendous mountains, roaring cataracts, silvery cascades, fantastic volcanic formations, magnificent landscapes, noble forests, and picturesque lakes . . .'.[30]

Bracken's fervid representation of New Zealand as a country of unsurpassingly romantic scenery and aesthetic satisfactions established a mode that has never gone out of fashion in promotional literature. It became a commonplace of guidebooks and promotional texts to compensate for New Zealand's 'youth in Art', or what the authors of *Maoriland* (see opposite) described as the lack of a 'human historic element', by extensive praise and description of 'the surpassing grandeur of her scenery'.[31] Bracken gears *The New Zealand Tourist* to a reader of 'refined mind, and of an elevated taste' whose desire is for 'rich fields for aesthetic realisation'.[32] He scatters the text with lumps of quotation, ranging from recycled chunks of *The Southern Guide* to lengthy passages from Wordsworth and Longfellow, and concentrates on scenic stops, panoramas and 'picturesque portions' of New Zealand. Practical advice about routes and transport gives way to descriptions of what is available for the 'naturalist' or the 'sketcher', and the tourist's objective is always seen as aesthetic and sentimental. New Zealand is the case study for sensibility.

Bracken is aware that his descriptive powers, if allowed 'full swing . . . might be taken by sceptical readers as a mere florid flight of fancy',[33] and there is some evidence that his readers did react unfavourably to his verbose, prescriptive and unpractical style. James Edge Partington, travelling in New Zealand in 1881, refers to *The New Zealand Tourist* as 'that most rubbishy of books':

> It seems strange that in a country so thoroughly adapted as it were for tourists, that there should be no decent guide-book. The one part mentioned is full of the most absurdly flowery descriptions of places, which don't assist you much . . .[34]

In one respect, though, *The New Zealand Tourist* indicated a travel market which was to become a major element of guidebooks and promotional literature generally by the turn of the century. At the end of Bracken's preface is half a page addressed 'To Anglers', which claims that New Zealand is 'beyond doubt the finest angling country in the Southern Hemisphere'. Field sportsmen will also find 'very extended scope' for their pastime, but, in a comparison which becomes standard in the writing of angler/tourists, 'trout and salmon are more prolific here than they are in Scotland, that country so famed for its fishing grounds'.

Maoriland

Five years later, in 1884, the Union Steam Ship Company lifted its sights again and produced *Maoriland*, an illustrated 'Handbook to New Zealand' by three men, Alexander Wilson, Rutherford Waddell and T. W. Whitson. Although twice the size and at 2s 6d more than twice the price of the two earlier guidebooks, *Maoriland* was still intended to be portable, with soft covers and octavo format, and affordable. It carried a significant increase in investment. Whereas *The Southern Tourist* concluded with sixteen pages of advertisements, mostly for hotels and local companies, and *The New Zealand Tourist* had none, *Maoriland* began and ended with substantial advertising sections, more than fifty-six pages in total, and supplied an index to advertisers under the headings Banks, Insurance Companies, Land and Finance Companies, Hotels and Miscellaneous. The impression of a society with a solidly established infrastructure and doing its best to replicate the security of the world from which the tourist has come is reinforced by the preface, which opens by alluding to the 'comforts, luxuries . . . and rapidity' of once-dreaded journeys. It then implicitly counteracts some of the features of *The New Zealand Tourist*. Explaining that the writers have concentrated on the noteworthy sights of the colony with descriptions 'faithful enough' to enable the tourist to recall them to mind and revive his impressions – a view of the guidebook as remembrancer – they go on to acknowledge the problem of textual representation and what Meaghan Morris has called the 'morbidity of description':[35]

> In reading a description of any scene as a preparation for seeing it, the danger lies in over-colouring. To the accusation of over-colouring most descriptions are more or less liable, according to the angle at which the various readers see the thing described. The writers of this work hope they may be accused rather of subduing than of heightening colour.[36]

Nevertheless, Rutherford Waddell uses literary and visual aesthetics to promote the South Island as a tourist destination. Gazing at a landscape 'almost entirely destitute of any human history', he supplies the referential tools with which to construct the landscape's 'emptiness' as inversely meaningful, viewing it through the tourist's well-stocked library:

> Wakatipu and Wanaka have no Lady of the Lake, no story of beauty and anguish walking hand in hand to death. Manapouri or Te Anau has no Lausanne or Ferney – no Rydal

Mount or Rotha Stream . . . The mountains and valleys are vacant, all, of those heroic records that weave their deathless memories around the Highlands of Scotland or the Alpine passes of Switzerland.[37]

Their motto is 'Excelsior'

In 1893 John Murray, pre-eminent publisher of travel and guidebooks, whose 'Murray's Handbook' series covered all the English counties, Scotland, Ireland and the countries of Western Europe as well as India, Egypt, Constantinople and the Holy Land, brought out *A Handbook to New Zealand* by F. W. Pennefather. Written mainly for people leaving from England and in response to a 'steady increase' in tourist numbers, Murray's *Handbook* has a standard format, with fold-out maps, bibliographies, classes of information (hotels, churches, clubs, population and conveyances) and suggested routes and excursions. Based principally on itineraries of scenery and what Frow has called 'an economy of looking',[38] this indicates what the reader's motivations and objectives in travelling might be, but it also presents New Zealand as a familiar product in a global tourist network. The handbook promises culturally specific pleasures achieved by means of the advice, plans and information it supplies.

In contrast, the *New Zealand Shipping Company's Pocket-Book*, supplied to passengers as a souvenir 'of a pleasant voyage' from 1908, is designed for a personalised traveller with a pocket full of cultural and economic wealth who wants to preserve memory and experience in a tasteful form. With a preface written by William Pember Reeves,[39] the pocket-book projects the travel space of the voyage as an intimate community, well schooled in aesthetics – there are colour prints of watercolours (by W. and F. Wright) of famous New Zealand scenes, including portraits of picturesque Maori engaged in pastoral tasks. It is a tool, as Susan Stewart has observed in relation to the postcard, for converting a 'public' event into a 'private' tourist object.[40] Autographed portraits of the captains are succeeded by blank pages for collecting autographs, daily distance tables, cash memoranda and notes.

In one respect the *Pocket-Book* takes the conventional idea of New Zealand as the Britain of the South to new lengths. In an extended comparison, the colony is seen as a brighter Britain, where there is 'no multitude of hungry and hard-driven poor for the rich to shrink from or regard as dangerous. . . . except for the comparative absence of frock-coats and tall silk hats . . . the middle class remain as a British middle class still'.[41] The *Pocket-Book* reimagines England as New Zealand to reinforce the constant claim of their interchangeability. If a New Zealand landscape and population were projected on to Britain, in a reverse mirroring of Wakefield's project, there would be about a million souls, of whom fifty thousand were brown and the rest white. The brown would be English-speaking and half-civilized and the whites just workaday Britons of the middle and labouring classes, a little taller and rather more tanned.[42]

With the population shrunk to a few people living around 'single piers in sheltered inlets like Falmouth', the traveller would note a 'comfortable race of small farmers established in the valley of the Thames but he would be struck by the almost empty look of the wide pastoral stretches in Berkshire and Oxford-shire'.[43]

In guidebooks generally, powerful connections are made between Britain and New Zealand as interchangeable geographies and cultures. The New Zealand Shipping Company's effort in the souvenir pocket-book to superimpose one geography on the other in an extended utopian fantasy says as much, perhaps, about the emotional and psychological baggage of an industrialised society as about the promotional effort to entice tourists to New Zealand. The *Pocket-Book*'s strategy is to induce travellers to complete what John Urry has called a 'kind of hermeneutic circle': to move from the descriptions of the guidebook to the 'experiential capture' of the tourist location by their own photography or writing, thus producing a kind of travel book with a commercially personalised format thoughtfully provided by the shipping company.[44]

A pocket-book has a special resonance as a souvenir. The small and intimate format, shaped for tucking away in the tourist's clothing, speaks of the relationship between reader and book – a relationship of high short-term use and particular experience. The pocket-book, warmed by its proximity to the body, is literally shaped by the tourist's activities, and records between its covers and in the marks of use they carry the object of memory, the tourist's visit to New Zealand.

The relationship between guidebooks and what tourists actually do is suggestively described by Lieutenant-Colonel Montagu Cradock, whose book about visiting New Zealand to go deerstalking was published in 1904:

the majority of [tourists] form a peculiar class of their own, whose one object in life is to see as much as they can possibly cram into the time they have set apart for their trip . . . they travel about loaded up with sheaves of tickets and volumes of guidebooks, and they know to a nicety what they have to do every day . . . Their motto truly is 'Excelsior', and a proud man is he who, stepping on board his ship for the return voyage home, can slap his chest and say he not only has seen all that any of his fellow-passengers have seen, but also can 'go one better' and enlarge on some unique spot he alone has visited! The Sounds and Mount Cook, Hot Lakes and Cold Lakes, all must have their turn, though the most transitory glimpse of each is sufficient so long as the itinerant 'tow row' can say *he has been there.*[45]

The 'souvenir' model of guidebook supplies for the 'itinerant "tow row"' a systematised tour conveniently amalgamated with the evidential record, full of photographic prompts and exhaustive description in case you forgot the sights you had seen.

The popular market for souvenir guides is suggested by C. N. Baeyertz's semi-official *Guide to New Zealand* ('authorised by the New Zealand Government'), which went through almost yearly editions between 1902 and 1912. Baeyertz was founder of the literary magazine *Triad* and music critic for the *Otago Daily Times*, and his guidebook is notable for its excessive claims to specular and spectacular aesthetics in a market already overflowing with eulogies to scenery. The title page of *Guide to New Zealand* extols 'the most wonderful Scenic Paradise in the World – Unequalled Fjords, Awe-Inspiring Geysers' and notes that the 'impotence of mere words' has been supplemented with 'copious' illustrations 'which will speak much more eloquently to the reader'. All the illustrations are photographs, mostly 'scenic' views of waterfalls, rivers and landscapes, with some picturesque portraits of Maori in native dress generically identified as 'A Maori Belle' or 'Maori Chief'. Such portraits illustrate Frow's comment on the photograph's ability to 'make readily available those aesthetic and observational competencies which had previously been the preserve of a cultural elite'.[46] The 'eloquence' of the photographic discourse of *Guide to New Zealand*, based on commodified aesthetic norms – all the photographs are commercially produced and composed as 'views' – is mirrored in Baeyertz's mechanistic application of adjectival phrases to every scenic feature: the text saturates the reader in exhausted vocabularies of sensibility.

Both the photographs and the text work to fix an aesthetic confirming the categories announced on the *Guide*'s title page: scenic paradise of the world and 'home of the Maori'. No Maori are shown actually at home. Most of the photographs display Maori in pre-European costume, posed and frozen in a romanticised ethnographic otherness – pensive, gazing out of the frame – associated with a natural landscape and an historical past distanced from the evidence of material and urban progress seen in photographs of colonial city streets and public buildings. A couple of casual shots of Maori in European clothes have them leaning on ponga fences or standing at the edge of a hot pool in landscapes presented as 'native'. Europeans, by contrast, are represented principally by their activities – rowing, fishing, driving coaches, hunting – and their works – ports, buildings, streetscapes, agriculture. Sections of print are broken into by images, reinforcing the ascendancy of the photographs: the guide offers 'an economy of looking' which suggests the aesthetic preconceptions, cultural authority and material possessions of the European reader/tourist. And in this scenic landscape of colonial activity and indigenous immobility, the presence of the tourist is suggested in the presentation of the book itself, with

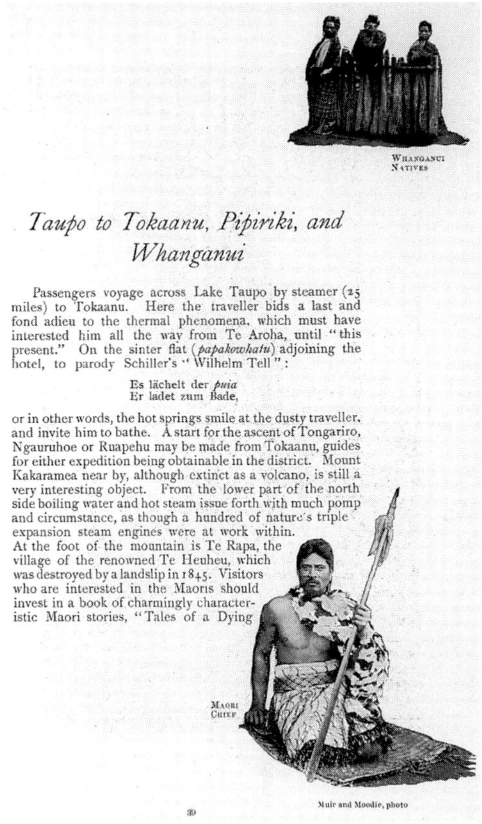

WHANGANUI NATIVES

Taupo to Tokaanu, Pipiriki, and Whanganui

Passengers voyage across Lake Taupo by steamer (25 miles) to Tokaanu. Here the traveller bids a last and fond adieu to the thermal phenomena, which must have interested him all the way from Te Aroha, until "this present." On the sinter flat (*papakowhatu*) adjoining the hotel, to parody Schiller's "Wilhelm Tell":

Es lächelt der *puia*
Er ladet zum Bade,

or in other words, the hot springs smile at the dusty traveller, and invite him to bathe. A start for the ascent of Tongariro, Ngauruhoe or Ruapehu may be made from Tokaanu, guides for either expedition being obtainable in the district. Mount Kakaramea near by, although extinct as a volcano, is still a very interesting object. From the lower part of the north side boiling water and hot steam issue forth with much pomp and circumstance, as though a hundred of nature's triple expansion steam engines were at work within. At the foot of the mountain is Te Rapa, the village of the renowned Te Heuheu, which was destroyed by a landslip in 1845. Visitors who are interested in the Maoris should invest in a book of charmingly characteristic Maori stories, "Tales of a Dying

MAORI CHIEF

Muir and Moodie, photo

39

'Taupo to Tokaanu, Pipiriki and Whanganui.' Page 39 from *Guide to New Zealand, the most wonderful scenic paradise in the world.* C. N. Baeyertz, 1902. ATL-B-K-173-39

its notes of appreciation, souvenired images, cut-outs and silhouettes, implying a personal record of tourist responses. A number of photographs in the *Guide to New Zealand* are cropped to outlines of people or significant landscape features; most are framed in a box. A broad view of Mitre Peak, Milford shows the top of the peak breaking through the box rule; other views of lakes or rivers or trees are clearcut, as if someone has used scissors and pasted a favourite snapshot decoratively on the page.

Photographing right and left

The perception of New Zealand as a country conveniently packaged for maximising tourism is revealing. Judith Adler has commented that by the nineteenth century the information-gathering focus of eighteenth-century travel had been replaced by a 'new discipline of connoisseurship for the eye, centring on the cultivation and display of "taste"'.[47] As John Frow has noted, it is this belief in aesthetic sightseeing that forms the basis of modern tourism and is xi.

THE CAMERA

IN THE

CORAL ISLANDS

⊶⊷⋙⊷⋙⊷⊶

A Series of Photographs illustrating the Scenery and the
Mode of Life in

THE FIJIS,
THE NAVIGATOR ISLANDS (Samoa),

AND

THE FRIENDLY ISLANDS (Tonga).

Taken during the two trips of the Union S.S. Co.'s "Wairarapa"
to the South Seas in June and July, 1884.

NEW ZEALAND

THROUGH

THE CAMERA.

⊶⊷⋙⊷⋙⊷⊶

Nearly Two Thousand Photographs of New Zealand Scenery

Thoroughly illustrating the natural beauties and wonders as well as
the material progress of the Colony.

☞ Catalogues of both Series sent post free to any address.

BURTON BROTHERS,
PORTRAIT, LANDSCAPE, & COMMERCIAL PHOTOGRAPHERS
DUNEDIN, N.Z.

'New Zealand through the camera.'
An advertisement published in
Maoriland; an illustrated handbook to New
Zealand, 1884, p.xi. ATL B-K-510-11

enabled and displayed by the development of photography.[48] The photograph,
like the printed book, was a primary tool of imperialism, bringing the world's
sights and peoples to the metropolitan audience and fixing them in a moment
and a mode of representation as 'ethnic' and 'exotic'. The development of photography occurred more or less contemporaneously with the heyday of European
imperialism and the colonisation of New Zealand, and the connections between
imperialism, travel and photography have been frequently discussed.[49] When
the tourist boom to New Zealand took place in the 1870s and 1880s, graphically
illustrated in the travel archive by a surge in the number of privately printed
travel books, there was a corresponding increase in the use of photography, both
as a tool for recording the experience of individual travellers (uniting, as Frow
notes, 'detached witnessing and aesthetic appreciation'),[50] and as the medium
for a new commodity market. Many travellers comment on photography and
photographers and use photographic images in their texts. Bertram Barton
noted in his letters to his family in 1884 that 'a photographer by the name of
Burton' was 'taking views of the country' near Bealey.[51] In Auckland, Froude

commented that photography was 'in fashion' and the shops full of 'landscapes, lakes, mountains, waterfalls . . . Maori chiefs and Maori villages'.[52]

When the Victorian journalist George Augustus Sala and his party arrived at the White Terrace in October 1885, they found a 'well-known photographer of Auckland, Mr Josiah Martin' camping out on the shores of Rotomahana. He had 'just concluded an exhaustive series of measurements of the dimensions of the Terrace and was now busy with his camera and dry plates, photographing right and left'.[53] Sala noted that Martin had paid the local Maori £5 'without murmuring for an artistic monopoly of Rotomahana':

> Just fancy the manner in which Americans or in which Frenchmen would act if the Indians in a Western 'Reserve' or the Arabs in Algeria insisted on the payment of so many dollars or so many francs before a photographer could be suffered to do his spiriting.[54]

Josiah Martin's willingness to pay for a 'monopoly' demonstrates the size of the market for photographs, which were widely reproduced in books and in the press as well as sold as art objects. Sala's reference to 'spiriting' shows he was aware of the widespread belief among indigenous peoples that a photographic image depleted their essence. It is not clear whether the insistence of the local tribe, the Tuhourangi, on the payment of fees at Rotomahana and Tarawera had anything to do with such beliefs, and the terms of their discussion with Constance Gordon Cumming – they wanted her to pay more for watercolour sketches as these were considered more true to life and therefore worth more[55] – suggests that hard-nosed business considerations were to the fore. Because of the volume of tourists visiting the Pink and White Terraces who objected to paying for the right to photograph or paint, there are many accounts of having to do so. Emile Wenz, a French tourist from Rheims, pointed out indignantly in his book *Mon Journal* (1886) that in other countries photographers were paid.

Broad and complex areas of cultural difference are revealed by the long-running dispute over reproducing the wonders of Rotomahana. The tendency of Europeans to universalise 'natural wonders' as the gift of God and available for everyone is disingenuous about who actually possesses the land they are found on, and about the mass-market potential of exotic images, quickly evident in the wide circulation of sketches, engravings, watercolours and photographs of Rotomahana and the Pink and White Terraces. The effects and expectations of increased tourist traffic produce a conflict between what travellers regard as an entitlement and the Maori perceive as a form of intellectual property right, and it is not the owner of the terrain who stands to gain from it. The large photographic archive of the terraces, Rotorua, Rotomahana and their indigenous inhabitants demonstrates the importance of the camera as an adjunct of the European presence. The accuracy of the Maori perception of photography's commercial potential is amply illustrated by the flood of images of the terraces reproduced in London papers both before and after the eruption of Mt Tarawera in June 1886.

The guidebook *Maoriland* is based on a set of defining assumptions about who is travelling, assumptions that are confirmed by the self-identification made by many travellers, or implied in the various ways in which travellers claim to be participants in culture – either through their own range of reference or their attention to aesthetics. James Clifford's association of travel with literariness and class is both self-evident and seminal. If, as Brian Musgrove argues, the art of travel is underscored by an anxious sense that to travel is to be 'nowhere',[56] the more the empty space into which the traveller is moving – the space 'destitute of human history' – has to be filled with cultural meaning and connections back to 'somewhere'. Photography is the tool which complements the traveller's assertion of cultural selfhood: not only can he or she bring to the new environment a head full of connecting comparisons, but also images of natural wonders can be carried home as a testimony to taste and beauty. You don't have to be able to sketch, or take your cumbersome painting equipment, to show the world at home what you have seen.

If travel books and photographs display the protocols and conventions which form travellers' experience of the world and allow the traveller to capture experience and dream of possession, they also suggest the difficulty of a personal response to scenery. It may be impossible to 'see' anywhere against the cultural grain, but the camera, as much as the guidebook, assists in standardising the 'views', 'prospects' and 'scenes' which adorn travel texts and travellers' experiences. Travel writing makes it very clear how few people – Thorpe Talbot is one – resist or vary their prepared role as a traveller seeing the sights in a foreign land.

CHAPTER 8

Exhausting the wonders

The heart of Wonderland

As the tourist traffic to New Zealand boomed in the 1870s, the accompanying publication of more and more books about where to go and what to see established an iconic cartography. As we have seen, most of the travel writing about New Zealand from the late 1870s was already overdetermined by the reiteration of travel routes, genre conventions and the expectations of a metropolitan reading public about what there is to see in the world and what to think about it. New Zealand and its indigenous people were compared with the already known world. The Wonderland of the Antipodes was compared with Yellowstone, the Southern Alps with Switzerland, the Canterbury plains with Kent, to form what Mary Louise Pratt has called the 'standard metonymic representation' of iconic images of nature:[1] a textual culture composed of layers of recorded journeys from which the topography and equivalence of New Zealand could emerge – revealed, recognised, mapped and brought home.

Most tourists arrived in New Zealand with a preconceived idea of what to see, primarily the 'hot water wonders' (in John Lawrence Lambe's phrase), and many did not travel further south than Rotorua. William Senior, an Englishman living in Queensland who was well known as an angler and fishing writer under the pseudonym 'Red Spinner', came to New Zealand in 1880 primarily to fish, but made the usual pilgrimage to 'Wonderland' or Rotomahana, the 'land of mystery'. Senior's metaphorical language, drawn from the vocabulary employed by all tourists, suggests that for most it was the exotic destination which produced the meaning of their journey:

> But it must be understood that Ohinemutu is, after all, but the means to an end. Rotorua is a fine lake, and the district, as we have seen, has its curiosities; but the Mecca of the pilgrim is Rotomahana and its terraces. It is there he will be in the heart of Wonderland.[2]

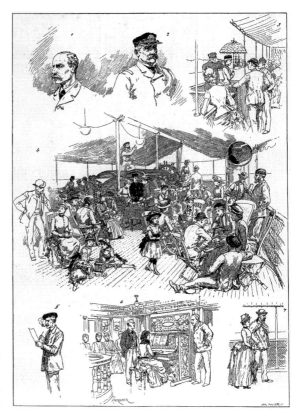

'The world of travellers', by 'our
special artist en route to Burmah',
Illustrated London News,
2 January 1886, p.4. ATL N-P-546-4

The heart of Wonderland, before 1886, was the Pink and White Terraces. The
gentleman explorer James Kerry-Nicholls may have an unusually broad range
of reference, but his comparative rhetoric and his judgement on the White
Terrace (Te Tarata) is typical of the traveller's reaction when he declares:

> I had seen the Himalayas and the Alps, the Blue Mountains of Tartary, the Rocky
> Mountains and the Sierra Nevadas. I had sailed over the principal lakes of Europe and
> America, floated down the Nile, the Ganges, the Yangtze Kiang, the Missouri and the
> Mississippi, through the thousand islands of the St Lawrence. I had beheld the giant
> marvels of Yosemite and stood by the thrilling waters of Niagara, but for delicate unique
> beauty, for chaste design and sublime detail of construction never had I gazed upon so
> wonderful a sight as Te Tarata.[3]

Despite universal agreement that Rotomahana and the terraces lived up to the
many descriptions of them circulating in travel books, guidebooks and London
illustrated papers by 1880, many writers perceived their skills as inadequate to
the task. James Hingston, author of *The Australian Abroad* (1879), represents a
common cluster of responses on arriving at Te Tarata:

We bid adieu altogether to the common sort of world we have known so many years, and enter upon that which, from our childhood, we had known only from the transformation scenes in pantomimes and the landscapes in fairy burlesques and extravaganzas. Before us now rises Te Tarata, and we think that, having written that much, we had better stop until we get the shade of J.W.M. Turner, that great painter of the mystic, to assist us. Our writing will be memoranda for our own reference merely – to be referred to hereafter as evidence of how barren our brains were in descriptive power in the year seventy-one.[4]

Like many travel writers who apostrophise the indescribability of the terraces, Hingston proceeds to describe them for several paragraphs. The Hon. James Inglis, who wrote under the pseudonym 'Maori' on the strength of having travelled through New Zealand in the 1860s, is typical when he remarks that 'words are all too feeble to give a just estimate of their many-sided wondrous beauty'.[5] Inglis also demonstrates the inability of most travellers who are not writers to produce descriptive language that is not already exhausted by overuse. C. E. R. Schwartze, one who identified himself as a recent Oxford BA, can only declare the White Terrace to be 'one of the most marvellous sights in the world' and the hot lakes district 'the wonderland of New Zealand and perhaps of the whole world'.[6] Charles Morton Ollivier resorts to apostrophising his reading culture:

To write an accurate account of these wonderful springs, and one that would convey such an impression as would enable the reader to picture these places in his mind, would be

'Pink Terraces, Roto Mahana', by John Philemon Backhouse, 1886. ATL G-452-3-2

impossible. Even a Walter Scott, or a Bulwer Lytton would fail in the task. That prince of romancers, Dumas, would not be equal to the occasion. Even he would have to admit that 'truth is stranger than fiction'.[7]

These natural wonders, an obligatory part of any travel narrative, developed standard descriptive modes through constant reiteration and aestheticisation, lodging in most travellers' texts as iconic representations of New Zealand. They sometimes quite literally mark the traveller's failure to negotiate them personally or textually. J. D.'s booklet *Ninety Days' Privilege Leave* (1886) explains that, owing to timetabling problems, he did not manage to go to Rotorua, so he inserts sixty pages from G. A. Sala's newspaper articles about the hot lakes as if they were part of his own experience.[8] Russell Colman's diary letters to his mother describe in detail crossing Lake Rotomahana in a boat with 'our four selves and three other tourists, six Maori rowers and a Maori guide', but when he arrives at the terraces, 'Here I must begin to take in outside help, my descriptive powers are not powerful enough . . .'.[9] Colman's 'outside help' was that extremely popular guidebook of the 1880s, *Maoriland*, co-written anonymously by Alexander Wilson. Wilson's account of the terraces brings orientalism into play, introducing the non-Western exotic into an already familiar and highly literary descriptive field with his reference to an 'Eastern fabulist':

> Could Eastern fabulist in his wildest flights imagine any work of the Genii to equal the exquisite workmanship of this range of sculptured fountains? One might talk of snow wreaths, of alabaster, of Parian marble, of any substance pure and rare, but all such comparisons would but mislead.[10]

O. W. Wight, an American whose *People and Countries visited in a winding journey around the world* (1888) sets out to 'draw faithful portraits of the leading civilized nations of the world as they exist today',[11] uses the same description. The frequent recycling of Wilson's description in the letter – and journal-based travel texts of tourists suggests a high level of agreement about what constitutes the exotic, including a convention of rhetorical practices. The overuse of this kind of descriptive language also leaves unpractised writers at a loss to express themselves.

An artist at the Hot Lakes

The well-known Victorian lady traveller Constance Gordon Cumming wrote professionally, selling articles to *Scribners*, the *Leisure Hour* and other English papers, and producing books (and paintings) that sold to large readerships. Her second book, *At Home in Fiji* (1881), described her visit to New Zealand as part of the entourage of Sir Arthur Hamilton Gordon, Governor of Fiji, and is based on

'The Kawau looking towards Auckland.' Watercolour by Constance Gordon Cumming, 9 January 1877. ATL D-022-010

her letters.[12] She published three books about her experiences in the Pacific within three years, exhibited numerous watercolours and sketches at the Colonial and Indian Exhibition in London in 1886, and published a stream of articles. In Dorothy Middleton's opinion, Gordon Cumming's books are 'almost unreadable, so informative are they', produced by someone who 'painted, observed, botanised, missionised and, above all, collected information as a duty'.[13] Despite their large readership, her books are represented as the product of a lady's leisure by preserving the form of letters to her sister, which throws a veneer of implied intimacy and domesticity over her professionalism and the idea of travel as a private activity.

Constance Gordon Cumming began her visit to New Zealand by staying with Sir George Grey on Kawau, where she enjoyed his 'cosy old English home' and 'beautified' island. She found 'the state of things existing in this country most extraordinary':

> Imagine that, within twenty miles of Auckland, there is a vast tract of land on which no white man dare set foot. Only outlaws, murderers and suchlike, are there allowed to take refuge, and justice cannot touch them.[14]

As a preamble to her trip to Rotorua, Gordon Cumming noticed an item in the *Times* which she copied out while revising a letter to her sister. Headed 'An English Lady Murdered in New Zealand', it was the story of the murder of Miss

Mary Dobie at Te Ngamu, in Taranaki, by a Maori man named Tuhi. Gordon Cumming had met Mary Dobie, who, like her, published sketches in the *Graphic*, and who was murdered at a bay where she had gone to sketch, in an uncomfortable reflection of Gordon Cumming's own travel practices. The latter observed:

> During ten years of travel among brown and yellow races of every hue, continually spending long days alone with my paint-box in most wild and remote places, I have always done so fearlessly, being convinced that among these people a white woman leads a charmed life. While revising these pages I have received awful proof to the contrary from the following paragraph in the 'Times'.[15]

Gordon Cumming's visit to the Pink and White Terraces was dominated by a disagreement with Maori about whether or not she should pay for sketching. Having left herself a little short of time to see the 'land of wonders', she tried to squeeze in as much as she could before the Pacific mail-steamer arrived in Auckland – visiting Taupo, Orakei-Korako, Ohinemutu and Rotomahana – 'and much as I had heard of it, the reality far surpasses my expectations'. Her first brush with the sketching problem occurred at Whakarewarewa, where she was fascinated by the cones and geysers and scrambled up a hill 'to sketch the whole group, in spite of the remonstrance of a picturesque Maori, who seemed to have some dim idea that he could exact payment for allowing me this privilege'.[16]

The whole of Gordon Cumming's engagement with volcanic wonders and Maori demonstrates what has been called the 'specularity of imperial ownership'.[17] Leonard Bell has suggested that a 'pictorialisation' of the world, such as Gordon Cumming describes in producing numerous sketches and watercolours, and in her text when comparing silica cones to wedding cakes and the terraces to wondrous marble staircases, produces 'an ordering of the "world" itself as an endless exhibition'.[18] When she writes to her sister about Te Tarata, she begins conventionally by despairing of 'being able, by any words, to give you a description', and refers her sister to the memory of other landscapes: 'perhaps you will best picture it to yourself as a steep hill-side . . . such as we see in mountainous parts of India'.[19] She begins what turns out to be an extended description of the terraces by noticing the depredations of the 'snobs of all nations'[20] who have written their names indelibly on the silica surface, and a printed English notice from the Maori asking visitors not to write on Te Tarata or break pieces off it. While she distinguishes herself from these 'barbarous tourists' and 'curiosity hunters', her relation to Maori is more equivocal. Their 'grave rebuke' to graffitists is one thing; their second printed notice, about the fees due for photography, is another.

Throughout Gordon Cumming's account of the beauty of the terraces, which confirms her aesthetic sensibility as an agency of ownership, Maori are adjuncts to her artistic role. Her tent is pitched by Maori 'lads', 'Old Mary' cooks their food and shows them the sights, 'the Maoris' have collective tastes and preferences. Aside from 'Old Mary' only one Maori is named, and he is first characterised by his relation to Gordon Cumming's work:

> it is no easy matter to hold a large block and work standing, even when a faithful Maori stands by to hold your colour-box. One man, Heme, is very good and helpful, but the others hold rather aloof.[21]

The restriction on photography is attributed to the 'instigation of a white man', which sets up rival alignments between 'faithful' and 'odious' Maori and their European connections. As the dispute continues, however, Maori slide into another register, becoming 'natives' who 'scented a possibility of extortion' from Gordon Cumming's sketch block. The dispute focuses on whether watercolour painting and photography 'are distinct arts', with Maori arguing that watercolours give a 'truer idea of the place and must therefore be more valuable'. Gordon Cumming's counter-argument is conducted in the market terms set by Maori:

> It was quite in vain to suggest that the sight of these pictures would induce fresh visitors to come and spend their much-coveted gold in the district. This only added fresh fuel to the fire. They said it was certain I should make a fortune by showing these pictures in Auckland, perhaps even in Britain, while they, the owners of the place would have no share in the profits.[22]

The Maori grasp of intellectual property and market issues evident in this reported discussion is framed by Gordon Cumming's assumptions about their property rights and her attitudes towards them. She dismisses their position as extortion – 'Of course I was determined not to pay the money . . . from a natural aversion to being done' – and the Maori themselves as 'noisy talkers'. Her eventual departure from Te Wairoa with her sketches hidden in a bundle of plaids and surrounded by a party of 'fourteen whites' is recounted as an increasingly fraught battle story – the 'wild Maori' are the 'foe' from whom Gordon Cumming is 'rescued'.[23] A few days later she leaves New Zealand for Fiji, a place where 'the people love to see themselves on paper, and will sit as still as a rock for hours to be sketched'.[24]

Both Gordon Cumming's travel writing and her *plein air* sketches represent the woman traveller primarily as a visual artist, surveying and reporting on natural wonders and their picturesque inhabitants. Leonard Bell has pointed out that Gordon Cumming's pictures 'imaged the Terraces both in terms of the spectacular and the everyday': the terraces are seen from close up as if 'pushing out into spectator space', with small Maori figures cooking and bathing, and

Portrait of C. F. Gordon
Cumming, published in her
autobiography *Memories*,
Edinburgh & London: William
Blackwood and Sons, 1904, p.196.
ATL B-K-403

small European figures gazing at the sights.[25] Her text replicates these spatial and power relations. Proprietorial bird's-eye descriptions of the terraces predominate over human activity; Maori are dominated by the artist–traveller's physical and aesthetic needs and her assumption of privilege, disturbed though it is by her increasingly aggressive encounters with the local Tuhourangi people. Narrating her dispute with Maori over her watercolours, Gordon Cumming proposes the right of the artist to paint and the traveller to write as inalienable intellectual property rights and the professional duties of a European, even when their subject, as she acknowledges, is a place owned by another people. The confrontational power and race relations which result are represented in her book and sketches as evidence of the lady traveller as artist and hero (a figure for whom poor Mary Dobie provides the other side) and as a story about entitlement. It is as 'natural' for Gordon Cumming to resent extortion as it is for her to regard the hot water wonders as universally owned.

The beau-ideal of a journalist

George Augustus Sala travelled to Australia and New Zealand in 1885 on a lecture tour intended to produce a 'nest egg' for his retirement. He sent home thirty-two articles, published in the *Daily Telegraph* under the general title *The Land of the Golden Fleece*, for which he earned £20 a week, and 'something like' £100 a week when they were syndicated in the Australian and New Zealand papers. The lectures were less of a sure thing. His audiences varied from state to state – he was popular in New South Wales but not in Victoria, though in New Zealand he was a 'bright success' – and some of his audiences rebutted him in the middle of speaking. Judy McKenzie has discussed the conditions under which Sala spoke in Australia, when the 'prevailing jingoistic mood' resulting from the decision of the New South Wales Premier to send an unsolicited contingent to the Sudan raised local imperialist feeling to fever pitch. McKenzie notes that Sala's tour was 'irrevocably shaped' by this crucial time in colonial politics, and concludes that his relative failure to make money on the scale he had hoped for resulted partly, and paradoxically, from his inability to subdue his own liberal sentiments enough to satisfy the imperial loyalties of the 'self-acclaimed classless societies of the antipodes'.[26]

The £100 he was paid to open the Blue Baths in Rotorua helped to defray his expenses, however, and by the time he returned home after the sudden death of his wife in Melbourne, the trip had been a financial success (though not on the scale of the *Daily News* war correspondent Archibald Forbes, whose £12,000 takings on an Australian lecture tour had given Sala the idea to do it himself). In his autobiography Sala described himself as 'a man whose only source of livelihood has been his pen'. From his first article in Charles Dickens's journal *Household Words* in 1851 to his death in 1895 he published forty books, several of them collections of travel articles, and had developed a devoted readership of hundreds of thousands of middle-class Victorians all over the world. In 1882 Charles Pebody, author of *English Journalism, and the Men Who Have Made It*, described his works as a 'library in themselves . . . found upon every bookstall and in every circulating library' and considered his 'sensibility', 'vivid and graphic writing' and 'great powers of expression . . . constitute him the beau-ideal of a journalist'.[27] Robert Dingley, who collected Sala's articles about Australia and New Zealand using his original title, *The Land of the Golden Fleece*, noted that they 'seem often the prose equivalent of flamboyant High Victorian design' and does not believe they can 'stand comparison with the more finished accounts of Trollope or of Froude'.[28] Sala not only was writing for a very different audience, the mass audience of newspaper readers, but saw authorship in a different way. His articles are professional copy priced by length, and their primary goal is to attract and retain the reader's attention no matter what the topic. As Nigel Cross has pointed out, between 1880 and 1895 'the world of publishing and journalism underwent a radical transformation', with the introduction of syndication and the expansion of the popular press being two of its features.[29] Sala was one of the first writers to write exclusively for the press, a deliberate choice he made in the 1850s 'fully cognisant of the fact that I learned my trade as a journalist and I could earn a handsome income by it'.[30] Compared with Froude and Trollope, whose books enunciate authorship as a product of education, cultivated skills, reputation and established readerships, Sala was in an openly competitive, commercial profession. He boasted that he was 'ready to write on anything from the price of beef to a coronation', and few details were too lowly for his attention. Matthew Arnold considered Sala's popularity a sign of the debasement of public taste, though, as Robert Dingley points out, compared with many Victorian travellers' tales, his are 'refreshingly short on political analysis, useful statistics and catalogues of approved "sights"'.[31] Nevertheless, even his most ardent critics agree about the extent of Sala's audience, which, as W. B. Maxwell observed, won him 'renown and praise all over the English-speaking world'.[32] His articles are tailored to this audience and the need to retain them over a meal or a snooze in the study, and his wordy, much – parodied style combines the intimacy of an after-dinner ramble with the rhetorical flourishes and dramatic construction of an experienced performer.

GAS, as he was known to cartoonists, wrote five articles on the 'Wonderland of New Zealand' that were published in the *Daily Telegraph*, then London's best-selling newspaper, from mid-January to the beginning of March 1886, almost ten years after Gordon Cumming's visit and just a few months before the eruption of Mt Tarawera which destroyed the terraces in June. His visit to New Zealand was explicitly professional, and his articles read as the marketing exercises they were. The spread of his attention tells its own story about his judgement of his readers' interest: one article each on Auckland, Wellington and Christchurch; three 'topical' articles (on the Auckland wharves, the Colonial Exhibition in Wellington and the 'Sad Depression' in Christchurch); and five detailed articles on different locations in the volcanic region, the 'Wonderland of New Zealand'. He is writing not for emigrants, and not really for travellers, but primarily for his large audience of faithful readers at home and a smaller, though more critical, colonial readership.

The articles based on Rotorua and its environs engage with famous natural wonders and the local indigenous population. Sala, like all tourists, encountered Maori principally at Rotorua, and he begins with a descriptive article which actually presents very little 'real' information about them. Sala's Maori are characters in the *Daily Telegraph*. From his 'very clean and comfortable' room at the Lake House Hotel he can see Mokoia island and reflect on the Maori legends and tales 'in the midst of a tribe of Maoris consistently loyal and friendly to the British Crown'. In his expansive, digressive, mock-serious and overblown style, Sala opens his tour of the hot lakes district with a portrait of race relations in which he negotiates the unstable territory of race and power, brought into focus, as it was for most Europeans, in the visibly unstable steamy landscape of

"THE NOBLEST ROAM UN OF THEM ALL."

Cartoon of George Augustus
Sala from the *Melbourne
Punch*, 19 March 1885.
STATE LIBRARY OF VICTORIA,
MELBOURNE, AUSTRALIA

Rotorua. Maori (specifically Te Arawa: Sala does not use the name of the iwi
though he is aware that the Maori he is describing are members of a particular
tribe; he quickly lets that distinction drop in favour of an unspecific collective)
are introduced by way of their dogs ('merriest, friendliest . . . grotesquely ugly
bow-wows') and compared serially with 'the Turk', 'the Arab', 'the Red Indian'
and 'a Spanish beggar'. They are represented as acquiescent in the proposition
that 'superiority in the arts of civilisation have made the "Pakeha" or European,
the dominant race, [but] he, the Maori is, as a man, your equal'. Equality is a
variable quantity, however. Maori are 'politically free' and not 'social pariahs' but
'strangest of all to relate, in some cases the Maori is the European's "boss", and
carries on matters not as the European but as he – the Maori – pleases'.[33]

The hierarchy of race which surfaces in Sala's article acts as a precautionary
preamble to the visitor's experience at the hot lakes, where, as Sala repeatedly
observes, the Maori are the territorial 'bosses'. Sala's rhetorical tactics undercut
any appearance – or fear – of Maori ascendancy by representing a reversal in
power relations as a comic mimicry of the norm. Sala notes that, if visitors
deface or damage the volcanic sites,

the stern Whakarewarewa Committee warn the Goths and Vandals from the so-called civilised parts of the world that they will be fined. Verily the noble savage . . . has learned something from his contact with the 'Pakeha'. That laudable solicitude for the safety of the 'incrustations' and the prohibitions against writing on or defacing them almost leads me to fancy that the framers of these rules and regulations must have been perusing the bye-laws of our Metropolitan Board of Works.[34]

Sala's representation of the noble savage as having stepped into a caricature of his role and mimicked the behaviour of a 'Metropolitan Board of Works' depends on a set of socially nuanced distinctions which configure Maori as already failing in their efforts to replicate 'civilisation'. His readers at breakfast in London are provided with a series of familiar and local comparisons which allows them to place Maori, and to replace them as 'lords paramount' with the image of the Metropolitan Board of Works. The substitution renders Maori as unimaginative, prescriptive, lower-middle-class bureaucrats, and reduces and 'naturalises' both them and their exotic landscape.

Sala's account of visiting the terraces covers what has become, by 1885, the usual range of tourist topics: the performance of a haka, meeting the famous guide Sophia ('La Belle Sauvage' he calls her), graffiti by 'brainless cads' and 'wonder at the hand of Nature'. Reflections on the corruption of Maori by tourist and European influences are also standard, usually sparked by the haka, seeing Maori people drinking or signs of wealth. Sala noticed that the 'grinning horrors of Wairoa', the tipuna, had 'eyeballs of shillings, sixpences and threepenny-bits. I was even told that some of these simulated organs of vision were sovereigns and half-sovereigns. To be sure, I noticed a good many empty orbits.'[35] His appreciation of the haka as a 'rhythmical stampede', picturesque and horrible, is interrupted by 'Bathos!' – a 'tall Maori with a short pipe, in his shirt-sleeves and "slop-pants" and a cabbage tree hat on his head, and bearing a zinc slop-pail full of beer'.[36]

Sala's writing persona is the jovial, much-travelled and experienced London club man, veteran of a thousand dinners and smoking parties in which the conversation like the wine flows freely from topic to topic and around the globe, secure in his assumptions and confidently opinionated. Every observation about New Zealand, Maori, the landscape, the climate, the food, the habits of the local population, is embedded in a stream of comparisons, asides and anecdotes; digression is his mode.[37] Sala depicts travel as a global activity centred on London, and his articles are a reflection of the place of New Zealand and its indigenous people in the thinking and reading of Londoners. The knowledge produced about New Zealand is always relational, and often reductively so.

The World – the more you travel, the more you grow convinced of the fact – is not 'such a very big village' after all. There is nothing new under the sun. . . to be sure, I have been told on all sides in New Zealand that the Pink and White Terraces of Rotomahana are undeniably and unchallengeably unique. I hope that such may be the case from the Wonders of the World point of view, but one becomes sceptical from long wanderings and experience of terrestrial matters, and you would not be so very much astonished at last to learn that there was more than one Great Wall of China; that the Colossus of Rhodes had several twin brethren of brass.[38]

Nature and the savage

The conflict noted by Constance Gordon Cumming and George Sala between a universalised claim to the thermal region as a site of natural wonders and the territorial ownership of the indigenous people began with the increasing tourist focus on the area in the 1870s. Encounters between travellers and Maori occurred mainly at the hot lakes, and the representation of Maori in travel writing moved ambivalently between Maori as the authentic and picturesque guardians of the wonders, legitimated by ethnicity, and Maori as the perpetrators of an illegitimate and sometimes threatening exploitation.

For most tourists to New Zealand, it was the thermal region which delivered foreignness, both geophysical and ethnic. On his world tour in 1884, C. E. R. Schwartze felt 'off the line' only while travelling there:

For once we were off the European track. For once we were clear of top hats and black coats. No Cook's tourists would meet us here, at any rate, and we were really and truly 'far from the madding crowd'.[39]

Thorpe Talbot declared on arriving in Rotorua in 1882: 'Groups of dusky figures standing or squatting wherever we turned our eyes made us feel that we were verily in Maoriland at last. Never before had we realised it.'[40] Almost all travellers comment on their feeling of having arrived in the heart of Maoriland, 'en plein pays de Maori' as Emile Wenz put it in 1885, when they reach Ohinemutu. Talbot's feeling of arriving in another culture is common from the 1880s, though in many texts the novelty is quickly succeeded by the opinion that contact with tourists has resulted in the degeneration of local Maori. J. Ernest Tinne compared the Maori of Rotorua unfavourably with the Hau Hau, who he claimed had a 'noble upright bearing that contrasted very favourably with the cringing manners of the semi-civilized scum of these lake districts'.[41] Talbot represents hundreds of Europeans who desire nativism and 'authenticity' when she wishes that Maori would not 'affect European attire . . . for the few that I have seen bareheaded, barelegged, and enveloped in the *korowai* looked so much more imposing', and besides the colours they choose are 'loud enough to make one's head ache'.[42]

'Sketches in New Zealand:
Maori civilization', from the
Illustrated London News,
2 October 1886, p.356.
ATL N-P-545-356

Schwartze at Te Wairoa, 'the very heart of the Maori country', is 'decidedly disappointed' with his observations of the 'habits of the natives':

> They have acquired all the European vices and none of the virtues, and are now, in the matter of bargaining, dealing and transacting business, *Ipsis Hibernis Hiberniores*. Their love of money is something appalling, and they will adopt any trickery to squeeze a few shillings out of you.[43]

Because, as John Frow has pointed out, for the tourist 'reality is figural rather than literal',[44] most tourists register disappointment that the encounter with Maori has not revealed to them the noble savage. Commercial exchange between tourists and Maori at the hot lakes became a sign of the degeneracy of Maori from some uncorrupted real state. Even when they recognised the forces driving change, which many of them did, the implication that Maori should maintain a cultural stasis while at the same time servicing the demands of tourism is always present. When Anthony Trollope finally arrived in a place with numerous

Maori, Rotorua, he asked how they lived. 'I was told that they were Friendlies, and that therefore the government fed them . . . I think I could see that the race was not progressing towards civilisation. The people are dying out, – and thus, and thus only, will the Maori difficulty be solved.'[45] Bathing in the hot pools on the Pink Terraces, Trollope imagines such a future:

> The time probably will soon come in which there will be a sprightly hotel at Roto Mahana, with a table d'hote, and boats at so much an hour, and regular seasons for bathing. As I lay there I framed the programme of such a hotel in my mind – and I did so, fixing the appropriate spot as I squatted in the water, and calculating how much it would cost and what return it would give.[46]

Alexander Wilson, anonymous co-author of *Maoriland*, described the transformation of the carved whare Hinemihi at Te Wairoa on Lake Tarawera:

> the natives point with considerable complacency and pride to the carved three fingered monsters with lolling tongues, whose eyes glare – not with the nacreous iridescence of the mutton-fish shell, as in ordinary whares – but with the genuine metallic lustre of half-sovereigns, florins, shillings, and sixpences.[47]

In the summer of 1885–86 the number of tourists visiting the 'Lake District', or Rotorua and its surrounding thermal region including the Pink and White Terraces, was estimated by the painter Charles Blomfield[48] at ten to thirty tourists arriving every weekday, 'mostly moneyed people from all parts of the world'.[49] Daily records for the Palace Hotel at Ohinemutu from early March to mid-May 1886 show between fifteen and thirty-five guests as resident. The Palace was one of four hotels at Ohinemutu, a Maori village on the shore of Lake Rotorua and the principal starting-point for the trip to Te Wairoa, Tarawera and the terraces. The local Maori, Te Arawa at Rotorua and Tuhourangi at Te Wairoa, owned the land leased for hotels and other buildings, and provided the transport, entertainment and technical knowledge of thermal terrain. Richard Tangye noted in May 1886 that the

> hotel at Wairoa is built on Maori land without any lease, and they will not sell it; they are at perfect liberty to eject the landlord whenever they like, and a few years ago, when Mr. C— was here with a party of ladies, they were just going to bed when a party of Maoris invaded the house, and drove everyone out on to the streets, where they had to stay until the landlord bribed the darkies to allow him to enter again.[50]

Most tourist writing records a similar range of activities: the performance of a haka, bathing at the terraces and eating local food are shared experiences which draw consistent responses. Being at home among Maori was also represented as a chance for tourists to go mildly native, as in the illustrations from the *Graphic* on 24 January 1880 (reprinted in a descriptive book for American children, *The Boy Travellers in Australasia* by Thomas Knox, published in 1889) showing tourists dressed in 'plaids',[51] walking among or reclining in hot pools, half naked. But most travellers articulated an unpassable racial and cultural boundary between them and the 'lords of the soil', a 'pigheaded people', as James Edge Partington put it, spoilt by 'our conciliatory treatment' of them: 'They consider themselves vastly superior to the white man. What black nation would not Exeter Hall and its nonsensical notions spoil?'[52]

Lords of the soil

Anna Vickers, a young Frenchwoman visiting in 1880 with her family, articulates an almost universal tourist attitude when she declares:

> Ah! les Maoris ne perdent jamais une occasion d'exploiter les voyageurs. Ils n'ont guère d'autres moyens d'existence, car ils travaillent peu, et le plus souvent, helas! pas du tout. Ils ne vivent donc, aux environs des lacs chauds, que de ce qu'ils attrapent à droite et à gauche; aussi ils ne laissent jamais passer une bonne occasion.[53]
>
> (The Maori never lose the opportunity of exploiting travellers. They have almost no other means of support as they work very little, or more often, alas, not at all. They live in the hot lakes region on what comes to hand, and never let a good opportunity pass them by.)

It has been estimated that, from boat fees alone, the annual income of the Tuhourangi people who controlled access to Rotomahana and the terraces was more than £6000.[54] An editorial in the *New Zealand Herald* for June 1886, just before the eruption of Mt Tarawera, castigated the Tuhourangi for their use of the money and suggested contact with tourists was corrupting and deracinating:

> For years past they have received a constant stream of money from tourists, have been plied with liquor to get up hakas and dances, and have been constantly drunk and idle. As a consequence notwithstanding all the money they receive, they live in a most wretched style and never have a sufficiency of nourishing food.[55]

Because negotiating with Maori was the only way to see the Pink and White Terraces and other thermal sights, the question of charges becomes for many tourists the point of tension at which cross-cultural contact is sharpened. A boundary expressed as a commercial transaction can be read from both sides: as an expression of the attitudes of travellers towards the world, how much its sights and wonders are worth, who they belong to and who is entitled to ask payment for them; and as a reciprocal recognition by Maori of what the travel

A visit to the Hot Lakes of New Zealand from the *Graphic*, 24 January 1880, p.92. ATL B-K 404-92

culture is based on and what kind of person travels for pleasure. Charles Morton Ollivier reported in 1871 that:

> The natives of Kariri have settled among themselves, or passed a law, that any party visiting Rota Mahana in a canoe from that pa, shall employ and take with them two Maoris for each white man forming the party, and shall pay five shillings per diem for the canoe, and a similar amount to each native. To this rule the natives adhere most rigidly . . . The Maories also demand a fee of £2 sterling, if they take the canoe up the creek between Tarawera and Rota Mahana. This charge is only demanded when the creek is taputapu and the £2 is supposed to have a magical effect upon this superstitious practice of theirs.[56]

The *Handbook to the Bay of Plenty* (1875), in advising that the cost of travelling in the thermal region should not exceed fifteen shillings a day, played to the reader conditioned by caricatures of non-European peoples in illustrated papers and travel writing with a satirical view of economic transactions with the Maori at Ohinemutu.

> There, may be seen in perfection the Maori Lord of the Soil in all his pristine glory, affable to a fault, and suffering from a chronic impecuniosity, which his instinct leads him to relieve at the expense of any confiding stranger who will part with a shilling on the strength of shaking hands with a soi disant Rangatira, who will manufacture for the occasion a genealogical descent from the Maori Noah.[57]

Much of J. Chantrey Harris's *The Southern Guide to the Hot Lake District of the North Island of New Zealand* (1878) is focused on Maori and what he perceives to be their shortcomings, configuring the reader as a colonist with an already established opinion on 'the Native Difficulty'. The 'Native Difficulty' is to do with land title, and Harris, who lived in Dunedin, has robust views on how it should be handled. At Ohinemutu it is thanks to the 'energy and pluck of the white settlers' that 'utter stagnation' of the horticultural potential of the land has been avoided, a reflection which leads him into a diatribe against the Native Land Court. At Te Wairoa Harris's commentary sets the ground for the innumerable tourists whose accounts recycle, usually in a less irascible vocabulary, the points of tension he identifies. Maori are a 'peculiar people', high handed, and 'think lightly of coming to blows for the possession of a pakeha tourist'.[58] They are 'inconsistent, short-sighted and illogical' in their treatment of tourists and extortionate in their charges, as 'all visitors are equally rich in the eyes of the Maori'. Harris gives detailed advice to tourists on how to negotiate charges with Maori, what and whom to pay. He recommends employing an 'intelligent white man rather than a Maori' as a guide and paying him 'liberally', partly because he will 'act fairly' and 'play a valuable intermediate part between tourists and the "lords of the soil"'.[59]

The Southern Guide represents the tourist's visit to Rotomahana as an economic contest. Repetition of Froude's description 'lords of the soil' through the guidebooks and travel texts of the late nineteenth century loads the phrase with a reverse significance. The idea of indigenous possession is seen as comically inappropriate, temporary and illegitimate, and this view underlies the accounts of struggles over charges and claims of extortion. The emphasis placed on Rotomahana and the terraces as the pre-eminent travel destination in New Zealand, resulting in a constant flow of tourists and thus stretching services and resources, makes tension over revenue and costs inevitable, but Harris's overtly contestatory model of negotiating relations with Maori ensures that his readers will respond in the same way.

Thorpe Talbot did recognise a reciprocity of exchange, however:

> The natives charge £2 for rowing one person across Tarawera to Rotomahana, and for every additional passenger 5s more. The guide costs 10s and the canoe fare across

Rotomahana another 10s. For permission to see the Terraces, there is another charge of 2s 6d for each tourist. This land belongs to the Wairoa natives, and they have learned from the pakeha to charge for admission to their show – small blame to them![60]

John Lawrence Lambe, who knew Edwin Bainbridge, the English tourist who died in the 1886 eruption, went to Rotomahana in order to visit the place of his death. He was so enraged by what he called the sharks 'lying in wait on every side to ensnare the unwary traveller' that he wrote a letter to the *New Zealand Herald* alleging that in a few years the 'intelligent British tourist, will be, like the moa, a thing of the past in this country'.[61] Lambe's objection to being charged pre-eruption prices to see the results of the eruption is the tail end of this constant stream of complaint by tourists about the charges levied by Tuhourangi for access to the Pink and White Terraces.

Looking at Maori – circulating stereotypes

Stereotypes about Maori as childlike, lazy, drunken and extortionate are relentlessly recycled by tourist writers. Some, like Anna Vickers, present their observations about Maori as self-evident and unexceptional. She speaks of 'les groupes de Maori qui se chauffent paresseusement au soleil' ('groups of Maori who lazily warm themselves in the sun'), Maori whose clothing displays a 'mélange de luxe et de misère' ('a mixture of luxury and misery').[62] Richard Waddington, whose 1887 *Notes of a Tour in the England of the Antipodes* was delivered first as a lecture at Sydenham, briefly described his interaction with Maori on the way to the 'object of my pilgrimage' as 'many squabbles, and being curiously inspected by numbers of idle, loafing Maoris who hung about the entrance of the hotel, where every penny they earned was spent in drink'.[63]

C. R. Sail (whose choice of pseudonym, 'an Anglo-Indian globe-trotter', indicates the attitudes expressed in his book) refers to the 'much-fleeced globe-trotter' having to 'fee a Maori for gazing' on the Hamarana spring. The statement introduces an extended description of Maori in the thermal regions as 'simply and inevitably detestable . . . idlers and drunkards of the most completely developed description'. In a telling synecdoche, their dress is compared to 'the broken down, shabby, dirty Europe clothes of a white navvy or of a half caste "loafer" in India'.[64] Sail's aim was to see the 'Maori unwesternized' but, after being disappointed in his expectation on a trip to Wanganui, he concludes that 'any remnant of the old Maori' will be found only in the 'Urewera country which is not easy to enter'. Anglo-India defines Sail's reaction to New Zealand and to Maori, particularly when he notes that even the Governor does not go into the Urewera unless asked. This point about Maori self-government is reiterated by tourists so often – usually about the King Country – that it expresses a widespread belief about race relations and British colonial administration. Sail asks his reader to:

> Fancy an Indian Raja – who is at least nominally independent, while these Maori home-rulers are at least nominally subject to the Queen and her representative – fancy one of our Native States signifying to an Indian Governor that he couldn't come to visit it just then because the chiefs were engaged upon business; but that he might, if he pleased, come later on, when their business was over.[65]

The behaviour of tourists in the presence of Maori and on their terrain displayed its own cultural volatilities. Bertram Barton, author of the privately published diary *Far From the Old Folks at Home* (1884), found the usual prelude to the terraces, the performance of a haka at a shilling per performer, 'very quaint and characteristic'. But it went on too long, so after ten minutes he 'astonished the house slightly in the middle of the proceedings by lighting a piece of magnesium wire which I happened to have put in my pocket. The "Oh's", the amazed silence, and then the shouts of applause were highly amusing.'[66]

When Froude was offered a performance of a haka, he was told gentlemen usually preferred the haka 'complete with its indecencies' for £3 10s. He commented:

> Tourists, it seems, do encourage these things, and the miserable people are encouraged to disgrace themselves, that they may have a drunken orgie afterwards. The tourists, I presume, wish to teach the poor savage "the blessings of civilisation".[67]

The Wealth of Nations

The great set-piece of travel writing about the hot lakes was a literal inscription, whereby the 'indescribably' beautiful terraces bore the names of countless tourists who expressed their appreciation of nature's wonders by writing indelibly on the silica. Charles Morton Ollivier, who published a guide based on his visit in 1869, notes that the autographs include those of Sir George Grey, Dr Hector, several army officers and a few notable government officials. Despite an extended account of the beauties of the terraces, especially the Pink Terrace (Otukapuarangi), whose 'lovely pink bloom' makes him reflect on its commercial cosmetic possibilities, Ollivier is uncritical of those who wrote their names on it. He reads the terraces like an upper-class visitors' book, noting with interest the 'notable personages that have written their autographs on this terrace' and anticipating the autograph of the Duke of Edinburgh, who wrote his name in silica on his second visit to New Zealand in the summer of 1870: 'This probably now bears that much respected name "Alfred", written by H.R.H.'s own hand, together with

'Old painkiller bath, Te Kauwhanga Point, Rotorua' by John Philemon Backhouse, ca 1880.
ATL E-053-004

the names of the gentlemen composing his suite.'[68] The Duke of Edinburgh did sign Te Tarata, but some eager patriot shortly after removed that entire chunk of terrace with an axe.[69]

In the next decade the reaction of visitors to the graffiti is reversed and the scribbled names are declassed. James Edge Partington observes there are 'Smiths, Browns and Robinsons innumerable'[70] whose names defile the 'crowning glory' of the lake district and result in a visible loss of immanence: the object of the romantic gaze, aesthetically authenticated by a royal signature, has been converted to a text of popular pleasure. The artist Edward Payton is typical:

> There is one feature about the Pink Terrace which is a disgrace to English tourists. The buttresses are covered with hundreds of names of people who probably thought the only way of letting the world know of their existence would be to write their names on this terrace – a piece of Nature's handiwork about which it has been written, and truly, 'anything so exquisite does not exist elsewhere in nature.' Unfortunately, instead of the constant stream of water washing the names out it has formed a transparent enamel over them, and rendered them indelible.[71]

What are these people doing? One aspect of graffiti is a record of presence left for an audience which is not present. In their books or articles, travel writers also sign their names on a composite textual artefact, New Zealand, recording their presence in time and space and affirming the complementary existence of a readership and a market.

So what, then, do travellers notice? This question lies at the heart of what they write, particularly in the construction of an 'other' people and place, the negotiation of space and race, and the attempt to produce meaning and fixity. The Pink and White Terraces lay at the heart of any traveller's wish to see New Zealand in the 1870s and 1880s. Represented again and again by travel writers, scientists, letter writers and diarists as a piece of nature's work too lovely to be reproduced in language, Te Tarata and Otukapuarangi were nevertheless climbed, bathed in, written over and looted by the floods of European tourists drawn to them. They stood at the centre of a borderland in which the physical features of the landscape, its unpredictability, dangers, the fluidity of its media – water in all its manifestations from steam to solidified silica flow, earth from edible mud to lava – represented the volatile cultural exchanges between peoples and the uncanny possibilities, the dark attractive heart of wonder at the centre of Euro-imperialism. All the contradictions, ambivalence, wounding and excitement of European expansionism flow through the travel narratives of late-nineteenth-century tourists.

The potency of a travelling culture whose important medium is print and whose expansion over the globe has the same volatile and unpredictable effects as superheated mud on the earth is metaphorically suggested in a little episode from John Lawrence Lambe's *Twelve Months of Travel*. After the eruption of Mt Tarawera in the early hours of 10 June 1886, which destroyed the Pink and White Terraces and the villages servicing the tourist trade, killing over 100 people, Lambe visited the scene where his friend, the tourist Edwin Bainbridge, had died. In a reprise of the standard trope of travel writing about the terraces, Lambe wrote:

> no words can describe the scene of desolation which now opened on our view, for on every side as far as the eye could see there was nothing but mud and ashes.[72]

Just outside the fatal verandah where Bainbridge had been crushed by the weight of mud, lava and ash thrown out in the eruption, Lambe found a book

> recently come to the surface. I picked it up. It was Adam Smith's 'Wealth of Nations', probably Bainbridge's property, but though I thought of taking a page for a memento, I could not for the life of me, and I replaced the book in the mud where I had found it.[73]

Texts of pleasure

For the great majority of British travellers, the ability to travel and the production and consumption of travel writing constitute part of their idea of themselves as an imperial nation, moving through their territories with the leisure to describe and characterise the new world within the assumptions, prejudices and knowledge systems of the old. In travel writing about New Zealand, what Paul Carter calls the double aspect of travelling is also emphasised in a tension between the familiar and the unfamiliar, and particularly the tension surrounding a *desire* for the unfamiliar – which, however, must not be too dangerous, uncomfortable or confrontational. The place towards which the traveller is journeying, and at which they come to rest, needs to satisfy a simultaneous desire for exoticism and familiarity. John Lawrence Lambe's travels in the South Island satisfied this double desire in a way that his North Island experiences did not. Riding through the West Coast bush and staying at stations and huts in remote areas around Okarito caused Lambe to resolve that, when he retired from public life, he would come back to New Zealand. When he travels by train from Wellington through the Manawatu Gorge, however, he finds the scenery bleak and uninteresting and the gorge not what it was cracked up to be. Lambe's responses partly reflect the difference he felt between the wilder, less developed and more conventionally aestheticised landscapes of the South Island and the more urbanised landscapes of the North, and partly what Paul Carter has described as the traveller's inability to see interest in the landscape if the object of the gaze does not correspond to their conditioned expectations of what constitutes a picturesque or dramatic landscape.[74]

Travel writing sits at the centre of various interests. Travelling and writing about travelling require financial investment and inevitably bring commercial opportunities and development, yet the point of travel, as represented to European readerships, is, as Trollope put it, to let 'the flavour of the dust of Pall Mall for the time depart from me altogether'.[75] Travel writing about New Zealand represents the country as seen in terms of a particular set of concerns and interests, to do with its status and history as a colony, its geographical location and ethnography, and its physical configuration. But for every traveller who works their way from one end to the other, or part of the way between, it is also a personal landscape of event and adventure. The production, circulation and reception of travel texts which bring New Zealand into the imaginative possession of a metropolitan readership also expand its relation to European imperialist development, and foster the alteration of the traveller's world to one that resembles the country they left behind. This is what tourists both do and do not desire, and travel writing about New Zealand in the later nineteenth century was always and inevitably shifting between a wish for the exotic and a fear of its being uncomfortable, expensive and foreign.

NOTES

Introduction

1 M. P. K. Sorrenson in 'Maori and Pakeha', in *The Oxford History of New Zealand*, estimates that by 1845 about half the adult Maori population could read a little in Maori (p.170), and there are numerous early accounts of Maori requesting books from missionaries.

2 Roger Chartier in *On the Edge of the Cliff: History, Language and Practices* (Baltimore: Johns Hopkins University Press, 1997, p.83), paraphrasing D. F. McKenzie, *Bibliography and the Sociology of Texts*.

3 Benedict Anderson, *Imagined Communities*, rev. ed., pp.37–46.

4 'On the Fine Perception of Colours possessed by the Ancient Maoris', a paper read before the Hawke's Bay Philosophical Institute, 10 October 1881. Published in *Transactions and Proceedings of the New Zealand Institute 1881*, Vol. XIV, pp.68–9.

5 Colonel J. R. Jackson, *What to Observe; or, The Traveller's Remembrancer*, 3rd ed., Preface.

6 Mary Louise Pratt, *Imperial Eyes: Travel Writing and Transculturation*, p.7.

7 Jackson, op. cit., Preface.

8 See Jill Steward, 'The Adventures of Miss Brown, Miss Jones and Miss Robinson: tourist writing and tourist performance from 1860 to 1914', *Journeys: the International Journal of Travel and Travel Writing* 1:1–2 (2000), pp.36–58.

9 I. R. Willison, 'Centre and Periphery in the Histories of the Book in the English-speaking world, and Global English Studies', a paper delivered to the 'Remembering Don McKenzie' conference in Wellington, New Zealand, 12–14 July 2001.

10 Pratt, op. cit., is a famous discussion, but the wealth of analysis of travel writing that has exploded through the past decade demonstrates the many ways in which imperial travel and travel writing advanced the appropriation of non-European knowledges, territories, resources, cultures and peoples. See *Journeys* 1 (2000) for recent examples, also Steve Clark (ed.), *Travel Writing and Empire* (1999).

11 See Simon Eliot, *Some Patterns and Trends in British Publishing 1800–1919*.

12 Joan-Pau Rubiés, 'Travel Writing as a Genre: Facts, Fictions and the Invention of a Scientific Discourse in Early Modern Europe', *Journeys* 1:1–2 (2000), p.7.

13 Anderson, op. cit., p.44.

14 Hilary Ericksen notes that Dieffenbach 'may have been a player … in colonization' but was 'not without concern for Maori and their welfare'. See '"Acting Proper": Encounter and Exchange on Tourism's Frontier', *Tourism, Culture & Communication* 2 (1999), pp.99–109.

15 John Frow, *Time and Commodity Culture: Essays in Cultural Theory and Postmodernity*, p.67.

16 Rubiés, op. cit., p.5.

Chapter 1: Captain Ceroni's watch

1 See Ross Gibson's discussion of the volatile mobile culture of the early colony in New South Wales in 'Ocean Settlement', *Meanjin* 4 (Summer 1994), pp.665–78.

2 A. S. Thomson, *The Story of New Zealand*, p.253.

3 D. F. McKenzie, 'Our Textual Definition of the Future: the New English Imperialism?', in *Printers of the Mind and Other Essays*, in press.

4 There is also an Otaheitan referred to as 'Jemmy' by Peter Dillon, Commander of the *Research*, who is said to be from the *City of Edinburgh* and certainly the same man (*Narrative and successful result of a voyage in the South Seas . . .*, p.213). G. L. Craik reports that J. L. Nicholas in New Zealand in 1815 'met with a Hindoo, who had made his escape from Captain Patterson's ship, the *City of Edinburgh* about five years before' (*The New Zealanders*, p.281).

5 See Greg Dening's discussion of the events in Tahiti in *Mr. Bligh's Bad Language: Passion, Power and Theatre on the Bounty*, 1992.

6 In the sense discussed by John Frow in *Time and Commodity Culture* that place is 'relational, historical and concerned with identity', p.75.

7 Anne Salmond, *Between Worlds*, p.387.

8 *The Philanthropist* (London: Longman &

Co.), 1811, Vol. 1, pp.265–8.

9 According to *The Oxford Companion to English Literature*, fifth edition (ed. Margaret Drabble), p.226, Archibald Constable went bankrupt in 1826 and began publishing Constable's *Miscellany*, 'a series of volumes on literature, art and science', in 1827, suggesting that the miscellany was a strategy to recoup the publisher's fortunes.

10 Alexander Berry, 'Particulars of the destruction of a British vessel on the coast of New Zealand, with anecdotes of some New Zealand chiefs', in Constable's *Miscellany, Adventures of British seamen in the Southern Ocean displaying the striking contrasts which the human character exhibits in an uncivilized state*, p.326.

11 Ibid., pp.326–7.

12 Ibid., p.329.

13 Ibid., p.331.

14 Ibid., p.338.

15 Ibid., p.345.

16 Ibid., pp.346–7.

17 Ibid., p.348.

18 Robert McNab, *Historical Records of New Zealand*, Vol. 1, p.312.

19 In his journal Marsden reported that the 'most awful calamity of the *Boyd* extinguished at once all hopes of introducing the Gospel into that country': *The Letters and Journals of Samuel Marsden*, ed. J. R. Elder, p.61.

20 J. L. Nicholas, *Narrative of a Voyage to New Zealand performed in the years 1814 and 1815, in company with the Rev. Samuel Marsden, Principal Chaplain of New South Wales*, p.323.

21 This quotation occurs in a footnote in Nicholas, pp.154–5, attributed to the *Missionary Register* for November 1816.

22 Nicholas, p.124.

23 Richard Cruise reports 'Tetoro's [Titore] suspicions of the soldiers on board the *Dromedary* in 1820': *Journal of a Ten Months' Residence in New Zealand*, p.25.

24 John Turnbull, *A voyage round the world*, second edition (1813), p.504.

25 *Narrative of the massacre of the crew of the ship Boyd, at New Zealand, by cannibals; embellished with a representation of the real head of Watangheon, the principal murderer, and a frontispiece copied from the grand painting exhibited in the Royal Liverpool Museum. To which are added accounts of the following extraordinary persons, viz. John Williams, a runaway convict at Norfolk Island, New South Wales; John Crossland, the Derby hangman, who executed his own brother and father; and Ravillac, who assassinated King Henry the fourth of France.* London: J. Meldon, c.1845.

26 The landscape shown in the frontispiece is clearly not New Zealand, and the people

depicted are not Maori.

27 See Timothy Mitchell, 'The world-as-exhibition', in *Comparative Studies in Society and History* 31 (1989), pp.217–36, and Derek Gregory's discussion of this idea in *Geographical Imaginations*, pp.34–52.

28 Alexander Berry, *Reminiscences of Alexander Berry*, p.104.

29 Nicholas, p.155.

Chapter 2: Adventures of the Printer

1 Colenso's account of this trip in *Fifty Years Ago in New Zealand* (pp.43–5) describes how the crowd who came and sat outside their tent at Hick's Bay to see the white men was so dense that the chief had to resort to head-butting to get them to move enough to allow Colenso and his companion out of their tent. The ship's steward was so sure he wouldn't see them again that he cried on dropping them off.

2 From 19 November 1841 to 22 February 1842.

3 Mary Louise Pratt, *Imperial Eyes: Travel Writing and Transculturation*, p.23.

4 William Colenso, 'Ancient Tide-Lore and Tales of the Sea from The Two Ends of the World', p.13.

5 Ibid., p.40, note C.

6 Autobiography 1, pp.10–11, quoted in A. G. Bagnall & G. C. Petersen, *William Colenso*, p.45.

7 Bagnall & Petersen, op. cit., p.72, report that Colenso in later life said he spent Christmas Day 1835 in Darwin's company.

8 Denis B. Walker has characterised Colenso as having a 'textual attitude towards reality' formed by exploration narratives and the 'poetry of Thomson, Wordsworth, Gray and Longfellow'. See 'At Home in the Wild: the Idea of Place and the Textualised Vision of William Colenso', in *Australian Canadian Studies, The Idea of Place: New Zealand Issue* Vol. 18, Nos 1 & 2 (2000), p.102. Pratt's *Imperial Eyes* also demonstrates that imperialism, including scientific imperialism, was conducted textually.

9 *Rovings in the Pacific from 1837–1849* by 'A Merchant' [Edward Lucett] (Vol. 1, pp.146–7) describes her progress to a meeting at Waikato, referring to her 'masculine spirit of adventure and travel'.

10 *Kew Gardens; or, A Popular Guide to the Gardens of Kew*, third edition (1848), p.6.

11 David Mackay, 'Myth, Science, and Experience', in *Voyages and Beaches*, ed. Alex Calder, Jonathan Lamb and Bridget Orr, p.103.

12 Op.cit., p.4.

13 Antarctic Journal of J. D. Hooker, 19 August 1841. Kew MS, cited in Bagnall and Petersen, p.85.

14 *Kew Gardens*, Preface, p.4.
15 Major Denham describes 'fine shady trees in the valleys, among which I saw several trees described in Mungo Park's Travels, under the name of Nutta'. See Denham, Dixon and Others, *Narrative of travels and discoveries in northern and central Africa, in the years 1822, 1823, and 1824 by Major Denham F. R. S., Captain Clapperton, and the late Doctor Cudney*, third edition (1828), Vol. 2, p.396.
16 Ibid., p.372.
17 For Pratt's discussion of her well-known term the 'anti-conquest', see *Imperial Eyes*, ch. 3, and for the 'narcissism of the sentimental' ch. 4, p.77.
18 Op. cit., Vol. 1, p.27.
19 See Peter Beilharz, *Imagining the Antipodes: culture, theory and the visual in the work of Bernard Smith*, p.76.
20 Walker, op. cit., describes Colenso's process as 'converting empty space into a place by bringing to it the repleteness of a pre-existing textuality' (p.100). I think Colenso's textual self-representation is also identity politics.
21 Colenso's frame of reference to African exploration is frequently evident in the casual asides he makes in his unpublished notebooks, like the note on 15 April 1839 as he travels to Cape Reinga: 'How often was I reminded, this day, of travelling in an Arabian desert!' (ATL, MS-0588).
22 Mungo Park, *Travels in the interior districts of Africa: performed in the years 1795–1796 and 1797, with an account of a subsequent mission to that country in 1805*, p.237.
23 Colenso, 'Journal of a Naturalist in some little known parts of New Zealand in a letter to Sir W. J. Hooker', *Journal of Botany*, 1844, p.6.
24 Pratt, op. cit., p.78.
25 *Excursion in the Northern Island of New Zealand; in the summer of 1841–2*, p.6.
26 William Hooker, quoting Allan Cunningham's *Florae insularum Novae Zelandiae precursor* (published in *Companion to the Botanical Magazine*, Vol. 2, p.230), in preface to the 'Journal of a Naturalist', p.2.
27 'Journal of a Naturalist', p.7.
28 Pratt, op. cit., p.201.
29 'Journal of a Naturalist', p.20.
30 Ibid., p.19.
31 *Epilobium* is the genus of willow-herbs. There are many New Zealand species.
32 The Maori name for *Coriaria* is tutu. 'Pteris esculenta' should be *Pteridium esculentum*, which is bracken fern, and *Leptospermum scoparium* is manuka.
33 'Journal of a Naturalist', p.21.
34 Mungo Park, op. cit., Vol. 1, pp.122–3.
35 This seems to me an instance of what Jonathan Culler has described as things read as signs of themselves: Colenso sees in the

physical scene a sign of beauty, a 'figural reality' (see 'Semiotics of Tourism', *American Journal of Semiotics* 1, 1 & 2 (1981), pp.127–40). Denis Walker, op. cit., has pointed out that Colenso's description is also 'Thomsonesque', deriving its self-consciously poetic qualities from Thomson's famous poem *The Seasons* (1730–46).
36 'Journal of a Naturalist', p.23.
37 Ibid., p.25.
38 See Rev. J. Hickson SM, *Catholic Missionary Work in Hawke's Bay from its Outset in 1841*. Colenso's unpublished journal for 23 December 1841 records that his party arrived at a tiny village at sunset where he learned that 'a R. C. Priest had preceded me by only a few hours, and that he was gone on to Waikare'.
39 Colenso, unpublished journals sent to the CMS, ATL Micro-MS-Coll-04, pp.531–3.
40 In his study of spatial history, *The Road to Botany Bay* (1987), Paul Carter has shown how the picturesque constitutes visibility. See particularly the discussion of the picturesque and how it 'discloses place', pp.240–1.
41 'Journal of a Naturalist', p.27.
42 *Excursion in the Northern Island of New Zealand*, p.49.
43 'Journal of a Naturalist', p.39.
44 Shef Rogers, '"Crusoe Among the Maori": Translation and Colonial Acculturation in Victorian New Zealand', in *Book History* 1 (1998), pp.182–95.
45 Pratt, op. cit., p.63.
46 'Journal of a Naturalist', p.36.
47 Ibid., p.47.
48 Ibid., p.43.
49 Ibid., p.49.
50 Ibid., p.54.
51 Allan Cunningham to William Colenso, 4 December 1838, ATL MS 90-253-1.
52 See A. L. Rowse, *The Controversial Colensos*, p.110. Rev. Henry Williams's refusal to allow Colenso to make an offer of marriage to his daughter reinforced the exclusion from the inner circle at Paihia already set in place through Colenso's being the printer and not an ordained missionary, and low church not High Anglican. Wade's letter is in ATL, Folder 88-103-1/14.
53 Cunningham wrote on 9 January 1839 in response to Colenso's enquiry about books: 'I am very sorry to find no botanical books are introd. to the Colony by the Booksellers. The Colonial public being not botanical readers, such works would not sell, it appears. You must I believe remain without those you wish for until I return home next year.' (ATL MS 90-253-1). Perhaps the most famous of Colenso's quarrels about being the first to discover and identify something is his claim to

the moa, discussed in Appendix D of Bagnall & Petersen, op. cit., pp.464–7. There are many such complaints and they provide an interesting tracking through the print culture of local professional relationships in the 1840s. Here are Colenso's views on Dieffenbach: 'The "Sphaeria Taylori" of Berkeley (Lond. Jour. Bot. Vol. 11., p210) has already been described and figured, by the Rev. R. Taylor, as Sph. Innominata, in the Tasmanian Journal vol.1., p308. I find Mr Berkeley, remarking on Sph. Robertsii, (p209) says, – "We are indebted to Mr Dieffenbach for the knowledge of the moth to which the Larva belongs"! O tempora, O mores! I mentally exclaimed, when I read this for I had not only described but actually shewn Dieffenbach (who up to that time knew nothing of the Animal which produced the Larvae), specimens of the Moth; one of which, of the very identical Moths which D. had handled – I subsequently sent you, and which you have mentioned in your Lond.Journ. Bot., Vol. 1 p.304. – published nearly a year before this paper of Mr Berkeley's!! and about the same time before Dieffenbach's 2 vols!!!' Letter to W. J. Hooker, 7 March 1844 (ATL MS 88-103-1/09).

54 Colenso to W. J. Hooker, 14 February, 1840 (ATL MS 88-103-1/09).

55 Cunningham to Colenso, 11 April 1839 (ATL MS 90-253-1).

56 Colenso to Cunningham, 1 March 1839 (ATL MS 90-253-1).

57 Colenso to W. J. Hooker, 31 July 1846 (ATL MS 88-103-1/09).

58 Colenso to Cunningham, 12 July 1839 (ATL MS 90-253-1).

59 Colenso to W. J. Hooker, 31 July 1846 (ATL MS 88-103-1/09).

60 Colenso to J. D. Hooker, 20 September 1847 (ATL MS 88-103-1/09).

61 Colenso to J. D. Hooker, 31 January 1853 (ATL MS 88-103-1/09).

62 Colenso to Cunningham, 13 November 1839 (ATL MS 90-253-1).

63 Colenso to Ronald Campbell Gunn, 4 September 1850 (ATL qMS-0491-0492). Ronald Gunn was a well-known naturalist and had been private secretary to Sir John Franklin.

Chapter 3: Swells' sons run out

1 Martin Green, *Dreams of Adventure, Deeds of Empire* (London: Routledge, 1980), p.3, cited by Catherine Hall, 'Missionary Stories: Gender and Ethnicity in England in the 1830s and 1840s', in Lawrence Grossberg, Cary Nelson, Paula A. Treichler, *Cultural Studies*, p.249.

2 Allan Cunningham to William Colenso, 9 January 1839, ATL MS 90-253-1.

3 Anthony Pagden, *European Encounters with the New World: from Renaissance to Romanticism*, p.148. Pagden describes a long tradition of using the noble savage as a point of critique on contemporary society.

4 Rod Edmond, *Representing the South Pacific Colonial Discourse from Cook to Gauguin*; Vanessa Smith, *Literary Culture and the Pacific: Nineteenth Century Textual Encounters*; Pagden, op. cit.

5 Edmond, op. cit., p.9.

6 For an extensive discussion of the status of Williams and his text after his death, see Edmond, op. cit., pp.119–20.

7 Rev. John Williams, *A Narrative of Missionary Enterprises*, Preface, p.vi.

8 Edmond, op. cit., Chapter 4.

9 Williams, op. cit., p.117.

10 John Campbell, *The Martyr of Erromanga*.

11 Samuel Smiles, *Self-Help; with illustrations of character and conduct.*

12 [John Campbell], *The Missionary's Farewell* (London: John Snow, 1838), p.21.

13 Approval of the heroic aspects of missionary activity was of course widespread. The only thing Charles Darwin and Robert FitzRoy agreed on during their voyage on the *Beagle* was the value of missionaries in changing the lives of savages (see Charles Darwin, *The Voyage of the 'Beagle'*, ed. Millicent Selsam (Kingswood, Surrey: World's Work, 1966), Introduction, p.xvi).

14 See James Wilson, *The Life and Dreadful Sufferings of Captain James Wilson . . . .* According to Wilson, the captain of *Le Grand Buonaparte*, Captain A. Carbonelle, said that if he had known who was on board the *Duff,* and 'in what they were engaged, he would sooner have given 500l. out of his own pocket than have met with them' (p.293). It didn't prevent him ransoming the ship at Rio de Janeiro, however.

15 Edmond, op. cit., makes the point that if the mutiny on the *Bounty* was 'essentially a European event, a distant echo of revolution' it also showed the 'anarchic appeal' of the South Pacific (p.9), and what Edmond calls the 'paradise regained narrative' of the alternative community established by the mutineers on Pitcairn Island (p.65).

16 Herman Melville, *Typee: a peep at Polynesian life, during a four months' residence in a valley of the Marquesas.*

17 Charles Darwin, op. cit., thought the greater part of the English the 'very refuse of society' and also made unfavourable comparisons between Tahitians and Maori. J. D. Hooker's *Antarctic Journal* (Kew MS) refers to Kororareka with its 'one bad hotel, three cheating stores, many grog shops and more houses of ill-fame'.

18 *Sydney Gazette*, 28 March 1837.

19 Smith, op. cit., pp.18, 31.

20 Ibid., p.28.

21 John Boultbee, *Journal of a Rambler: the Journal of John Boultbee*, ed. June Starke, p.3.

22 Introduction to Boultbee, op. cit., p.xx.

23 John Rochfort, *The Adventures of a Surveyor*, Preface.

24 Edward Lucett, *Rovings in the Pacific from 1837–1849 with a glance at California by a merchant long resident in Tahiti*, Preface.

25 Barnet Burns, *A Brief Narrative of a New Zealand Chief, being the Remarkable History of Barnet Burns, An English Sailor, with a faithful account of the way in which he became A Chief of one of the Tribes of New Zealand, together with a few remarks on the manners and customs of the people, and other interesting matter. Written by himself* (1848).

26 George Bayly, *Sea-Life Sixty Years Ago: a record of adventures which led up to the discovery of the relics of the long-missing expedition commanded by the Comte de la Perouse*, Preface.

27 Stephen Greenblatt, *Marvelous Possessions: the Wonder of the New World*, p.126.

28 F. E. Maning, *Old New Zealand: a tale of the good old times by a Pakeha Maori*, p.vii.

29 Greenblatt, op. cit., p.9.

30 Lucett, op. cit., Preface, p.v.

31 Archibald Campbell, *A Voyage Round the World from 1806 to 1812*, ed. James Smith, p.10.

32 Ibid., p.11.

33 Boultbee, op. cit., p.1.

34 J. G. A. Pocock, 'Nature and History, Self and Other: European Perceptions of World History in the Age of Encounter', in *Voyages and Beaches*, ed. Calder, Lamb and Orr, p.36.

35 Henry Morton, travelling in Taranaki in 1872, claimed in *Notes of a New Zealand Tour* that a Pakeha–Maori who was attending a Native Land Court hearing with a group from his tribe stayed in the same hotel as Morton: 'I afterwards learned [he] had been forwarded to Australia many years ago under the auspices of the Imperial Government'.

36 Boultbee, op. cit., p.3.

37 Herman Melville, *The Works of Herman Melville*, Vol. 2: *Omoo: a narrative of adventures in the South Seas*, p.95.

38 Lucett, op. cit., p.293.

39 Boultbee, op. cit., pp.3–10

40 Ibid., p.11.

41 Recounting his passage to Bass Strait in the *Sally* and a gale the ship encountered, Boultbee quotes from *Henry IV Part 2* describing the size of the waves and the crew's conditions. Reference to this most English of plays may also be an implied assertion about his place in an alien world. He later quotes from *Macbeth* and *Henry VI*

Part 1.

42 Boultbee, op. cit., p.16.

43 Ibid., p.31.

44 Edward Markham, *New Zealand or Recollections of It*, ed. E. H. McCormick. Introduction, p.22, in which McCormick transcribes from the Hobart section of Markham's journal. The query is McCormick's.

45 Ibid., p.59.

46 Ibid., p.52.

47 Ibid., p.51.

48 Ibid., pp.41–2.

49 Ibid., p.43.

50 Ibid., p.79.

51 Ibid., p.30.

52 Ibid., p.58.

53 Ibid., pp.57–61.

54 Ibid., p.69.

55 Ibid., pp.47–8.

56 Ibid., p.66.

57 Ibid., p.27.

58 Ibid., p.38.

59 Ibid., p.41.

60 Herman Melville, *The Works of Herman Melville*, Vol. 5: *Redburn, his first voyage; being the sailor-boy confessions and reminiscences of the son of a gentleman in the merchant service*, p.1.

61 Ibid., p.4.

62 Augustus Earle, *A narrative of a nine months' residence in New Zealand in 1827*, p.1.

63 Ibid., p.82.

64 Richard Helgerson, *Forms of Nationhood: the Elizabethan Writing of England*, p.13.

65 Earle, op. cit., p.58.

66 Ibid., p.71.

67 Ibid., p.59.

68 Ibid.

69 Brian Musgrove, 'Travel and Unsettlement', in Steve Clark (ed.), *Travel Writing and Empire*, p.32.

70 Earle, op. cit., pp.57–8.

71 Helgerson, op. cit., p.191.

72 Earle, op. cit., p.60.

73 See Peter Hulme, Introduction to *Cannibalism and the Colonial World*, ed. Francis Barker, Peter Hulme and Margaret Iversen, p.3, for a discussion of a 'typical' scene of a witness stumbling across the remains of a cannibal feast.

74 Earle, op. cit., p.61.

75 Ibid., p.132.

76 Ibid., p.138.

77 Ibid., p.139.

78 Ibid., p.157.

79 Ibid., p.193.

80 *Edinburgh Review* lvi (1833), pp.333–49.

81 *Quarterly Review* xlviii (1832), pp.132–65; *Protestant Journal* (London, 1833), pp.1–46.

82 Lucett, op. cit., p.2.

83 Ibid., p.27.
84 Ibid., p.14.
85 Ibid., p.40.
86 Ibid., p.44.
87 Ibid., p.63.
88 Ibid., p.67.
89 Ibid., p.73.
90 Ibid., p.79.
91 Ibid., p.82.
92 Ibid., p.124.
93 Ibid., p.105.
94 Ibid., p.127.
95 Ibid., p.142.
96 George Lillie Craik, *The New Zealanders*, The Library of Entertaining Knowledge, Vol. 5, pp.93–7.
97 Ibid., p.86.
98 Ibid., p.94.
99 Ibid., p.99.
100 Ibid. (emphasis added).
101 Ibid., p.159.
102 Ibid., p.275.
103 Ibid.
104 Ibid., p.278.
105 Dennis Porter, *Haunted Journeys: Desire and Transgression in European Travel-Writing*, p.9.

Chapter 4: Travel with interest
1 J. G. A. Pocock, 'Nature and History, Self and Other: European Perceptions of World History in the Age of Encounter', in *Voyages and Beaches*, ed. Calder, Lamb and Orr, p.28.
2 All quotations are from the unnumbered title and dedication pages of W. R. Wade, *A Journey in the Northern Island of New Zealand*.
3 D. F. McKenzie, *Bibliography and the Sociology of Texts*, p.12.
4 W. R. Wade to Rev. John Saunders, 24 August 1839, in DUHO Misc MS-0323, Hocken Library, Dunedin. I owe this reference to Phil Parkinson.
5 Peter Gibbons, 'Non-fiction', in *The Oxford History of New Zealand Literature in English* (second edition), ed. Terry Sturm, p.37.
6 Wade, *A Journey in the Northern Island of New Zealand*, p.17.
7 Ibid., p.14.
8 Ibid., p.21.
9 Ibid., p.26.
10 Ibid., p.23.
11 Ibid., p.74.
12 Ibid., p.123.
13 Ibid.
14 Ibid., Chapter 2, pp.38–53.
15 Unpublished review by W. R. Wade of the second edition of *An Account of New Zealand* by William Yate, CMS Records in the Webster Collection, WTU Micro-MS-0239, 10 October 1836. I owe this information to Phil

Parkinson.
16 William Yate, *An Account of New Zealand* was published without the knowledge of his fellow workers at the mission while Yate was in London in 1835. Judith Binney's entry on Yate in the *Dictionary of New Zealand Biography*, Vol. 1, notes the other mission workers thought Yate had over represented himself in the mission's activity.
17 Judith Binney, Introduction to William Yate, *An Account of New Zealand* (Wellington: Reed, 1970), p.xii.
18 Edward Markham refers to seeing 'a book published by Yates the Missionary' at the Cape on his way home from New Zealand, 'but did not read it': *New Zealand or Recollections of It*, ed. E. H. McCormick, p.40.
19 Richard Davis, diary extracts in Davis to Secretaries, 24 April 1837, ATL Micro-MS-Coll-04-08 (CMS Archives CN/M v.9 pp.546). I owe this reference to Phil Parkinson and his monumental work on early missionaries.
20 B. Y. Ashwell to the Secretary, 27 December 1836, ATL Micro-MS-Coll-04-32 (CMS Archives CN/M v.10 p.26). Again I owe this reference to Phil Parkinson.
21 A. G. Bagnall, *New Zealand National Bibliography to the Year 1960*, p.6205.
22 Gibbons, op. cit., p.36.
23 Yate, op. cit., p.5.
24 Yate's book perfectly conforms to the recommended Royal Society model as laid out in Colonel Julian Jackson's *What to Observe; or, The Traveller's Remembrancer* (London: James Madden & Co, 1841; previously published in Paris in 1822 under the title *Guide du Voyageur*). The Royal Society model begins with geographical position (longitude, latitude) and moves through a set list of descriptive categories, from geology and topography to climate, mineral resources, flora, fauna, indigenous peoples, their physiology, customs, religion, society and history of encounter. Jackson instructs his readers on how to produce useful scientific information, such as measuring the height of mountains, analysing rock and soil types, etc.
25 Yate, op. cit., p.19.
26 Describing the denseness of New Zealand forests, Yate observes (p.19): 'The jungles of India, or the forests of America, cannot yield a more secure retreat for beasts of prey than these vast woods; yet none are found to exist here.'
27 Ibid., p.199.
28 When Edward Lucett was travelling at East Cape in 1840 he met a tall young chief named 'Ne-pere' who brought several books out from his hut and asked Lucett and his

companion to read them. Lucett noted that when he used a wrong pronunciation 'all would call out to correct us': *Rovings in the Pacific from 1837-1849*, pp.75–6.

29 See the work of Simon Eliot, *Some Patterns and Trends in British Publishing 1800–1919*.

30 In a letter to the Secretaries of the CMS from Waimate in 1832, Yate refers to Volume 2 of Ellis's *Polynesian Researches* on the issue of indigenous customary rights in marriage. I owe this information and that in the following paragraph to Phil Parkinson.

31 Proceedings of the Church Missionary Society, 36th year (1835/36), p.45.

32 Mary Louise Pratt, *Imperial Eyes*, p.35.

33 William Barrett Marshall, *A Personal Narrative of Two Visits to New Zealand in His Majesty's Ship 'Alligator' A. D. 1834*, [p.ii].

34 Glenelg was Principal Secretary of State for the Colonies.

35 Marshall, op. cit., Preface, p.xii.

36 Ibid., p.59.

37 Baron Karl von Hugel, who wrote *Der Stille Ocean* (Vienna, 1860, privately circulated).

38 Marshall refers to Tyerman and Bennet's *Journal of Voyages and Travels* (London: Frederick A. H. Davis, London Missionary Society, 1831) and Augustus Earle, among others.

39 Marshall, op. cit., p.57.

40 Ibid., p.71.

41 Ibid., p.72.

42 In Marshall's account of the second visit of the *Alligator* to New Zealand, he reflects on the naming practises of the British and criticises the 'propriety of giving arbitrary names at all to places not connected with us': see pp.154–5.

43 Ibid., p.109.

44 Ibid., p.192.

45 Ibid., p.194.

46 Ibid., p.204.

47 Richard Cruise, *Journal of a Ten Months' Residence in New Zealand*, Preface, p.v.

48 Pratt, op. cit., p.35.

49 See Anne Salmond, *Two Worlds* (pp.78–83), for an account of the ambush on Tasman's boat crews at Taitapu, in which three Dutch sailors were killed and one died later from injury. Salmond notes it was the first time Maori 'experienced the crackle and flash of firearms'.

50 See R. D. Crosby, *The Musket Wars: a History of Inter-Iwi conflict 1806–45*, p.19: 'The first and primary factor was the spread of muskets throughout the country.'

51 Cruise, op. cit., p.6.

52 Ibid., p.8.

53 Ibid., p.67.

54 Ibid., p.13.

55 Crosby, op. cit. (p.56), notes that by 1818 Ngapuhi had accumulated so many muskets through trading they could produce two armed taua comprising 'many hundreds of men each'.

56 Pratt, op. cit., p.7.

57 A. G. Bagnall, Introduction to his 1957 edition of Cruise, *Journal of a Ten Months' Residence in New Zealand* (Christchurch: Pegasus Press), p.7.

58 Cruise, op. cit., p.179.

59 Ibid., p.261.

60 The distinction between symbolic and material cannibalism, or 'good' (eating flesh as a cultural practice) and 'bad' (eating for appetite) cannibals, is crucial to the maintenance of New Zealand as a suitable site for 'civilisation' and most early writers about New Zealand attempt a distinction between Maori as cannibals and savagery.

61 *Quarterly Review LXI*, December 1824, Article 111, pp.52–65.

62 Lieutenant H. F. McKillop, *Reminiscences of twelve months' service in New Zealand*.

63 Ibid., p.52.

64 Ibid., pp.154–5.

65 Ibid., p.91.

66 Ibid., pp.96–99, 102.

67 McKillop's reason for publishing despatches was to defend Colonel Despard, whose defeat by Hone Heke at Waimate in 1845 resulted in a loss of a quarter of his men. 'Christianity in Melanesia and New Zealand', in *Quarterly Review CLXXXIX* (June 1854), p.194, describes the fighting of that year as a 'series of partial military disasters'.

68 McKillop, op. cit., p.89.

69 Ibid., pp.274–5.

70 G. C. Mundy, *Our Antipodes; or, residence and rambles in the Australasian Colonies*, Vol. 1, p.v.

71 Ibid., p.vi.

72 Ibid., p.vii.

73 Earl Grey, Secretary of State for the Colonies, had proposed a complex constitution, conferring representative parliamentary institutions on the settlers, which Governor Grey refused to implement on the ground that it would give Europeans minority rule. See Keith Sinclair, *Dictionary of New Zealand Biography*, Vol. 1, p.161.

74 Mundy, op. cit., Vol. 2, p.49.

75 Ibid., p.68.

76 Ibid., p.71.

77 Ibid., p.82.

78 These descriptions occur in Mundy, op. cit., Vol. 2, Chapter IV, pp.70–101.

79 Ibid., p.86.

80 Ibid., p.102.

81 Ibid., p.104.

82 Ibid., p.110.

83 Ibid., p.150.

84 Ibid., p.152.
85 Ibid., p.90.
86 Ibid., p.92.
87 Ibid., p.178.
88 Ibid., p.213.
89 Ibid., p.82.
90 J. C. Bidwill, *Rambles in New Zealand*.
91 Ibid., p.26.
92 Ibid., p.26.
93 Ibid., p.77.
94 Ibid., p.43.
95 Ibid., pp.79, 85.
96 Allan Cunningham to William Colenso, 9 January 1839, ATL MS 90-253-1.
97 A. G. Bagnall *New Zealand National Bibliography to the Year 1960*, p.4589.
98 J. S. Polack, *New Zealand: Being a Narrative of Travels and Adventures during a residence in that country between the years 1831 and 1837*.
99 Ibid., p.276.
100 L. M. Goldman, *The History of the Jews in New Zealand*, p.41. John Israel Montefiore was a Jewish Londoner who came to the Bay of Islands in 1831 as a trader.
101 Ibid., pp.38–9.
102 Polack's second book, also published in 1838, was *Manners and Customs of the New Zealanders and Remarks to Intending Emigrants*. It uses the same materials but excludes the personal narrative.
103 Polack, p.89.
104 Mungo Park and Major Denham describe similar scenes. Denham has a charming description of being examined by half a dozen women in Sockna who were especially amazed when he put his hands into the pockets of his trousers: 'my hands were pulled out, and those of three or four of the ladies thrust in'. Denham et al, *Narrative of travels and discoveries*, pp.15–16
105 Polack, *New Zealand*, p.115.
106 Ibid., p.60.
107 Ibid., p.126.
108 Gibbons, op. cit., p.37.
109 He uses poetic archaisms ('betook', 'yonder'), uncommon words ('interfluing', 'juncous'), French and Latin expressions and numerous classical references.
110 Eliot, op. cit., p.45. The figure dropped to about twelve percent for the rest of the century but remained significant. Eliot cites a study by Paul Kaufman, 'Some Reading Trends in Bristol 1773–84' (in *Libraries and Their Users: Collected Papers in Library History* (London, 1969) pp.28–35), which shows that works on travel and geography were the most frequently borrowed category during that period. Eliot's time span reflects the huge surge in European exploration and colonisation that occurred up to 1840.
111 Ernst Dieffenbach, *Travels in New Zealand,*

with contributions to the geography, geology, botany and natural history of that country, p.9.
112 Ibid, pp.iii–iv.
113 In his Preface Dieffenbach makes these interests very clear: 'I have entered, on several occasions, upon questions intimately connected with the capabilities of the country as a home for Europeans. In a time pregnant with the universal desire for search for employment, and to open a new field for exertion, foreign and unoccupied countries, previous to colonization, should be explored with a view of making ourselves acquainted with their soil and natural productions. Natural history and the affiliated sciences should, in that case, be merely the helpmates to noble enterprise; and even more than that they should guide and lead it.'
114 Barnet Burns refers to 'a gentleman, of the name of Montifore, who had just at that time [February 1829] formed an establishment for the flax trade': *A Brief Narrative of a New Zealand Chief*, p.6.
115 Alexander Marjoribanks, *Travels in New Zealand* (1846), Preface.
116 Hocken's adjective in *A Bibliography of the Literature Relating to New Zealand* (Wellington, 1909), p.124.
117 *New Zealand Journal*, 26 April 1845, pp.105–7.
118 Ibid., p.106.
119 A. G. Bagnall, *National Bibliography*, p.1078.
120 Patricia Burns, *Fatal Success: a History of the New Zealand Company*, p.261.
121 Ibid.
122 Marjoribanks, op. cit., p.11.
123 *New Zealand Journal*, 24 May 1845, p.129.
124 Ibid., p.131.
125 Marjoribanks, op. cit., p.174.
126 The publishers were Smith Elder & Co., who were prominent in publishing travel writing and published a number of works connected with the New Zealand Company.
127 See Harold Smith, *The Society for the Diffusion of Useful Knowledge 1826–46: a Social and Bibliographical Evaluation* (Dalhousie University Libraries and Dalhousie University School of Library Services, Occasional Paper No. 8, 1974).

Chapter 5: Empire travellers, 1: writers who travel

1 John Shaw's *A Gallop to the Antipodes* (1858) opens with the reflection that 'science has shortened in a most wonderful manner the voyage from these shores to the antipodes; no stronger proof can be produced than the following – that on my way to that region in 1850, I spent 150 days on the water: in 1857 but 72 days only' (p.1).
2 *A Boy's Journey Around the World*, ed. Samuel

Smiles (London: John Murray, 1871), p.210. Smiles describes going to the Auckland parade ground in the evening and the 'Prince's elephant was there too, and afforded a good deal of amusement. How the poor brute was slung out of the "Galatea", got on shore, and got back on ship-board again, was to me a mystery'. I have been unable to confirm the presence of an elephant on the *Galatea*.

3 Benedict Anderson, *Imagined Communities* (rev. ed., p.93).

4 G. W. Lyttelton, 'Two Lectures on a visit to the Canterbury Colony in 1867–8'. ATL, NZ Pamphlets Collection, Vol. 13, No. 8.

5 Michel de Certeau, *The Practice of Everyday Life*, trans. Steven Rendall, p.118.

6 Lyttelton, op. cit., p.7.

7 Ibid., p.18.

8 Ibid., p.37.

9 Ibid., p.24.

10 Geoffrey Blainey (ed.), *Greater Britain: Charles Dilke visits her new lands 1866 & 1867*, Foreword.

11 C. W. Dilke, *Greater Britain: A Record of travel in English-speaking countries during 1866 and 1867*, p.vii.

12 See Roy Jenkins, *Sir Charles Dilke: A Victorian Tragedy*. Dilke was cited as co-respondent in a divorce case which became a *cause célèbre* and resulted in his resignation from public life. Jenkins argues it was a conspiracy.

13 *The British Army* (1888) and *Imperial Defence* (1892) both carried the byline 'by the author of *Greater Britain*'. He also wrote *Problems of Great Britain* (1890) and published a collection of essays on foreign policy.

14 What has been referred to as Sir Charles Dilke's 'banana blunder' received considerable publicity. Charles Hursthouse wrote a letter to the *Taranaki Herald*, published 12 April 1872 under the heading 'The Terrible Effects of Sir C. W. Dilke's New Zealand Banana!!', in which he claimed that, because where '*it* flourishes the Briton will fade', the 'terrible effects' of 'the Banana in *New Zealand* appearing in so popular a book, as "Greater Britain" may seriously damage Her "Capitalist-Immigrationary" Interests'.

15 Dilke, *Greater Britain*, p.27.

16 Ibid., p.394.

17 James Clifford, 'Traveling Cultures', in *Cultural Studies*, ed. Lawrence Grossberg, Cary Nelson and Paula A. Treichler, p.110.

18 Dilke, *Greater Britain*, p.318.

19 Ibid., p.330.

20 Ibid., p.332.

21 Ibid., p.344.

22 Ibid., pp.353–4.

23 Ibid., pp.365–6.

24 Jenkins, op. cit., p.43.

25 Dilke, *Greater Britain*, pp.391–2.

26 One of Trollope's biographers, T. H. S. Escott in *Anthony Trollope: His Work, Associates and Originals*, notes (p.274) that 'a new interest in the Greater Britain beyond the seas had deeply stirred the popular imagination and reflected itself in the writings of [Trollope's] best known contemporaries'.

27 Anthony Trollope, *Australia and New Zealand*, 2nd ed., Vol. 2, p.342.

28 Ibid., pp.321–2.

29 Ibid., p.322.

30 J. Ernest Tinne, *The Wonderland of the Antipodes; and Other Sketches of Travel in the North Island of New Zealand*, p.1.

31 A great many of these publications were emigration handbooks, manuals for settlers, settler writing, descriptive books driven by colonisation.

32 Trollope, op. cit., Vol. 1, p.15.

33 Victoria Glendinning, *Anthony Trollope*, p.414.

34 Escott , op. cit., p.286.

35 Ibid., p.275.

36 Trollope, op. cit. Vol 2, p.324.

37 Quoted in Brian Musgrove, 'Travel and Unsettlement: Freud on Vacation', in *Travel Writing and Empire*, ed. Steve Clark, p.40.

38 Quoted in Marcie Muir, *Anthony Trollope in Australia*, p.88.

39 Trollope is far less sympathetic to Aboriginal people than to Maori, and declared: 'It is their fate to be abolished.' Op. cit., Vol. 1, p.75.

40 Ibid., Vol. 2, p.378.

41 Ibid., pp.589–608.

42 Ibid., p.422.

43 Anderson, op. cit., p.7.

44 See Muir, op. cit., p.87.

45 A. H. Reed (ed.), *With Anthony Trollope in New Zealand*, p.145.

46 Ibid., p.146, quoting a report of Trollope's farewell speech from the *Daily Southern Cross*, 3 October 1872.

47 *Edinburgh Review*, April 1886, pp.407–8.

48 J. A. Froude, *Oceana or England and Her Colonies*, p.230.

49 Ibid., p.73.

50 Sir James Harrington, *The Commonwealth of Oceana*. 'Oceana' was Harrington's name for England and his introduction declares: 'The Sea giveth law unto the growth of *Venice*, but the growth of *Oceana* giveth law unto the Sea'.

51 Froude, op. cit., p.277.

52 Ibid., p.275.

53 Ibid.

54 Ibid., p.279.

55 Ibid., p.282.

56 Ibid.

57 Ibid., p.300.

58 Anderson, op. cit., p.188.

59 Edward Wakefield, 'New Zealand and Mr. Froude', *Nineteenth Century*, CXIV (August 1886), pp.171–82. Wakefield, who was the MP for Selwyn, was famous for his wit, power of argument and sarcasm (see entry on Edward Wakefield by Edmund Bohan in *Dictionary of New Zealand Biography*, Vol. 2.)

60 Ibid., p.171.

61 Ibid., p.172.

62 Geoffrey Blainey (ed.), *Oceana: the tempestuous voyage of J. A. Froude, 1884 & 1885*, pp.199–206.

63 Wakefield, op. cit., p.172.

64 Ibid.

65 Ibid., p.174.

66 Froude's biographer, Waldo Dunn, wrote in 1930 that it was 'doubtful whether any other man of letters in Great Britain has been the object of such bitter misrepresentation and such organised opposition as has Froude.' See *Froude and Carlyle*, p.3.

67 These figures are taken from Blainey's introduction to his edition of *Oceana*.

68 John MacGregor, *Toil and Travel*, p.56.

69 William Westgarth, *Personal Recollections of Early Melbourne and Victoria*, p.2.

70 J. L. Lambe, *Twelve Months of Travel*, p.131.

71 Froude, *Greater Britain*, p.319.

72 Ibid., p.311.

73 Ibid., p.307.

74 Ibid., p.308.

Chapter 6: Empire travellers, 2: travellers who write

1 J. H. Kerry-Nicholls *The King Country or Explorations in New Zealand*, p.14.

2 Ibid., p.268.

3 Ibid., p.272.

4 [Miss Muller], *Notes of a Tour Through Various Parts of New Zealand Including a Visit to the Hot Springs by a German Lady*, p.26.

5 J. A. Froude, *Oceana*, pp.231–2.

6 Ibid., p.243.

7 Ibid., p.261.

8 Ibid., pp.270–1.

9 J. L. Lambe, *Twelve Months of Travel*, p.96.

10 Froude, op. cit., p.237.

11 [Muller], op. cit., p.3.

12 Alice M. Frere, *The Antipodes and Round the World, or Travels in Australia, New Zealand, Ceylon, China, Japan and California* (1870), p.1.

13 James Edge Partington, *Random Rot* (Altrincham: for private circulation only), 1883.

14 James Coutts, *Vacation Tours in New Zealand and Australia* (1880), Preface.

15 Frank Henley, *Bright Memories; being reminiscences of Frank Henley compiled directly from letters, containing an account of his visits to Australia and New Zealand* (1887).

16 Annie R. Butler, *Glimpses of Maoriland*, p.43.

17 Mrs Muter, *Travels and Adventures of an Officer's Wife in India, China and New Zealand*, Preface, p.v.

18 Claudia Knapman, 'Western Women's Travel Writing about the Pacific Islands', in *Pacific Studies* 20:2 (June 1997), pp.31–51.

19 Ibid., p.34.

20 C. R. Sail, *Farthest East, and South and West: Notes of a Journey Home Through Japan, Australasia, and America by an Anglo-Indian Globe-Trotter* (1892), p.v.

21 Edward Payton, *Round about New Zealand: Being Notes from a Journal of Three Years' Wanderings in the Antipodes*, Preface.

22 Stephen Greenblatt, *Marvelous Possessions: the Wonder of the New World*, p.122.

23 B. H. Barton, *Far from the Old Folks at Home: My Journal Letters Home during a Twenty-One Months' Tour Round the World* (privately printed, 1884), Preface.

24 W. Towers Brown, *Notes of Travel 1879–1881* (printed for private circulation, 1882), p.vi.

25 Lambe, op. cit., p.139.

26 James Clifford, *Routes: Travel and Translation in the Late Twentieth Century*, p.66.

27 Payton, op. cit., p.10.

28 J. Ernest Tinne, *The Wonderland of the Antipodes; and Other Sketches of Travel in the North Island of New Zealand*, p.1.

29 Ibid., p.38.

30 Ibid.

31 Ibid., p.39.

32 Ibid., p.77.

33 Ibid., p.82.

34 Mrs Howard Vincent, *Forty Thousand Miles Over Land and Water: The Journal of a Tour through the British Empire and America*, p.107.

35 J. A. Froude, *Oceana*, p.262.

36 Froude, reflecting on the difficulty of 'making acquaintants at the *table d'hote*', comments: 'You may make my hairdresser's vote as good as mine, but you cannot make me ask him to dinner, or speak to any casual companion who . . . may claim me afterwards as a friend.' Op. cit., p.276.

37 Butler, op. cit., p.134.

38 Vincent, op. cit., p.205.

39 [Muller], op. cit., p.3.

40 W. Little, *Round the World; notes by the way, by a 'Commercial'*, p.99.

41 In a letter to her sister, Isabella Bird said she was 'appalled by the drunkenness everywhere' (quoted in Anna M. Stoddart, *The Life of Isabella Bird (Mrs. Bishop)*, 3rd ed., p.79). Annie R. Butler mentioned the driver of an omnibus she travelled in, whose 'speech betrayed him' as a member of a higher social class. She observed 'To send an idle, dissipated young man to the colonies is the quickest way to ruin him completely . . .

This man who might have been an ornament to our universities, but whose sole talk was of drink and horses. . . . '(op. cit., p.117).

42 Henry Selden Young's diary was published in 1999 by his granddaughter as 'a precious piece of history from the nineteenth century': *Diary of a Voyage to Australia and New Zealand 1885*.

43 'A young fellow named Reid is out here travelling for the World Publishing Co, a Canadian firm of publishers that does business on a scale quite undreamed of by English publishers and booksellers. The firm publishes a great number of books and it has agencies and travellers in every English-speaking country or colony in the world.' Young gives a long description of Reid's work practices and how he induces working people to buy the books: 'when he knew I was a bookseller, he was not unwilling to tell me anything I asked' (p.42).

44 Young, op. cit., p.93.

45 Clifford, op. cit., p.67.

46 Paul Carter, *The Road to Botany Bay: An Essay in Spatial History* (London: Faber & Faber, 1987), p.232.

47 See Knapman, op. cit., p.44.

48 Clifford, op. cit., p.68

49 Marianne North, *Recollections of a Happy Life: being the autobiography of Marianne North, edited by her sister Mrs John Addington Symonds*, Vol. 2, pp.183–4. North also reported a remark made by the Governor, Sir Arthur Hamilton Gordon, when she was staying with him that has resonance for the exhaustion of the vocabulary of sightseeing and also New Zealand's long history of self-promotion: 'I moved into his house and heard him abuse the island and all belonging to it with as much heartiness as I did. He said, justly, something must be wrong with a country which required so much laudation. Everyone was asserting its supreme beauty and superiority wherever I went.' (pp.189–90).

50 Richard Tangye, *Notes of my fourth voyage to the Australian Colonies, including Australia, Tasmania and New Zealand* (1886), p.89.

51 John MacGregor, *Toil and Travel*, p.54.

52 Count Fritz von Hochberg, *An Eastern Voyage: a Journal of the Travels of Count Fritz von Hochberg through the British Empire in the East and Japan* (1910), p.82.

53 [Muller], op. cit., p.54.

54 David Kennedy Jnr, *Kennedy's Colonial Travel: a Narrative of a Four Years' Tour through Australia, New Zealand, Canada &c* (1876), p.255.

55 Edward Wakefield, 'New Zealand and Mr Froude', *Nineteenth Century* CXVI (August 1886), p.173.

56 G. W. Lyttelton, *Two Lectures on a visit to the Canterbury Colony in 1867–8* (1868), p.18.

57 Vincent, op. cit., p.149.

58 Kennedy, op. cit., p.190.

59 Vincent, op. cit., p.139.

60 W. Towers Brown, *Notes of Travel 1879–1881* (London: printed for private circulation, 1882), pp.83–4.

61 Jeff Guy says that, by the time the Battle of Ulundi was fought, the 'intensity of Zulu resistance had already persuaded London that the cost of ending Zulu independence was too high'. The Battle of Ulundi was promoted to a 'major military victory' to wipe out the 'stain' on Britain's honour of the Isandlawhna defeat. Jeff Guy, *The Destruction of the Zulu Kingdom: the Civil War in Zululand 1879–1884*, cited in James Belich, *The New Zealand Wars and the Victorian Interpretation of Racial Conflict*, pp.331–3.

Chapter 7: The business of travel

1 *Fifty Years in New Zealand 1888–1938: Travel reminiscences and early history of Cook's Travel Service in New Zealand* (1939), pages not numbered.

2 Quoted in 'An Epoch in the History of the Colony', *Thomas Cook New Zealand Centenary: a Special Publication to Celebrate Thomas Cook's New Zealand Centenary* (1988), pages not numbered.

3 James Clifford, *Routes: Travel and Translation in the Late Twentieth Century*, p.65.

4 *New Zealand Herald*, quoted in 'An Epoch in the History of the Colony', op. cit.

5 Count Fritz von Hochberg, *An Eastern Voyage: a Journal of the Travels of Count Fritz von Hochberg through the British Empire in the East and Japan*, p.100.

6 E. Brodie Hoare, *Impressions of New Zealand: an antidote to Mr Froude by an experienced London banker, who has travelled from one end of New Zealand to the other* (1887).

7 Constance F. Gordon Cumming, *At Home in Fiji*, p.154.

8 William Towers Brown, *Notes of Travel 1879–1881*, p.110.

9 John Frow, *Time and Commodity Culture: Essays in Cultural Theory and Postmodernity*, p.75.

10 Frow, op. cit., discusses Jonathan Culler's argument that 'for the tourist gaze, things are read as signs of themselves . . . giving on to a *type* of the beautiful, or the extraordinary or the culturally authentic. Hence the structural role of disappointment in the tourist experience.' (p.67).

11 Charles Baeyertz, *Guide to New Zealand, the most wonderful scenic paradise in the world*.

Dunedin:1902.

12 G. T. Chapman, *Chapman's Traveller's Guide Through New Zealand*, Preface, p.iii.

13 See note 24 in Chapter 4.

14 Chapman, op. cit., p.30.

15 Ibid., p.41.

16 Ibid., p.40.

17 Ibid., p.39.

18 Charles Morton Ollivier, *A Visit to the Boiling Springs of New Zealand; including a trip to White Island*.

19 Ibid., p.6.

20 Frow, op. cit., p.70. Frow discusses Dean McCannell's distinction between the 'back' region of tourism and the 'front' region set up for display. Nineteenth-century tourist accounts of Rotorua reflect this distinction in their perception of the 'front' historical display at Gate Pa, and the 'back' actuality of Rotomahana, where the effects of colonisation mostly confirm entrenched views about Maori people. Authentic Maoriness is historical, and visibly retreating, and what is left behind is corrupted, unheroic and dying out.

21 Langbridge & Edgecumbe, publishers, *The Handbook to the Bay of Plenty and Guide to the Hot Lakes, the Boiling Springs, the Healing Baths, the Geysers, the Intermitting Fountains &c in the Rotomahana and Taupo districts (Province of Auckland) New Zealand*. Tauranga (1875).

22 Ibid., Preface, [p.3].

23 Ibid., p.16.

24 Thorpe Talbot, *The New Guide to the Lakes and Hot Springs and A Month in Hot Water*, 'Prefatory Remarks', p.vi.

25 Judith Adler, 'Origins of Sightseeing', in *Annals of Tourism Research* 16:1 (1989), pp.7–29, cited in Frow, op. cit., p.91.

26 T.T.H., *The Newest Guide to the Hot Lakes by a Man Constantly in Hot Water*, Preface, [p.1].

27 Ibid., p.17.

28 Ibid., p.9.

29 J. Chantrey Harris, *The Southern Guide to the Hot Lake District of the North Island of New Zealand*, Preface, [p.iii].

30 Thomas Bracken, *The New Zealand Tourist*, p.vii.

31 [Alexander Wilson, Rutherford Waddell and T. W. Whitson], *Maoriland; an illustrated handbook to New Zealand*, issued by the Union Steam Ship Company of New Zealand Ltd, pp.17–19.

32 Bracken, op. cit., p.vii.

33 Ibid., p.53.

34 James Edge Partington, *Random Rot* (1883), p.310.

35 Meaghan Morris, 1988: Quoted in Brian Musgrove, 'Travel and Unsettlement: Freud on Vacation', in *Travel Writing and Empire*,

ed. Steve Clark, p.40.

36 [Wilson et al.], op. cit., p.1.

37 Ibid, pp.17–18.

38 Frow, op. cit., p.92. 'It is this economy, the "belief in the restorative effects of happily constituted scenes, and an increasingly romantic orientation to aesthetic sightseeing" that forms the basis of modern tourism.' (Frow is quoting Malcolm Andrews, *The Search for the Picturesque: Landscape, Aesthetics and Tourism in Britain, 1760–1800.* Stanford: Stanford University Press, 1990.)

39 William Pember Reeves, lawyer, journalist and politician, became New Zealand's Agent-General in London in 1896. He published an extremely influential celebration of New Zealand, *The Long White Cloud*, in 1898.

40 Susan Stewart, *On Longing: Narratives of the Miniature, the Gigantic, the Souvenir, the Collection.* Baltimore: Johns Hopkins University Press, 1984. Quoted in Frow, op. cit., p.93.

41 *New Zealand Shipping Company's Pocket-Book: an interesting guide for passengers by the Company's steamers, and containing information of general interest to all travellers to the Dominion*, p.v.

42 Ibid., pp.37–8.

43 Ibid., p.39.

44 John Urry, *The Tourist Gaze: Leisure and Travel in Contemporary Societies*, p.140.

45 Lieutenant-Colonel Montagu Cradock, *Sport in New Zealand*, p.39.

46 Frow, op. cit., p.93.

47 Adler, op. cit., cited in Frow, op. cit., p.92.

48 Frow, op. cit., p.93.

49 See, for example, two recent books: Anne Maxwell, *Colonial Photography and Exhibitions* (1999); Peter D. Osborne, *Travelling Light: photography, travel and visual culture* (2000).

50 Frow, op. cit., p.93.

51 B. H. Barton, *Far From the Old Folks At Home*, p.344.

52 J. A. Froude, *Oceana*, p.248.

53 G. A. Sala, *The Land of the Golden Fleece*, ed. Robert Dingley (1995), p.179.

54 Ibid., p.180.

55 Cumming, op. cit., p.224.

56 Musgrove, op. cit., p.32.

Chapter 8: Exhausting the wonders

1 Mary Louise Pratt, *Imperial Eyes: Travel Writing and Transculturation*, p.125.

2 William Senior, *Travel and Trout in the Antipodes: a Traveller's Sketches in Tasmania and New Zealand*, p.221.

3 J. H. Kerry-Nicholls, *The King Country or Explorations in New Zealand*, pp.95–6.

4 James Hingston, *The Australian Abroad*,

pp.218–9.

5   Hon. James Inglis ('Maori'), *Our New Zealand Cousins* (1887), p.47.

6   C. E. R. Schwartze, *Travels in Greater Britain*, p.126.

7   Charles Morton Ollivier, *A Visit to the Boiling Springs of New Zealand; including a trip to White Island*, p.21.

8   J. D., *Ninety Days' Privilege Leave to Australia, Tasmania and New Zealand*, p.19: 'As I committed a crime in the eyes of a New Zealander, of passing through the country without visiting the Hot Lakes, I feel it my duty to expiate my fault in a measure by giving the following account of the Lake District and the Maoris from the description of Mr. G. A. Sala.'

9   Russell James Colman, *Trifles from a Tourist* (1887), p.78.

10 [Alexander Wilson, Rutherford Waddell and T. W. Whitson], *Maoriland; an illustrated handbook to New Zealand*, p.282.

11 O. W. Wight, *People and Countries visited in a winding journey around the world*, p.vii.

12 Claudia Knapman comments that the use of letter or diary styles by women writers amounts to a gendered subgenre, constructing the travel writing of women as more 'domestic and personal … [it] generally conformed to topics and stylistic conventions suitable for ladies … [T]he masculinist heroic discourses of exploration, discovery and colonialism were unavailable to women.' (See 'Western Women's Travel Writing About the Pacific Islands', *Pacific Studies* 20:2 (June 1997), p.34.)

13 Dorothy Middleton, *Victorian Lady Travellers*, p.4.

14 Constance F. Gordon Cumming, *At Home in Fiji*, Vol. 2, p.164.

15 Ibid., p.163.

16 Ibid., p.200.

17 Phrase used by Brian Musgrove in his discussion of Stephen Greenblatt's *Marvelous Possessions*: see 'Travel and Unsettlement', in *Travel Writing and Empire*, ed. Steve Clark, p.35.

18 Leonard Bell, 'Travel art and its complications: Constance Frederica Gordon Cumming's 1877 visit to New Zealand, and the Colonial and Indian Exhibition of 1886', *Bulletin of New Zealand Art History*, Vol. 16 (1995), p.37. See also Timothy Mitchell, 'The world-as-exhibition', pp.314–28, cited in Derek Gregory, Chapter 1.

19 Gordon Cumming, op. cit., p.209.

20 The charge that the graffitists were 'snobs' is frequently made. T. T. H., author of *The Newest Guide to the Hot Lakes by a Man Constantly in Hot Water*, talks of 'snobs who will insist on writing their names on these lovely terraces … cads like these get cheap immortality.' (p.15).

21 Gordon Cumming, op. cit., p.223.

22 Ibid., p.224.

23 Alfred Maudslay, private secretary to Sir Arthur Gordon, wrote in his memoir of their trip to New Zealand, *Life in the Pacific Fifty Years Ago* (London, 1930), this description of Gordon Cumming, which serves as a gloss on the personality traits which contributed to the situation: 'A very tall plain woman, a regular globe-trotter, wonderfully good-tempered, no tact, very pushy when she wants anything done.' (p.84).

24 Gordon Cumming, op. cit., p.232.

25 Bell, op. cit., p.37.

26 Judy McKenzie 'G. A. S. in Australia: Hot-Air Down Under?', *Australian Literary Studies*, Vol. 15 (1992), pp.313–22.

27 Charles Pebody, *English Journalism, and the Men Who Have Made It* (London: Cassell, 1882), pp.143–4, quoted by Robert Dingley (ed.), *The Land of the Golden Fleece*, Editorial Preface, p.vii.

28 Dingley, op. cit., p.v.

29 Nigel Cross, *The Common Writer: Life in Nineteenth Century Grub Street*, p.114.

30 *The Life and Adventures of George Augustus Sala written by himself*, p.435.

31 Dingley, op. cit., p.ix.

32 W. B. Maxwell, quoted in Lord Burnham, *Peterborough Court: The Story of the* Daily Telegraph (London: Cassell, 1955), p.34, cited by Dingley, op. cit., p.vii.

33 George Augustus Sala, *The Land of the Golden Fleece*, ed. Robert Dingley, pp.147–8.

34 Ibid., p.149.

35 Ibid., pp.171–2.

36 Ibid., p.174.

37 Marcus Clarke parodied Sala's style and these features of it in an article for the *Australasian* in August 1868 called 'Arcadia in the Colonies', quoted in Dingley, op. cit., p.vii.

38 Sala, op. cit., p.155.

39 C. E. R. Schwartze, *Travels in Greater Britain*, p.127.

40 Thorpe Talbot, *The New Guide to the Lakes and Hot Springs and A Month in Hot Water*, p.10.

41 J. Ernest Tinne, *The Wonderland of the Antipodes; and Other Sketches of Travel in the North Island of New Zealand*, p.19.

42 Talbot, op. cit., p.11.

43 Schwartze, op. cit., pp.123–4.

44 John Frow, *Time and Commodity Culture*, p.67: 'A place, a gesture, a use of language are understood not as given bits of the real but as suffused with ideality, giving on to the *type* of the beautiful, or the extraordinary, or the culturally authentic. Their reality is figural rather than literal.'

45 Anthony Trollope, *Australia and New Zealand*, 2nd ed., Vol. 2, pp.478–9.

46 Ibid., p.484.

47 [Wilson et al.], *Maoriland*, p.270.

48 Roger Blackley, 'Blomfield's Terraces', *Turnbull Library Record* 20:1 (May 1987), pp.9–16, describes how Blomfield sold more than 200 replicas of a series of twelve canvases painted in 1884–85, while on a camping trip at Rotomahana with his daughter. The market potential of the terraces was realised in various ways.

49 Blomfield's unpublished diary, quoted in S. B. Reggett, 'The Tarawera Eruption, its effects on the tourist industry'. MA thesis, Massey University (1972), p.91.

50 Richard Tangye, *Notes of my fourth voyage to the Australian Colonies, including Australia, Tasmania and New Zealand*, p.113.

51 In his very influential book, *The Art of Travel or Shifts and Contrivances Available in Wild Countries* (London: John Murray, 1872), Sir Francis Galton notes several uses of the plaid indispensable to travellers, and many travel books refer to them.

52 James Edge Partington, *Random Rot*, p.366.

53 Anna Vickers, *Voyage en Australie et en Nouvelle-Zélande*, p.418.

54 Peter Waaka, *Tarawera Eruption Centennial Exhibition*, p.12.

55 *New Zealand Herald*, 1 June 1886, cited in Ron Keam, *Tarawera*, p.58.

56 C. M. Ollivier, *A Visit to the Boiling Springs of New Zealand*, p.19.

57 Langbridge & Edgecumbe, *The Handbook to the Bay of Plenty and Guide to the Hot Lakes, the Boiling Springs, the Healing Baths, the Geysers, the Intermitting Fountains &c in the Rotomahana and Taupo districts (Province of Auckland) New Zealand*, p.11.

58 J. Chantrey Harris, *The Southern Guide to the Hot Lake District of the North Island of New Zealand*, p.60.

59 Ibid., p.63.

60 Talbot, op. cit., pp.4–5.

61 *New Zealand Herald*, 4 October 1887.

62 Vickers, op. cit., p.333.

63 Richard Waddington, *Notes of a Tour in the England of the Antipodes*, p.31.

64 C. R. Sail, *Farthest East, and South and West: Notes of a Journey Home Through Japan, Australasia, and America by an Anglo-Indian Globe-Trotter*, p.216.

65 Ibid., p.222.

66 B. H. Barton, *Far from the Old Folks at Home*, p.335.

67 J. A. Froude, *Oceana*, p.283.

68 Ollivier, op. cit., p.31.

69 Prince Albert, the Duke of Edinburgh was escorted to Rotomahana by Captain Gilbert Mair. A few weeks later the Mair family returned to the terraces and noticed that the royal signature had been removed. See Reggett, op. cit., pp.37–8.

70 Partington, op. cit., p.371.

71 Edward Payton, *Round about New Zealand: Being Notes from a Journal of Three Years' Wanderings in the Antipodes* (1888), pp.128–9.

72 Lambe, op. cit., p.121.

73 Ibid., p.122.

74 Carter discusses travellers' perceptions of the monotony of the Australian bush landscape and how their discovery of 'picturesque' scenes made the country pleasant and desirable: *The Road to Botany Bay*, Chapter 8: 'A More Pleasing Prospect', pp.230–60.

75 Anthony Trollope, op. cit., p.322.

SELECT BIBLIOGRAPHY

Adams, C. Warren. *A Spring in the Canterbury Settlement*. London: Longman, Brown, Green & Longmans, 1853.

Adler, Judith. 'Origins of Sightseeing', *Annals of Tourism Research* 16:1 (1989), pp.7–29.

Adorno, T. and M. Horkheimer. *The Dialectic of Enlightenment*, trans. J. Cumming. London: Allen Lane, 1973.

Anderson, Benedict. *Imagined Communities*, rev. ed. London & New York: Verso, 1991.

Angas, George French. *The New Zealanders Illustrated*. London: Thomas M'Lean, 1847.

Arnold, Thomas. *New Zealand Letters of Thomas Arnold the younger with further letters from Van Diemen's Land and letters of Arthur Hugh Clough, 1847–1851*, ed. James Bertram. Auckland: Auckland University Press, 1966.

Baeyertz, Charles N. *Guide to New Zealand, the most wonderful scenic paradise in the world*. Dunedin: [Mills, Dick & Co], 1902.

Bagnall, A. G. *New Zealand National Bibliography to the Year 1960*. Wellington: A. R. Shearer, Government Printer, 1969.

Bagnall, A. G. and G. C. Petersen. *William Colenso*. Wellington: A. H. & A. W. Reed, 1948.

Barker, Francis, Peter Hulme and Margaret Iversen (eds). *Cannibalism and the Colonial World*. Cambridge: Cambridge University Press, 1998.

Barton, Bertram Hugh. *Far from the Old Folks at Home: My Journal Letters Home during a Twenty-One Months' Tour Round the World*. Privately printed, 1884.

Bayly, George. *Sea-Life Sixty Years Ago: a record of adventures which led up to the discovery of the relics of the long-missing expedition commanded by the Comte de la Perouse*. London: Kegan Paul, Trench & Co., 1885.

Beilharz, Peter. *Imagining the Antipodes: culture, theory and the visual in the work of Bernard Smith*. New York: Cambridge University Press, 1997.

Belich, James. *The New Zealand Wars and the Victorian Interpretation of Racial Conflict*. Auckland: Auckland University Press, 1987.

Bell, Bill. 'Bound for Australia: shipboard reading in the nineteenth century', in *Journey Through the Market: Travel, Travellers and the Book Trade*, ed. Robin Myers and Michael Harris. Delaware: St Paul's Bibliographies, 1999, pp.119–140.

Bell, James Mackintosh. *The Wilds of Maoriland*. London: Macmillan & Co, 1914.

Bell, Leonard. 'Travel art and its complications: Constance Frederica Gordon Cumming's 1877 visit to New Zealand, and the Colonial and Indian Exhibition of 1886', *Bulletin of New Zealand Art History* 16 (1995), pp.29–43.

Berry, Alexander. 'Particulars of the destruction of a British vessel on the coast of New Zealand, with anecdotes of some New Zealand chiefs', in Constable's Miscellany 4: *Adventures of British seamen in the Southern Ocean displaying the striking contrasts which the human character exhibits in an uncivilized state*. Edinburgh: Constable, 1827, pp.323–53.

—— *Reminiscences of Alexander Berry*. Sydney: Angus & Robertson, 1912.

Bidwill, John Carne. *Rambles in New Zealand*. London & Exeter: W. S. Orr & Co, 1841.

Bird, Isabella. *The Hawaiian Archipelago: Six Months among the Palm Groves, Coral Reefs and Volcanoes of the Sandwich Islands*. London: John Murray, 1875.

Blainey, Geoffrey (ed.). *Greater Britain: Charles Dilke visits her new lands 1866 & 1867*. Sydney: Methuen Haynes, 1985.

—— (ed.). *Oceana: the Tempestuous Voyage of J. A. Froude 1884 & 1885*. Sydney: Methuen Haynes, 1985.

Boultbee, John. *Journal of a Rambler: the Journal of John Boultbee*, ed. June Starke. Auckland: Oxford University Press, 1986.

Bracken, Thomas. *The New Zealand Tourist*. Dunedin: Mackay, Bracken & Co for Union Steamship Company of New Zealand Ltd, 1879.

Bradshaw, John. *New Zealand As It Is*. London: Sampson Low, Marston, Searle & Rivington, 1883.

Broad, Lucy. *A Woman's Wanderings the World Over*. London: Headley Bros, 1909.

Brown, Henry. *Diary during a Tour Round the World: written and posted for my wife during absence*. Torquay: printed by the Directory Office, 1874.

Brown, William Towers. *Notes of Travel 1879–1881*. London: printed for private circulation, 1882.

Bruce, James. *Travels to Discover the Sources of the Nile in the years 1768, 1769, 1770, 1771, 1772 & 1773.* Edinburgh and London: Manners & Miller, 1805.

Bundey, W. H. *Notes of a return voyage from England to South Australia, via Ceylon, Singapore, China, Japan, California, Honolulu and New Zealand.* Adelaide: Webb, Vardon and Pritchard, 1882.

Burns, Barnet. *A Brief Narrative of a New Zealand Chief, being the Remarkable History of Barnet Burns, An English Sailor, with a faithful account of the way in which he became A Chief of one of the Tribes of New Zealand, together with a few remarks on the manners and customs of the people, and other interesting matter. Written by himself.* Kendal: printed by H. B. Graham, 1848.

Burns, Patricia. *Fatal Success: a History of the New Zealand Company.* Auckland: Heinemann Reed, 1980.

Butler, Annie R. *Glimpses of Maoriland.* New York: American Tract Society, 1887[?].

Byles, Marie Beuzeville. *By Cargo Boat and Mountain: the unconventional experiences of a woman on a tramp round the world.* London: Seeley, Service & Co., 1931.

Calder, Alex, Jonathan Lamb and Bridget Orr (eds). *Voyages and Beaches: Pacific Encounters, 1769–1840.* Honolulu: University of Hawai'i Press, 1999.

Campbell, Archibald. *A Voyage Round the World from 1806 to 1812,* ed. James Smith. Edinburgh: A. Constable & Co., 1816.

Campbell, John. *The Martyr of Erromanga, or the philosophy of missions, illustrating the labours, death and character of the late Rev. John Williams.* London: John Snow, 1842.

Carter, Paul. *The Road to Botany Bay: an Essay in Spatial History.* London: Faber & Faber, 1987.

Chapman, G. T. *Chapman's Traveller's Guide Through New Zealand.* Auckland: G. T. Chapman, 1872.

Chartier, Roger. *Cultural History,* trans. Lydia G. Cochrane. Ithaca: Cornell University Press, 1988.

Chartier, Roger. *On the Edge of the Cliff: History, Language, and Practices,* trans. Lydia G. Cochrane. Baltimore and London: Johns Hopkins University Press, 1997.

Clark, Steve (ed.). *Travel Writing and Empire: Postcolonial Theory in Transit.* London and New York: Zed Books, 1999.

Clifford, James. *The Predicament of Culture: Twentieth century ethnography, literature, and art.* Cambridge, Massachusetts: Harvard University Press, 1988.

—— *Routes: Travel and Translation in the Late Twentieth Century.* Cambridge, Massachusetts: Harvard University Press, 1997.

—— 'Traveling Cultures', in *Cultural Studies,* ed. Lawrence Grossberg, Cary Nelson and Paula Treichler. New York and London: Routledge, 1992, pp.96–116.

Colenso, William. *Ancient Tide-lore and Tales of the Sea, from The Two Ends of the World.* Napier: R. C. Harding, 1889.

—— *Excursion in the Northern Island of New Zealand; in the summer of 1841–2.* Launceston: printed at the Office of the *Launceston Examiner,* 1844. Reprinted in the *Tasmanian Journal of Natural Science* 2 (1845), pp.210–34, 241–308.

—— *Fifty Years Ago in New Zealand.* Napier: R. C. Harding, 1898.

—— 'Journal of a Naturalist in some little known parts of New Zealand in a letter to Sir W. J. Hooker'. *Journal of Botany,* London, 1844.

—— 'On the Fine Perception of Colours possessed by the Ancient Maoris': paper read before the Hawke's Bay Philosophical Institute, 10 October 1881, in *Transactions and Proceedings of the New Zealand Institute 1881,* Vol. XIV, pp.49–76.

Unpublished sources::

Letters between Allan Cunningham and William Colenso, Alexander Turnbull Library Manuscripts (ATL MS) 90-253-1.

Letters between J. D. Hooker, W. J. Hooker and Colenso, ATL MS 88-103-1/109.

Bush Journal, Vol. 1, October–December 1847, A. G. Bagnall Collection, Box 2, Acc. 88-103-2/01.

Memoranda of journies (ATL MS-0589).

Notebook (ATL MS-0588).

Colman, Russell. *Trifles from a Tourist.* Norwich: for private circulation, 1887.

Cook, Thos & Son. *New Zealand as a Tourist and Health Resort,* compiled and edited by W. T. Cunningham. Auckland: 1893.

Coutts, James. *Vacation Tours in New Zealand and Australia.* Melbourne: George Robertson, 1880.

Cradock, Lieutenant-Colonel Montagu. *Sport in New Zealand.* London: Anthony Treherne & Co., 1904.

Craik, George Lillie. *The New Zealanders.* The Library of Entertaining Knowledge, Vol. 5. London: C. Knight, 1830.

Crawford, James Coutts. *Recollections of Travel in New Zealand and Australia.* London: Trubner, 1880.

Crosby, R. D. *The Musket Wars: a History of Inter-Iwi Conflict 1806–45.* Auckland: Reed, 1999.

Cross, Nigel. *The Common Writer: Life in Nineteenth Century Grub Street.* Cambridge: Cambridge University Press, 1985.

Cruise, Richard Alexander. *Journal of a Ten Months' Residence in New Zealand.* London: Longman, Hurst, Rees,

Orme & Brown, 1823.

Cumming, Constance F. Gordon. *At Home in Fiji*. Edinburgh: William Blackwood & Sons, 1881.

Cunningham, Allan. *Florae insularum Novae Zelandiae precursor or A Specimen of the Botany of the islands of New Zealand*. London: 1836–39[?].

Darwin, Charles. *The Voyage of the 'Beagle'*, ed. Millicent Selsam. Kingswood, Surrey: World's Work, 1966.

Denham, Dixon and Others. *Narrative of travels and discoveries in northern and central Africa, in the years 1822, 1823, and 1824 by Major Denham F.R.S., Captain Clapperton, and the late Doctor Cudney*, 3rd ed. London: John Murray, 1828.

Dening, Greg. *Islands and Beaches: Discourse on a Silent Land: Marquesas 1774–1880*. Melbourne: Melbourne University Press, 1980.

—— *Mr. Bligh's Bad Language: Passion, Power and Theatre on the Bounty*. Cambridge: Cambridge University Press, 1992.

Derrida, Jacques. *Of Grammatology*, trans. Gayatri Charavorty Spivak. Baltimore: Johns Hopkins University Press, 1976, pp.165–6, cited in David Spurr, *The Rhetoric of Empire*. Durham and London: Duke University Press, 1993, pp.109–110.

Dictionary of New Zealand Biography, Volume One: 1769–1869, ed. W. H. Oliver. Wellington: Allen & Unwin/Dept of Internal Affairs, 1990.

Dictionary of New Zealand Biography, Volume Two: 1870–1900, ed. Claudia Orange. Wellington: Bridget Williams Books/Dept of Internal Affairs, 1993.

Dieffenbach, Ernst. *Travels in New Zealand, with contributions to the geography, geology, botany and natural history of that country*. London: John Murray, 1843.

Dilke, Charles Wentworth. *Greater Britain: a Record of travel in English-speaking countries during 1866 and 1867*. London: Macmillan and Co., 1868.

Dillon, Peter. *Narrative and successful result of a voyage in the South Seas … to ascertain the actual fate of La Perouse's expedition*. London: Hurst, Chance & Co., 1829.

Dingley, Robert (ed.). *The Land of the Golden Fleece*, articles by George Augustus Sala. Canberra: Mulini Press, 1995.

Doak, Wade. *The Burning of the 'Boyd': a saga of culture clash*. Auckland: Hodder & Stoughton, 1984.

Drabble, Margaret (ed.). *The Oxford Companion to English Literature*, 5th ed. Oxford: Oxford University Press, 1985.

Dunn, Waldo. *Froude and Carlyle*. London: Longmans, Green & Co., 1930.

Earle, Augustus. *A narrative of a nine months' residence in New Zealand in 1827; together with a journal of a residence in Tristan d'Achuna, an island situated between South America and the Cape of Good Hope*. London: Longman, Rees, Orme, Brown, Green & Longman, 1832.

Edmond, Rod. *Representing the South Pacific: Colonial Discourse from Cook to Gauguin*. Cambridge: Cambridge University Press, 1997.

Eliot, Simon. *Some Patterns and Trends in British Publishing 1800–1919*. Occasional Papers of the Bibliographic Society 8, 1994.

Ellis, William. *Polynesian Researches during a residence of nearly eight years in the Society and Sandwich Islands*, 2nd ed. London: Fisher, Son and Jackson, 1831.

—— *The Missionary's Farewell: Valedictory Services of the Rev. John Williams*. London: [J. J. Campbell], 1838.

Elsner, Jas and Joan-Pau Rubiés (eds). *Voyages and Visions: Towards a Cultural History of Travel*. London: Reaktion Books, 1999.

Elsner, John and Roger Cardinal (eds). *The Cultures of Collecting*. Melbourne: Melbourne University Press, 1994.

Escott, T. H. S. *Anthony Trollope: His Work, Associates and Originals*. London: John Lane, 1913.

Feather, John. *A History of British Publishing*. London: Croom Helm, 1988.

Ferguson, John. *To The Antipodes, the Orient, and the West 1900–1*. Privately published, 1903.

Frere, Alice M. *The Antipodes and Round the World, or Travels in Australia, New Zealand, Ceylon, China, Japan and California*. London: Hatchards, 1870.

Froude, James Anthony. *Oceana, or England and Her Colonies*. London: Longmans, Green & Co., 1886.

Frow, John. *Time and Commodity Culture: Essays in Cultural Theory and Postmodernity*. Oxford: Clarendon Press, 1997.

Foucault, Michel. *Power/Knowledge: Selected Interviews and Other Writings 1972–1977*, ed. Colin Gordon. Brighton: Harvester Press, 1980.

Gibbons, Peter. 'Non-Fiction', in *The Oxford History of New Zealand Literature in English*, ed. Terry Sturm, 2nd ed. Auckland: Oxford University Press, 1998, pp.31–118.

Glendinning, Victoria. *Anthony Trollope*. New York: Knopf, 1993.

Goldman, L. M. *The History of the Jews in New Zealand*. Wellington: A. H. & A. W. Reed, 1958.

Greenblatt, Stephen. *Marvelous Possessions: the Wonder of the New World*. Chicago: Chicago University Press, 1991.

Greene, A. M. *A Voyage to New Zealand and Back through the United States of America*. Bromley, Kent: printed by S. Bush and Son, 1898.

Gregory, Derek. *Geographical Imaginations*. Oxford: Blackwell, 1994.

Grimshaw, Beatrice. *In The Strange South Seas*. London: Hutchinson & Co., 1907.

Grossberg, Lawrence, Cary Nelson and Paula A. Treichler. *Cultural Studies*. New York: Routledge, 1992.

Hall, Mary. *A Woman in the Antipodes and the Far East*. London: Methuen, 1914.

Harris, J. Chantray, *The Southern Guide to the Hot Lake District of the North Island of New Zealand*. Dunedin: printed at the *Daily Times* Office, 1878.

Haughton, S. *Sport and Travel*. Dublin: printed for the author, 1916.

Head, Hugh Stanley. *The Journals and Letters of Hugh Stanley Head, Edited by His Mother*. London: Rankin, Ellis & Co., 1892.

Heaphy, Charles. *Narrative of a Residence in various parts of New Zealand*. London: Smith, Elder & Co., 1842.

Helgerson, Richard. *Forms of Nationhood: the Elizabethan Writing of England*. Chicago: Chicago University Press, 1992.

Henley, Frank. *Bright Memories; being reminiscences of Frank Henley compiled directly from letters, containing an account of his visits to Australia and New Zealand*. Torquay: W. H. Goss, 1887.

Hickson, Rev. J., SM. *Catholic Missionary Work in Hawke's Bay from its Outset in 1841*. Auckland: Whitcombe & Tombs, 1924.

Hingston, James. *The Australian Abroad*. London: Sampson Low, Marston, Searle & Rivington, 1879.

Hoare, E. Brodie. *Impressions of New Zealand: an antidote to Mr Froude by an experienced London banker, who has travelled from one end of New Zealand to the other*. Christchurch: Christchurch Press Co., 1887.

Hochberg, Count Fritz von. *An Eastern Voyage: a Journal of the Travels of Count Fritz von Hochberg through the British Empire in the East and Japan*. London: J. M. Dent & Sons, 1910.

Hodgskin, Richard Jnr. *A Narrative of Eight Months' Sojourn in New Zealand*. Coleraine: printed for the author, 1841.

Hooker, Sir Joseph Dalton. *The Botany of the Antarctic Voyage of H.M. discovery ships 'Erebus' and 'Terror', in the years 1839–1843*. London: Reeve, 1844–61.

—— *Handbook of the New Zealand Flora*. London: Lovell, Reeve and Co., 1864.

Hooker, Sir W. J. *Kew Gardens; or, A Popular Guide to the Royal Botanical Gardens of Kew*, 3rd ed. London: Longman, Brown, Green & Longmans, 1848.

Hulme, Peter. *Cannibalism and the Colonial World*. Cambridge: Cambridge University Press, 1998.

Humboldt, F. H. Alexander, Baron von. *Personal narrative of travels to the equinoctial regions of the new continent during the years 1799–1804*, trans. Helen Maria Williams. London: Longman, Hurst, Rees, Orme & Brown, 1814.

Inglis, Hon. James ('Maori'). *Our New Zealand Cousins*. London: Sampson Low, Marston, Searle & Rivington, 1887.

Jackson, Carlton. *Zane Grey*, rev. ed. Boston: Twayne Publishers, 1989.

Jackson, Colonel Julian R. *What to Observe; or, The Traveller's Remembrancer*, 3rd ed., revised and edited by Dr Norton Shaw. London: Houlston & Wright, 1861.

Jameson, R. G. *New Zealand, South Australia and New South Wales: A Record of Recent Travels in these Colonies, with Especial Reference to Emigration and the Advantageous Employment of Labour and Capital*. London: Smith, Elder & Co., 1841.

J. D. *Ninety Days' Privilege Leave to Australia, Tasmania and New Zealand*. Allahabad: printed at the Pioneer Press, 1886.

Jordan, John O. and Robert L. Patten (eds). *Literature in the Marketplace: Nineteenth Century British Publishing and Reading Practices*. Cambridge: Cambridge University Press, 1995.

Kabbani, Rana. *Europe's Myths of Orient: Devise and Rule*. London: Macmillan, 1989.

Keam, Ron. *Tarawera: the volcanic eruption of 10 June 1886*. Auckland: R. F. Keam, 1988.

Kennedy, David Jnr. *Kennedy's Colonial Travel: a Narrative of a Four Years' Tour through Australia, New Zealand, Canada &c.* Edinburgh and London: Simpkin, Marshall & Co., 1876.

Kerry-Nicholls, J. H. *The King Country or Explorations in New Zealand*. London: Sampson Low, Marston, Searle & Rivington, 1884.

Knapman, Claudia. 'Western Women's Travel Writing about the Pacific Islands', *Pacific Studies* 20:2 (June 1997), pp.31–51.

Knights, John. *The Journal of John Knights*. Salem, Massachusetts: Marine Research Society, 1925.

Knox, Thomas W. *The Boy Travellers in Australasia*. New York: Harper & Bros, 1889.

Lambe, J. L. *Twelve Months of Travel*. Manchester: A. Ireland & Co., printed for private circulation only, 1888.

Langbridge & Edgecumbe (publishers). *The Handbook to the Bay of Plenty and Guide to the Hot Lakes, the Boiling Springs, the Healing Baths, the Geysers, the Intermitting Fountains &c in the Rotomahana and Taupo districts (Province of Auckland) New Zealand*. Tauranga: 1875.

Little, W. *Round the World; notes by the way, by a 'Commercial'*. Heckington: printed by F. G. Locke [c.1875].

Loftie, W. J. (ed.). *Orient Line Guide.* London: Sampson Low, Marston, Searle & Rivington, 1888.

[Lucett, Edward]. *Rovings in the Pacific from 1837–1849 with a glance at California by a merchant long resident in Tahiti.* London: Longman, Brown, Green & Longmans, 1851.

Lyttelton, George William, Fourth Baron. *New Zealand and the Canterbury Colony.* London: W. H. Dalton, 1859.

—— *Two Lectures on a visit to the Canterbury Colony in 1867–8.* Stourbridge: T. Mark, 1868.

MacGregor, John. *Toil and Travel.* London: T. Fisher Unwin, 1892.

Mackay, David. *In the Wake of Cook: exploration, science and empire, 1780–1801.* London: Croom Helm, 1981.

—— 'Myth, Science, and Experience', in *Voyages and Beaches*, ed. Calder et al. Honolulu: University of Hawai'i Press, 1999, pp.100–13.

McKenzie, D. F. *Oral Culture, Literacy and Print in Early New Zealand: The Treaty of Waitangi.* Wellington: Victoria University Press, 1985.

—— *Bibliography and the Sociology of Texts: The Panizzi Lectures 1985.* London: British Library, 1986.

McKillop, Henry Frederick. *Reminiscences of twelve months' service in New Zealand as a midshipman, during the late disturbances in that colony.* London: Richard Bentley, 1849.

McNab, Robert. *Historical Records of New Zealand*, Vol. 1. Wellington: Government Printer, 1908.

Maning, F. E. *Old New Zealand: a tale of the good old times by a Pakeha Maori.* Auckland: R. J. Creighton & A. Scales, 1863.

Marjoribanks, Alexander. *Travels in New Zealand.* London: Smith, Elder & Co., 1846.

Markham, Edward. *New Zealand or Recollections of It*, ed. and introduced E. H. McCormick. Wellington: Government Printer, 1963.

Marsden, Samuel. *The Letters and Journals of Samuel Marsden 1765–1838*, ed. J. R. Elder. Dunedin: Coulls, S. Wilkie & A. H. Reed, 1932.

Marshall, W. B. *A Personal Narrative of Two Visits to New Zealand in His Majesty's Ship 'Alligator' A.D. 1834.* London: James Nisbet, 1836.

Martin, John. *An Account of the Natives of the Tonga Islands in the South Pacific Ocean compiled and arranged from the Extensive Communications of Mr. William Mariner, several years resident in those islands.* 2nd ed., with additions. London: John Murray, 1818.

Martineau, Harriet. *How to Observe: Morals and Manners.* London: C. Knight, 1838.

Maxwell, Anne. *Colonial Photography and Exhibitions: Representations of the 'Native' and the Making of European Identities.* Leicester: Leicester University Press, 1999.

Meade, Herbert. *A Ride through the Disturbed Districts of New Zealand, together with some account of the South Sea Islands, edited by his brother.* London: J. Murray, 1870.

Melville, Herman. *Typee: a peep at Polynesian life, during a four months' residence in a valley of the Marquesas,* rev. ed. with sequel. London: George Routledge, 1850.

—— *The Works of Herman Melville.* Vol. 2: *Omoo: a narrative of adventures in the South Seas.* Vol. 5: *Redburn, his first voyage; being the sailor-boy confessions and reminiscences of the son of a gentleman in the merchant service.* London: Constable & Co., 1922.

Middleton, Dorothy. *Victorian Lady Travellers.* London: Routledge & Kegan Paul, 1965.

Mills, Sara. *Discourses of Difference: an Analysis of Women's Travel-writing and Colonialism.* London: Routledge, 1991.

Missionary Register, Church Missionary Society, London, 1813–55.

Mitchell, H. J. T. (ed.). *Landscape and Power.* Chicago: University of Chicago Press, 1994.

Mitchell, Timothy. 'The world-as-exhibition', *Comparative Studies in Society and History* 31 (1989), pp.314–28.

Money, Charles. *Knocking About in New Zealand.* Melbourne: Samuel Mullen, 1871.

Morris, Meaghan. 'Panorama: The Live, the Dead, and the Living', in Paul Foss (ed.), *Islands in the Stream: Myths of Place in Australian Culture.* Sydney: Pluto, 1988, pp.160–87.

Morton, Henry Bruce. *Notes of a New Zealand Tour.* Auckland: printed by W. C. Wilson, *New Zealand Herald* Office, 1878.

Muir, Marcie. *Anthony Trollope in Australia.* Adelaide: Wakefield Press, 1949.

[Muller, Miss]. *Notes of a Tour Through Various Parts of New Zealand Including a Visit to the Hot Springs by a German Lady.* Sydney: Lee & Ross Printers, 1877.

Mundy, Godfrey Charles. *Our Antipodes; or, residence and rambles in the Australasian Colonies.* London: Richard Bentley, 1852.

Muter, Mrs. *Travels and Adventures of an Officer's Wife in India, China and New Zealand.* London: Hurst & Blackett, 1864.

[Nesfield, H. W.] *A Chequered Career: or, fifteen years in Australia and New Zealand.* London: Richard Bentley & Son, 1881.

New Zealand Shipping Company. *New Zealand Shipping Company's Pocket-Book: an interesting guide for passengers by the Company's steamers, and containing information of general interest to all travellers to the Dominion.* London: Adam & Charles Black, 1908.

Nicholas, John Liddiard. *Narrative of a voyage to New Zealand performed in the years 1814 and 1815, in company with the Rev. Samuel Marsden, Principal Chaplain of New South Wales*. London: James Black & Co., 1817.

North, Marianne. *Recollections of a Happy Life: being the autobiography of Marianne North, edited by her sister Mrs John Addington Symonds*. London: Macmillan, 1893.

Ollivier, Charles Morton. *A Visit to the Boiling Springs of New Zealand; including a trip to White Island*. Christchurch: J. Hughes, 1871.

Osborne, Peter D. *Travelling Light: photography, travel and visual culture*. Manchester: Manchester University Press, 2000.

Pagden, Anthony. *European Encounters with the New World: from Renaissance to Romanticism*. New Haven: Yale University Press, 1993.

Park, Mungo. *Travels in the interior districts of Africa: performed in the years 1795–1796 and 1797, with an account of a subsequent mission to that country in 1805*. London: J. Murray, 1816.

Partington, James Edge. *Random Rot*. Altrincham: for private circulation only, 1883.

Payton, Edward. *Round about New Zealand: Being Notes from a Journal of Three Years' Wanderings in the Antipodes*. London: Chapman & Hall, 1888.

Pennefather, F. W. *A Handbook for Travellers in New Zealand*. London: John Murray, 1893.

Pocock. J. G. A. 'Nature and History, Self and Other: European Perceptions of World History in the Age of Encounter' in *Voyages and Beaches*, ed. Calder et al. Honolulu: University of Hawai'i Press, 1999.

Polack, Joel Samuel. *New Zealand: Being a Narrative of Travels and Adventures during a residence in that country between the years 1831 and 1837*. London: Richard Bentley, 1838.

Porter, Dennis. *Haunted Journeys: Desire and Transgression in European Travel-Writing*. Princeton: Princeton University Press, 1991.

Power, W. Tyrone. *Sketches in New Zealand with pen and pencil*. London: Longman, Brown, Green & Longmans, 1849.

Pratt, Mary Louise. *Imperial Eyes: Travel Writing and Transculturation*. London: Routledge, 1992.

Rabinow, Paul (ed.). *The Foucault Reader*. Harmondsworth: Penguin, 1984.

Reggett, S. B. 'The Tarawera Eruption, its effects on the tourist industry'. MA thesis, Massey University, 1972.

Roberts, J. Herbert. *A World-Tour; being a year's diary written 1884–85*. Liverpool: printed for private circulation, 1886.

Rochfort, John. *The Adventures of a Surveyor*. London: David Bogue, 1853.

Rogers, Shef. '"Crusoe Among the Maori": Translation and Colonial Acculturation in Victorian New Zealand', *Book History* 1 (1998), pp.182–95.

Rowse, A. L. *The Controversial Colensos*. Truro, Cornwall: Dyllanso, 1989.

Rubiés, Joan-Pau. 'Travel Writing as a Genre: Facts, Fictions and the Invention of a Scientific Discourse in Early Modern Europe', *Journeys: the International Journal of Travel and Travel Writing* 1:1–2 (2000), pp.5–35.

Said, Edward. *Orientalism*. Harmondsworth: Penguin, 1985.

—— *The World, the Text and the Critic*. Cambridge, Massachusetts: Harvard University Press, 1983.

Sail, C. R. *Farthest East, and South and West: Notes of a Journey Home Through Japan, Australasia, and America by an Anglo-Indian Globe-Trotter*. London: W. H. Allen, 1892.

Sala, George Augustus, *The Land of the Golden Fleece*, ed. Robert Dingley. Canberra: Mulini Press, 1995.

—— *The Life and Adventures of George Augustus Sala written by himself*. London: Cassell, 1896.

Salmond, Anne. *Between Worlds: Early Exchanges between Maori and Europeans 1773–1815*. Auckland: Viking, 1997.

—— *Two Worlds: First Meetings between Maori and Europeans 1642–1772*. Auckland: Viking, 1993.

Schwartze, C. E. R. *Travels in Greater Britain*. London: printed for the author by Cassell & Co., 1885.

Senior, William. *Travel and Trout in the Antipodes: a Traveller's Sketches in Tasmania and New Zealand*. London: Chatto & Windus, 1880.

Shaw, Dr John. *A Gallop to the Antipodes Returning Overland Through India*. London: J. F. Hope, 1858.

Simpson, Tony. *Art and Massacre: Documentary Racism in the Burning of the 'Boyd'*. Wellington: Cultural Construction Company, 1993.

Sinnema, Peter. *The Dynamics of the Pictured Page Representing the Nation in the Illustrated London News*. Aldershot and Brookfield: Ashgate, 1998.

Smiles, Samuel. *Self-Help; with illustrations of character and conduct*. London: John Murray, 1862.

—— (ed.). *A Boy's Journey Around the World*. London: John Murray, 1871.

Smith, Vanessa. *Literary Culture and the Pacific: Nineteenth Century Textual Encounters*. Cambridge: Cambridge University Press, 1998.

Sorrenson, M. P. K. 'Maori and Pakeha', in *The Oxford History of New Zealand*, ed. W. H. Oliver. Auckland: Oxford University Press, 1981.

Spurr, David. *The Rhetoric of Empire: Colonial Discourse in Journalism, Travel Writing and Imperial Administration*. Durham and London: Duke University Press, 1993.

Steward, Jill. 'The Adventures of Miss Brown, Miss Jones and Miss Robinson: tourist writing and tourist performance from 1860 to 1914', *Journey: the International Journal of Travel and Travel Writing* 1:1–2

(2000), pp.36–58.

Stoddart, Anna M. *The Life of Isabella Bird (Mrs. Bishop)*, 3rd ed. London: John Murray, 1908.

Talbot, Thorpe. *The New Guide to the Lakes and Hot Springs and A Month in Hot Water*. Auckland: Wilson & Horton Printers, 1882.

Tangye, Richard. *Notes of my fourth voyage to the Australian Colonies, including Australia, Tasmania and New Zealand*. Birmingham: White & Pike, 1886.

—— *Reminiscences of Travel in Australia, America and Egypt*. London: Sampson Low, Marston, Searle and Rivington, 1883.

Tinne, J. Ernest. *The Wonderland of the Antipodes; and Other Sketches of Travel in the North Island of New Zealand*. London: Sampson Low, Marston, Low & Searle, 1873.

Thomas, Nicholas. *Colonialism's Culture: Anthropology, Travel and Government*. Princeton: Princeton University Press, 1994.

Thomson, A. S. *The Story of New Zealand, past and present, savage and civilised*. London: John Murray, 1859.

Trollope, Anthony. *Australia and New Zealand*, 2nd ed. London: Dawson's of Pall Mall, 1968 [first published 1873].

—— *Anthony Trollope in New Zealand in 1872: contemporary newspaper extracts*. Wellington: Alexander Turnbull Library, 1971.

T. T. H. *The Newest Guide to the Hot Lakes by a Man Constantly in Hot Water*. Auckland: Wilson & Horton, c.1885.

Turnbull, John. *A voyage round the world, in the years 1800, 1801, 1802, 1803 and 1804; in which the author visited the principal islands in the Pacific Ocean, and the English settlements of Port Jackson and Norfolk Island*. London: Richard Phillips, 1805.

Tyerman, Rev. Daniel and George Bennet. *Journal of Voyages and Travels*. London: Frederick A. H. Davis, London Missionary Society, 1831.

Urry, John. *The Tourist Gaze: Leisure and Travel in Contemporary Societies*. London: Sage, 1990.

Vickers, Anna. *Voyage en Australie et en Nouvelle-Zélande*. Paris: Librairie Ch. Delagrave, 1883.

Vincent, Mrs Howard. *Forty Thousand Miles Over Land and Water: The Journal of a Tour through the British Empire and America*. London: Sampson Low, Marston, Searle & Rivington, 1885.

Waaka, Peter. *Tarawera Eruption Centennial Exhibition 1886–1986*. Rotorua: Rotorua District Council, 1986, pp.11–13.

Waddington, Richard. *Notes of a Tour in the England of the Antipodes*. London: Warren, Hall & Lovett Printers, 1887.

Wade, William Richard. *A Journey in the Northern Island of New Zealand, interspersed with various information relative to the country and people*. Hobart: G. Rolwegan, 1842.

Wakefield, Edward Jerningham. *Adventure in New Zealand from 1839 to 1844; with some account of the British colonization of the islands*. London: J. Murray, 1845.

Walker, Denis B. 'At Home in the Wild: the Idea of Place and the Textualised Vision of William Colenso', *Australian Canadian Studies, The Idea of Place: New Zealand Issue* 18:1–2 (2000), pp.99–112.

Westgarth, William. *Personal Recollections of Early Melbourne and Victoria*. Melbourne & Sydney: George Robertson & Co., 1888.

Wenz, Emile. *Mon Journal*. Paris: Nourrit et Cie, 1886.

Wight, O. W. *People and Countries visited in a winding journey around the world*. Boston and New York: Houghton, Mifflin & Co., 1888.

Williams, Rev. John. *A Narrative of Missionary Enterprises in the South Sea Islands*. London: J. Snow, 1838.

[Wilson, Alexander, Rutherford Waddell and T. W. Whitson]. *Maoriland; an illustrated handbook to New Zealand*, issued by the Union Steam Ship Company of New Zealand Ltd. Melbourne: Robertson, 1884.

Wilson, Captain James. *The Life and Dreadful Sufferings of Captain James Wilson in various parts of the globe including a faithful narrative of every Circumstance during the voyage to the South Sea islands in the Missionary ship 'Duff' for the propagation of the Gospel; with an authentic and interesting account of the sufferings and calamities of the missionaries from the year 1797, to the present period*. Portsea: T. Chapman, 1810.

Yate, William. *An Account of New Zealand; and of the formation and progress of the Church Missionary Society's mission in the northern island*. London: Seeley & Burnside, 1835.

—— *An Account of New Zealand*, ed. Judith Binney. Wellington: Reed, 1970.

Young, Henry Selden. *Diary of a Voyage to Australia and New Zealand 1885*. Auckland: Polygraphia, 1999.

INDEX